THE FOREIGN POLICY OF
JAMES G. BLAINE

THE FOREIGN POLICY OF
JAMES G. BLAINE

By

ALICE FELT TYLER

ARCHON BOOKS
HAMDEN, CONNECTICUT
1965

Library of Congress Catalog Card Number: 65-16899

Printed in The United States of America

FOREWORD

JUST as it is said that each generation needs to re-write the history of past events, so it is necessary from time to time to evaluate again the contributions of past leaders in politics. The generation that knew James G. Blaine — and all of his contemporaries felt sure they knew him whether they had ever seen him or not — that generation has nearly disappeared, so that his name no longer awakens a thrill of pride or arouses a flash of anger. But with the passing of time and the achievement of a certain perspective, Blaine's place can be fixed with more assurance than was possible two or three decades ago.

Those who had reached maturity while Blaine's name was still something to conjure with, and those whose youthful impressions were reflections of their elders' strongly expressed opinions are more than likely to associate with him the spectacular events of his career in the game of national politics. His name, to those who distrusted him, calls to mind the Mulligan Letters, the charges of using his official position to promote legislation to favor railroads he was inter-ested in, the defection of Republicans into the Mug-wump camp in the presidential campaign of 1884, the circumstances under which he left Harrison's Cabinet. To those who gave him their unquestioning devotion

— and their name was legion — Blaine meant the "Plumed Knight," the incomparable orator, the man who was cheated out of the Republican nomination in 1880 by the Machiavellian tactics of Roscoe Conkling, the leader defeated by the Reverend Mr. Burchard's "Rum, Romanism, and Rebellion."

There is, however, another aspect of Blaine which, although not unnoticed by his contemporaries, was certainly overshadowed. Blaine, as Secretary of State for a period of less than four years, split between two administrations, stands out in perspective as one of the men who have set distinctive marks on American diplomacy. In this study there has been made for the first time an adequate and dispassionate examination of what Blaine did and what he tried to do as Secretary of State. Mrs. Tyler's work is a contribution to the history of American foreign relations and to the biographical material on an outstanding American, and as such enriches the historical literature dealing with the past half-century.

LESTER BURRELL SHIPPEE

ACKNOWLEDGMENTS

IT is peculiarly fitting that, in the publication of this book, there should be some acknowledgment of my indebtedness to those who have been my teachers and guides in the field of history as well as to those who have given more direct aid in the preparation of this study. I am sure that there are many who have as students worked with Professor John Leonard Conger, of the Department of History of Knox College, who would join with me in giving to him credit for much of the work, and more of the joy of the work, done since that time.

I wish to make acknowledgment, also, of my great indebtedness to Professor Lester Burrell Shippee, of the Department of History of the University of Minnesota, whose advice and assistance have, in large measure, made this book possible. He has been in every way "guide, counselor, and friend." He spent many weary hours reading the manuscript and aided in all changes and revisions.

Professor C. D. Allin, of the Department of Political Science of the University of Minnesota, read the entire manuscript and made many valuable suggestions, especially for the chapters dealing with the relations of Canada and the United States. Professor Guy Stanton Ford, Dean of the Graduate School of the University of Minnesota, read the manuscript and made valuable criticisms.

My gratitude is due to Mrs. Natalia Summers for her kindness, interest, and assistance in the Archives of the Department of State during one very torrid Washington summer. I owe much also to Mrs. Margaret S. Harding, who prepared the manuscript for the press, and who has done much of the exacting work of reading proof.

ALICE FELT TYLER

MINNEAPOLIS
  JUNE, 1927

CONTENTS

CHAPTER I

INTRODUCTION

THE man who became President Garfield's Secretary of State in 1881 had been his friend for nearly twenty years and had been a prominent figure in public affairs for an even longer time. James Gillespie Blaine was elected to the state legislature in Maine in 1858, and in 1859 became chairman of the Republican state committee, which position he held until 1881. In 1862 he was elected to Congress, where he served brilliantly for seventeen years. In 1869 he was chosen Speaker of the House of Representatives over which he was to preside until he was elected to the Senate in 1876.

More than twenty years of the most active political life could scarcely have given opportunity for close study of foreign affairs, especially since those years came in a period when Congress and the country as a whole were interested, almost solely, in the many and varied problems of Civil War and Reconstruction and in the economic questions resulting from an unprecedented industrial development. Without any vestige of training in diplomacy, Mr. Blaine had a keen and very real interest in the relations of the United States with other nations and that sensitiveness to the desires and interests of the people of the United States which many years of legislative service can give to the true political leader.[1]

Brilliant, versatile, successful, he was in 1880 the outstanding figure in the Republican party. His charm of personality and his possession in a great degree of that indefinable quality known as magnetism made him the object of the affection and admiration, almost of the adoration, of a large body of followers, many of whom had never seen him nor heard him speak. Charges of dishonesty and double dealing in financial matters brought against him at critical times in his political career, never proved but never completely refuted, caused him to be regarded by other large bodies of voters as absolutely unsafe. This distrust was used by Blaine's political enemies, cultivated, played upon, until by many men he was felt to be the associate of the Prince of Darkness himself. Few political leaders in this country have been at the same time so popular and so feared and hated. Five times his name appeared in presidential nominating conventions, and once, in 1884, he was nominated in spite of the opposition of factions within the party, and was defeated in the campaign by one of the narrowest margins known in the history of presidential elections. Twice he was

[1] Since the days of Jacksonian Democracy and the end of the line of early statesmen, it has not been the practice of the United States to give the office of Secretary of State to men of diplomatic training. Time after time it has gone to an outstanding leader of the incoming party. The appointment of Blaine in 1881 and 1889 were no exceptions to what may almost be considered the rule in American politics.

the almost inevitable choice for the leading post in the Cabinet of a president elected largely through his influence and effort. He was Secretary of State through Garfield's short term of office in 1881 and again when Harrison was President in 1889-1892.

The Republican convention in the summer of 1880 was the scene of a long contest. The movement for a third term for General Grant met defeat, but the circumstances were such that Blaine, the candidate whose strength was nearly as great, could not obtain a majority. Conkling and the Stalwarts, who were supporting Grant, were opposed to Blaine and refused to cast the vote of the New York delegation in his favor. Upon the thirty-sixth ballot a stampede began which gave the nomination to General Garfield. Blaine and Garfield were intimate friends, and the former enthusiastically entered the campaign, using all of his well-known political ability, first in Maine where his leadership was unquestioned, and later in the West. He not only was of assistance in the canvass before the election but was called upon for aid and advice at every step of the way. In June Garfield wrote asking for suggestions on the letter accepting the nomination, particularly requesting paragraphs on the questions of Chinese exclusion, the South, the civil service, and the silver issue.[2] The letters between the two men all bear evidence to the intimacy of their friendship and to their mutual confidence in each other. There seems to be no reason for thinking that either dominated or controlled the other. They

[2] Gail Hamilton, *Biography of James G. Blaine*, 486.

belonged to the middle section of the party, their views on many questions were similar, they were in accord.

It was, therefore, a matter of course that very soon after the election Garfield offered Blaine the office of Secretary of State. In recording the conversation in his journal, Garfield wrote:

At first he spoke as if he could not exchange his place in the Senate for the one in the cabinet. I pointed out the career which executive work offered and told him I thought it would be better for his fame and for the health of the party in Maine if he would resign the leadership for a time.[3]

The offer was not accepted at once. On December 10, Blaine wrote:

The more I think of the State Department the more I am inclined thereto, though up to this time, and still continuing, my mind is the theatre of conflicting arguments and even emotions. I believe with you as President, and in your full confidence, I could do much to build up the party as the result of a strong and wise policy. I find myself drawn towards it, and possibly by the date you fixed as a limit I may be wholly and enthusiastically disposed thereto.[4]

Ten days later the decision was reached, and a warmly personal letter accepting the Secretaryship was sent to Garfield:

In accepting this important post I shall give all that I am, and all that I can hope to be, freely and joyfully to your service. You need no pledge of my loyalty both in heart and in act. I should

[3] Theodore Clark Smith, *James Abram Garfield — Life and Letters,* II, 1049.

[4] Blaine to Garfield, December 10, 1880, Hamilton, *Blaine,* 490.

be false to myself did I not prove true to the great trust you confide to me and to your own personal and political fortunes in the present and in the future.[5]

In this letter also, Blaine showed himself as first and foremost the party man, a political leader of congressional stamp and training, and only potentially the statesman, for he made his decision,

. . . not for the honor of the promotion it gives me in the public service but because I believe I can be useful to the country and the party, — useful to you as the responsible head of the party and the great head of the government.

The letter ended on a note of friendly intimacy:

I hail it as one of the happiest circumstances connected with this important affair, that in allying my political fortunes with yours — or rather in merging mine in yours — my heart goes with my head and that I carry to you not only political support, but personal and devoted friendship. . . . For however much I might admire you as a statesman, I would not enter your Cabinet if I did not believe in you as a man and love you as a friend.[6]

Garfield answered this letter with one equally friendly in tone, saying:

Our long and eventful service together, and our friendship, never for a moment interrupted, but tested in so many ways, gives assurance that we can happily unite in working out the important problems which confront us.[7]

Despite the perfect sincerity of this statement, it is

[5] Blaine to Garfield, December 20, 1880, *ibid.*, 494.
[6] *Ibid.*, 495.
[7] Garfield to Blaine, December 23, 1880, *ibid.*, 495.

apparent that Garfield saw clearly the difficulties which might attend giving the first place in his Cabinet to a political leader so brilliant and dynamic, whose enemies in the party were nearly as numerous and active as his friends.[8] The uncontradicted rumor of the offer and of Mr. Blaine's acceptance of it brought forth a storm of criticism as well as many expressions of satisfaction. The New York politicians did not like it, for they felt it presaged difficulties over the control of New York patronage. The President-elect seemed to have tied himself up with the anti-Conkling wing of the party. Such leaders of the party as President Hayes and Senator John Sherman of Ohio felt that the choice was necessary and inevitable, and that Blaine would make a brilliant member of the Cabinet provided Garfield could "restrain his immense activity and keep him from meddling with other departments."[9] It must be said, moreover, that, despite the intimacy of the two men and the keen interest in all political affairs, which was characteristic of Blaine, Garfield did maintain his independence of judgment and of action. The President viewed the policies of his Secretary of State with sympathy, understanding, and approval in those few months in which they were permitted to work together.

When James G. Blaine became Secretary of State in March of 1881, a new era in American foreign relations began. The United States adopted for the first

[8] Smith, *James Abram Garfield*, II, 1052.

[9] Smith, *James Abram Garfield*, II, 1059, quoting from a letter from Sherman.

time since the days of Seward an aggressive American policy, which was to have a very real influence upon the relations of this country with the Central and South American Republics, with Hawaii and the islands of the Caribbean, from that date to this. Blaine's successors in the office have frequently disavowed his policies, but they have again and again come back to them, until today the principles which he so earnestly upheld for the relations of the United States to the other States of this hemisphere have been accepted as maxims of American policy. Little by little the ends he sought in 1881 have been achieved, and if that friendly feeling, that attitude of mutual trust and confidence, for which he worked, have not grown up between the United States and the other American Republics it is not entirely the fault of the man who initiated the policy.

James G. Blaine became Secretary of State with a definite purpose. He was one of the few holders of that office who were not entirely opportunists. This purpose was the adoption of an American continental system. The policy comprehended the prevention of wars between countries in this hemisphere and the development of better commercial relations between the United States and the Latin American nations. The United States was to play the part of friendly counselor, was to mediate, advise, but not forcefully intervene. In other words the Monroe Doctrine was to be extended to mean a positive aid to the development of that part of the world which it affected.[10]

[10] Edward Stanwood, *James G. Blaine*, 241 ff.

This conception of an American continental system, with peaceful relations and steadily increasing commercial development among the states forming that system, was the mainspring of Secretary Blaine's policy, but there were two or three other matters about which he had already formed definite opinions, which were to carry over and color his policy both in 1881 and in his later term of office. He had, in 1879, delivered two speeches in the Senate on the subject of Chinese exclusion and had written a long letter to the New York *Tribune* in answer to criticisms of his point of view.[11] The platforms of both parties in 1880 contained exclusion planks. When asked by Garfield for an expression of opinion on the subject as an aid to the formulation of his letter of acceptance, Blaine wrote: "You will, I think, be compelled to take the ground that a servile class — assimilating in all its conditions of labor to chattel slavery — must be excluded from free immigration."[12] The preceding administration had concluded a treaty with China on November 17, 1880, which had not yet been ratified, which provided for the desired exclusion of Chinese laborers.[13] Very soon after President Garfield's inauguration, Secretary Blaine submitted a draft for a special message to the Senate on the subject of this treaty, and on May 5, after

[11] These speeches and the letter are reprinted in Blaine, *Political Discussions Legislative, Diplomatic and Popular.*

[12] Hamilton, *Blaine*, 487.

[13] *U. S. Foreign Relations*, 1881, negotiations of the treaty commission. See also Tyler Dennett, *Americans in Eastern Asia*, 542 ff.

the Senate had resumed executive sessions, the treaty was finally ratified.[14]

The relations between the United States and England, especially where they touched Canada, were of much interest to Blaine. He had taken the position in 1877 that Great Britain acted unfairly in the matter of the selection of a third arbitrator for the commission which was to carry out the Fisheries Treaty of 1871. This commission was to fix the amount to be paid by the United States, if it was decided that the benefits accruing to the United States from the treaty were greater than the market privileges for her fish, secured by Canada. He had held that the award of five and a half million dollars to Canada was grossly unfair, but that it was good policy to pay the amount awarded while calling the attention of Great Britain to the fact that, in the opinion of Congress, the award was an unfair one.[15] After he had been offered the position of Secretary of State, but before he had accepted that offer, he wrote Garfield to call his attention to the fact that the

concessions and guarantees contained in XVIII to XXV, and in articles XXVIII, XXIX and XXX, have a ten-year limit for notice and two years after notice. This throws the whole subject open for fresh and I hope more lasting adjustment during *your "first term."* The subjects involved are the Fisheries, the navigation of the St. John and the right of transit for Can-

[14] Smith, *Garfield*, II, 1165.
[15] Stanwood, *Blaine*, 201-202. See also, Blaine, *Twenty Years in Congress*, II, 620.

adian goods through our territory, the free international use of the Welland canal, the St. Clair flats canal, and many other topics. In short it opens the whole Canadian question and gives a splendid opportunity to achieve some things of which we have already spoken. . . . Can't you quietly drop a note to Hayes suggesting that the whole question of a readjustment of Canadian matters should be left without embarrassment to your administration? [16]

Garfield wrote to Hayes, as suggested, but the desired opportunity to bring about a readjustment of all the irksome questions relating to Canada was not permitted Secretary Blaine in his few brief months of office in 1881. Some of these questions he met again later in 1889-1892, but at no time was he able to advance the solution of the problems.

The attitude of Blaine toward England and toward Canada, always suspicious, sometimes hostile, never entirely friendly, is an interesting field for speculation. Strain after strain of Scotch, of Irish, and of Scotch-Irish composed his ancestry. Of Revolutionary stock he had grown up during the days of "54° 40′ or fight" and of the Aroostook wars. For more than twenty years he had been a citizen of the state of Maine. It is, perhaps, not surprising that he was not always entirely unbiased in his attitude toward England and her daughter, Canada.

Such, then, was the situation in March of 1881. The President and his Secretary of State were in complete

[16] Blaine to Garfield, December 13, 1880, quoted in Hamilton, *Blaine*, 492.

accord on matters of foreign policy. They had an earnest desire to take a positive, forward-looking position in regard to Latin America, to inaugurate a new version of the Monroe Doctrine. At the same time, there is nothing to indicate that they contemplated any change of policy in regard to the relations of the United States to any European country.

CHAPTER II

THE CONTROVERSY WITH ENGLAND OVER THE CLAYTON-BULWER TREATY

THE question of the attitude of the Garfield administration toward Latin America and toward the Monroe Doctrine is bound up with the action taken by Secretary Blaine in the enunciation of the American position in regard to the question of an interoceanic canal and with the controversy with Great Britain arising out of that action. Ever since the period of expansion by "Manifest Destiny" in the 1840's and 1850's, the possibility of an interoceanic canal through Panama, through Nicaragua, or through the Isthmus of Tehuantepec had been recurringly of importance to the Department of State.[1]

[1] The diplomatic correspondence, treaties etc., for the entire period from 1840 on, was gathered together about 1900 and reprinted as "Correspondence Relating to the Interoceanic Canal," *Senate Documents* Nos. 161 and 237, 56 Congress, 1st Session, (Serial No. 3853). One of the reprints, *Senate Executive Document* No. 194, 47 Congress, 1st Session, is the most comprehensive. There is a great deal of secondary material on the subject. The best accounts are probably Mary W. Williams, *Anglo-American Isthmian Diplomacy, 1815-1915*; Lindley M. Keasbey, *The Nicaragua Canal and the Monroe Doctrine*; and Ira D. Travis, "The History of the Clayton-Bulwer Treaty," *Publications of the Michigan Political Science Association*, III.

By Article 35 of the treaty negotiated with New Granada (Colombia) in 1846, the United States was given the right of transit by "any mode," without tolls or charges other than those which citizens of New Granada might pay. The United States formally recognized New Granada's rights of sovereignty over the State of Panama, promised to defend such sovereignty, and guaranteed the neutrality of the Isthmus and of any routes over or through it. The treaty was ratified in 1848, and the Panama railroad was built in the years immediately following. The duration of the treaty was stipulated at twenty years, and it was renewed by Secretary Fish for another twenty. It was, therefore, in force when Blaine became Secretary of State.

Great Britain also had many interests in the general region of Central America through her ownership of British Honduras and her influence along the Mosquito coast. Because of the development of the Pacific coast of British North America, England was interested in any canal project. These interests of England would come into contact, if not into conflict, with those of the United States, which were of rapidly increasing importance after the war with Mexico. It seemed the wisest plan, therefore, to come to terms with Great Britain and to make some arrangement for a joint control of the canal route, especially since it was apparent that English capital must be sought for the construction of any canal which might be built in the immediate future. The Clayton-Bulwer Treaty was negotiated to satisfy the needs of this situation and was signed on April 19, 1850. The treaty referred especially to the Nicaragua route, but in its eighth and last clause a general principle was deduced, extending the joint protection and guarantee clauses to any route which might be constructed across any part of Central America.[2] A

[2] Clayton-Bulwer Treaty, April 19, 1850, 56 Cong., 1st Session, *Senate Document* No. 161, Art. I. — "The governments of the United States & Great.Britain declare that neither the one nor the other will ever obtain or maintain for itself any exclusive control over the said ship canal; agreeing that neither will ever erect or maintain any fortifications commanding the same or in the vicinity thereof, or occupy, or fortify, or colonize, or assume, or exercise any dominion over Nicaragua, Costa Rica, the Mosquito coast, or any part of Central America; nor will either make use of any protection which either affords or may afford, or any alliance which either has or may have, to or with any state or people, for the purpose of erecting or maintaining any such fortifications or of occuying, fortifying, or colonizing Nicaragua, Costa Rica, the Mosquito coast, or any part of Central America, or of assuming or exercising dominion over the same; nor will the United States or Great Britain take advantage of any intimacy, or use any alliance, connection or influence that either may possess with any state or government through whose territory the said canal may pass, for the purpose of acquiring or holding, directly or indirectly, for the citizens or subjects of the one, any rights or advantages in regard to commerce or navigation through the said canal which shall not be offered on the same terms to the citizens or subjects of the other." Art. VIII. — "The Governments of the United States and Great Britain having not only desired, in entering into this convention, to accomplish a particular object, but also to establish a general principle, they hereby agree to extend their protection, by treaty stipulations to any other practicable communications, whether by canal or railway, across the isthmus which connects North and South America, and especially to the interoceanic communications, should the same prove to be practicable, whether by canal or railroad,

canal so constructed was to be neutralized by the joint action of Great Britain and the United States, and neither power was to fortify or colonize the route chosen.   An invitation was to be extended to other nations to accede to the joint guarantee, thus making it a collective one.[3]

The Clayton-Bulwer Treaty was not felt by the United States to be entirely satisfactory, for it did not bring to an end the activities of Great Britain in Central America, but by 1860 arrangements were made which led President Buchanan to declare the treaty "entirely satisfactory." [4]   He thus caused an estoppel for further protests against the treaty, which was to be used against the United States at a later period.   There was, in the years after the Civil War, considerable activity on the part of officers of the United States Navy in the making of maps and surveys.   President

which are now proposed to be established by the way of Tehuantepec or Panama. In granting, however, their joint protection to any such canals or railways as are by this article specified, it is always understood by the United States and Great Britain that the parties constructing or owning the same shall impose no charges or conditions of traffic thereupon than the aforesaid governments shall approve of as just and equitable; and that the same canals or railways, being open to the citizens and subjects of the United States and Great Britain on equal terms, shall also be open on like terms to the citizens and subjects of every other state which is willing to grant thereto, such protection as the United States and Great Britain engage to afford."

[3] No other nation did so accede.

[4] Annual Message, December, 1860, J. D. Richardson, *A Compilation of the Messages and Papers of the Presidents of the United States, 1789-1897*, V, 639.

Grant appointed an Interoceanic Canal Commission, and interest was increasing yearly in the United States.

The Clayton-Bulwer Treaty was not questioned again, however, until the actual construction of the canal seemed imminent. In 1878 Ferdinand de Lesseps secured a concession from Colombia permitting him to construct a canal across the Isthmus of Panama.[5] From that moment public opinion and congressional action began to evidence the growth of a new and distinctly American point of view in regard to the whole interoceanic canal project. By the spring of 1880 Evarts, the Secretary of State, and President Hayes had both placed themselves on record as in favor of a distinctly American canal under the control of the United States.[6] The House of Representatives in December, 1879, appointed a special committee to examine the questions, and this committee held protracted hearings, at which appeared Mr. Dichman, the United States minister to Colombia, who was an ardent supporter of an American-controlled canal, M. de Lesseps himself, Mr. Eads, who was fathering a scheme

[5] The story of the Wyse Concession, the organization of the De Lesseps Company, and the meeting at Paris of the International Scientific Congress in 1879 cannot be given here. They may be studied in the report of Lieutenant John T. Sullivan, U. S. N., *The Problem of Interoceanic Communication by way of the American Isthmus*, published by the Bureau of Navigation in 1883 and in J. C. Rodrigues, *The Panama Canal, Its History, Its Political Aspects and Financial Difficulties*. Keasbey, *Nicaragua Canal and the Monroe Doctrine* gives a good summary.

[6] Hayes' Message, December, 1879, in Richardson, *Messages and Papers*, VII, 569 and the Special Message of March 8, 1880, *ibid.*, 585.

for a ship-railroad across the Isthmus of Tehuantepec, and a group of American capitalists who were interested in the Nicaragua route.[7] The Senate also discussed the canal question, but in that house the discussion turned chiefly on the Clayton-Bulwer Treaty, the existence of which seemed to many to block the United States in an endeavor to assume exclusive control of any route. The congressional interest in the question culminated in April, 1880, in a resolution in the House, authorizing the President to take "immediate steps for the formal and final abrogation of the convention of April 19, 1850, between the United States and Her Britannic Majesty." [8]

The presidential campaign and election of 1880 occupied the attention of the politicians and the public through the rest of the year, but Secretary Evarts did not diminish his watchfulness and activity. He asked and received the assurance of the French Government that it was in no way concerned in the De Lesseps project and was not giving it any support.[9] He corresponded extensively with Mr. Dichman in Colombia, and in February of 1881 he negotiated with the Colombian minister at Washington a protocol to be added to the Treaty of 1846, which would give the United

[7] *House Miscellaneous Document* No. 16, 46 Congress, 3rd Session. For testimony before the committee see *House Report* No. 390, 46 Cong., 3rd Session; *Congressional Record*, Vols. 10 and 11. See also, Williams, *Life of Hayes*, II, 219, for extracts from Hayes' diary.

[8] *House Report* No. 1121, 46 Cong., 2nd Session.

[9] M. Outrey to Mr. Evarts, March 22, 1880, *U. S. Foreign Relations, 1880*, No. 385.

States such extensive rights over the Isthmus of Panama as to limit Colombian sovereignty and practically nullify the Clayton-Bulwer Treaty.[10]   This scheme to reduce Colombia to little more than a vassal state so far as its foreign relations were concerned was a failure, for Colombia promptly refused to ratify the treaty and even manifested a desire to be released from the provisions of the Treaty of 1846.   She expressed herself as willing to invite the powers of Europe to guarantee the sovereignty and neutrality of the canal.[11]

Congress, again in session, took up the matter of an interoceanic canal in both the Senate and the House. On February 14, 1881, a joint resolution was introduced in the House, stating that the construction of a canal by foreign capital and under foreign auspices would be hostile to the policy of the United States and would be a violation of the Monroe Doctrine.[12]   Two days later the Senate passed a resolution with the concurrence of the House to the effect that the United States would insist that its consent be obtained before the construction of any interoceanic waterway should be attempted, and that the United States must be consulted as to rules and regulations under which the canal should be operated in peace and in war.[13]   On March 3 the House Committee on the Interoceanic Canal (appointed a year earlier) reported on all of its investiga-

[10] *Sen. Exec. Doc.* No. 237, 56 Cong., 1st Session, "Correspondence not heretofore communicated to Congress," 473 ff.   See also *U. S. Foreign Relations*, 1881, 361 ff.

[11] See note 18 below.

[12] *House Report* No. 224, 46 Cong., 3rd Session.

[13] *Senate Miscellaneous Document* No. 42, 46 Cong., 3rd Session.

tions, giving a long discussion of the Monroe Doctrine and its applicability to the situation. The report ended by recommending "prompt and energetic action to protect the interests of this country." [14]

The new President and his Secretary of State had been in Congress during the years when public opinion in the United States developed on the canal issue. They had watched the shift from acquiescence in the Clayton-Bulwer Treaty to a desire for its abrogation. Neither seems to have taken a prominent part in the discussion of the various resolutions and measures proposed in Congress, but Mr. Blaine, at least, must have been conversant with them. His interest in Latin America was of long standing, and it is probable that one of his first interests upon being appointed Secretary of State was to familiarize himself with the correspondence upon the question.

Their ideas on the subject received their first opportunity for expression in the inaugural address of President Garfield. In a passage referring to the canal, the new President said:

We will urge no narrow policy nor seek peculiar or exclusive privileges in any commercial route; but, in the language of my predecessor, I believe it to be the right and duty of the United States to assert and maintain such supervision and authority over any interoceanic canal across the isthmus that connects North and South America as will protect our national interests.[15]

This was the sort of noncommittal statement which

[14] *House Report* No. 390, 46 Cong., 3rd Session.
[15] Richardson, *Messages and Papers*, VIII, 11.

might have been expected in such a paper. The first clause of the passage quoted might not seem inconsistent with a continuance of the limitations of the Clayton-Bulwer Treaty,[16] but the spirit of the latter part of the passage animated the first dispatches which set forth Secretary Blaine's ideas on the subject. His fundamental policy of an American continental system with the benevolent but dominating influence of the United States permeating the entire structure could not permit an isthmus with a canal under French control and a Clayton-Bulwer Treaty hampering every move.

If ever a man came into office with a clear mandate to inaugurate a policy, Mr. Blaine was that man. Through both houses of the national legislature, through the executive, in the utterances of the President and the Secretary of State, the preceding administration had declared the policy of the party. The public had expressed itself in numerous petitions to Congress, coming from Pacific coast and Gulf states, and lobbyists for one scheme or another had been active in Washington for the past three years. The issue was not of Blaine's seeking, he was to pronounce no view unheard before, but with thorough knowledge of the Congressional activities, he was armed and ready for the fray.[17]

Early in May Mr. Dichman, the ever-watchful minister to Colombia, reported to the State Department

---

[16] T. J. Lawrence, *Essays on Some Disputed Questions in Modern International Law*, 104.

[17] Hector Pétin, *Les États-Unis et la doctrine de Monroe*, 135.

that Colombia was seeking from the European powers some sort of joint declaration of the neutrality of the Isthmus of Panama and a guarantee of Colombian sovereignty.[18] Rumors had reached Blaine earlier than this, indicating that there was a desire on the part of some of the European powers to undertake such a guarantee.[19] Believing that the Treaty of 1846, which was still in force, offered Colombia ample guarantees, Blaine determined to nip in the bud any such movement on the part of Colombia and any European powers.[20]

[18] Dichman to Blaine, May 9, 1881, MS. Dispatches, Colombia, Vol. 35, No. 269. "It has been reported to me confidentially that the Colombian government has sent copies of the protocol signed by Mr. Trescott and General Santadomingo at New York, to its ministers at London and Paris with instructions to bring the 'unusual pretensions' . . . of the government of the United States . . . to the knowledge of the governments of Great Britain and France and to invite them as well as the governments of Germany, Spain and Italy, to join in due execution of a treaty guarantying the neutrality of the Isthmus of Panama and the sovereingty of Colombia over that territory." In a dispatch (MS. Dispatches, Colombia, Vol. 36, No. 306) of August 27, 1881, Mr. Dichman again commented upon the precarious condition of the treaty, stating that Colombia would like to give the required notice for its termination but did not dare to do so. "The existence of the treaty wounds their pride and what is worse checks them from establishing the policy of spoliation at the Isthmus; but without it they fear to lose the State of Panama and the benefits which they reap at present and which the future has in store."

[19] *U. S. Foreign Relations*, 1881, 356.

[20] *Sen. Exec. Doc.* No. 5, 47 Cong., Special Session. In answer to a Senate Resolution of October 14, 1881, asking if the United States had taken any measures to protect the interests of the United States at Panama, Mr. Blaine wrote: ". . . The Secretary of State has the honor to report that having learned since the adjournment of Congress of the rejection by Colombia of the protocol negotiated by the

President Garfield was in complete agreement with his Secretary of State on this policy, which amounted in effect to a new interpretation or extension of the Monroe Doctrine, and recorded in his journal for June 14, "Cabinet full today for the first time in two weeks. Blaine read an important identic note to several of our leading ministers in Europe on the neutrality of the South American isthmus, holding that the United States has guaranteed its neutrality and denies the rights of other, especially European powers, to take any part in the guarantee." [21]

On June 24 the circular letter was dispatched to the ministers of the United States in Europe for informal transmission to the foreign secretaries of the Governments to which they were accredited.[22] In it Blaine took

representatives of the United States and that republic, which was hoped would secure a treaty satisfactory to both, and being informed by the Minister of the United States in Colombia that the Government of Colombia by its public acts was avowing its desire to terminate the Treaty of 1846 and appeal to the powers of Europe for a joint guarantee of the neutrality of the isthmus and the sovereignty of Colombia, this Department addressed the following letter of instructions to the United States Minister in London." There follows the identic note of June 24, 1881.

[21] Quoted in Smith, *Garfield*, II, 1167.

[22] This note and the later correspondence between Blaine and Frelinghuysen and Lord Granville may be found in *Sen. Exec. Doc.* No. 194, 47 Cong., 1st Session. The diplomatic controversy has been treated in detail by many writers whose main interest was the development of the Monroe Doctrine. The most able presentations are probably, Kraus, *Die Monroedoktrin*; Pétin, *Les États-Unis et la doctrine de Monroe*; Keasbey, *Nicaragua Canal and the Monroe Doctrine*; Lawrence, *Essays on Some Disputed Questions in Modern International Law*; Travis, *Clayton-Bulwer Treaty*; and Williams, *Anglo-American Isthmian Diplomacy, 1815-1915*.

a positive position against any European action in the way of a guarantee. The Treaty of 1846 between the United States and the Republic of New Granada was a sufficient guarantee, which, he maintained, "does not require re-inforcement or accession or assent from any other power" and any attempt to supplement it would be regarded as an

uncalled-for intrusion into a field where the local and general interests of the United States of America must be considered before the interests of any other power save those of the United States of Colombia alone.

Blaine re-affirmed Evarts' idea that the United States did not wish to interfere with any commercial management of the canal nor to seek exclusive privilege in time of peace, but that the United States was determined to maintain a political control over the route of any canal that might be constructed.

During any war to which the United States of America or the United States of Colombia might be a party, the passage of armed vessels of a hostile nation through the canal would be no more admissable than would the passage of the armed forces of a hostile nation over the railway lines joining the Atlantic and Pacific shores of the United States or of Colombia. The United States of America will insist upon her right to take all needful precautions against a possibility that the Isthmus transit shall be in any event used offensively against her interests upon the land or upon the sea.

Mr. Blaine ended his argument in language still more vigorous:

Any attempt to supersede that guaranty by an agreement

between European powers which maintain vast armies and patrol the seas with immense fleets and whose interests in the canal and its operations can never be so vital and supreme as ours, would partake of the nature of an alliance against the United States.

The Monroe Doctrine was called upon in the following language:

While observing the strictest neutrality with respect to complications abroad, it is the long-settled conviction of this government that any extension to our shores of the political system by which the great powers have controlled and determined events in Europe would be attended with danger to the peace and welfare of this nation.

In closing Blaine advised the respective ministers to be careful not to present the position of the United States as the development of a new policy.

It is nothing more than the pronounced adherence of the United States to principles long since enunciated by the highest authority of the government and now, in the judgment of the President, firmly interwoven as an integral and important part of our national policy.

Leaving for later consideration the merits of Blaine's argument, it is of interest to examine the response received from the European powers. As Blaine undoubtedly expected, there was little exception taken to his dispatch, for De Lesseps had already abandoned his plan of joint European protection of the Panama route.[23] The minister to France reported that the

[23] Lindley M. Keasbey, *The Nicaragua Canal and the Monroe Doctrine*, 394.

French Foreign Office had had no official intimation of the intention of Colombia but was glad to know the views of the Secretary of State.[24] Italy made no reply; Russia had no knowledge of the affair, no interest in it, and would take no initiative.[25] Sweden expressed interest, objected to the minister's likening the interoceanic canal to the Gotha Canal, but expressed a willingness for the United States to police any canal that might be constructed, provided all nations had commercial equality.[26] Austria manifested no interest in the subject and hoped there would be no difficulty.[27] The Spanish minister "listened attentively to the reading of the official note of Mr. Blaine and said . . . that the case was important, very interesting and merited serious examination." There was some interest in the Spanish Cortes due to the alarm lest the new policy of extension of the Monroe Doctrine might affect the Spanish possessions. The Foreign Minister was interpolated and reassured the Cortes that "Spain was in accord with the other powers and Spanish interests were safeguarded." [28]

The case of Great Britain was quite different. She had had interests in the canal zone since the seventeenth century, and by the terms of the Clayton-Bulwer Treaty

[24] Pomeroy to Blaine, July 14, 1881, *U. S. Foreign Relations*, 1881, 416.

[25] Foster to Blaine, July 19, 1881, *ibid.*, 1027.

[26] Stevens to Blaine, September 23, 1881, *ibid.*, 1073.

[27] Phelps to Blaine, July 15, 1881, *ibid.*, 60.

[28] Antoine S. de Bustamante, "Le Canal de Panama et la droit international," *Revue de droit international*, 1895, 136.

her rights were as distinctly set forth as those of the United States. The formal response of Lord Granville, foreign secretary, was not sent until November, but the newspapers protested with vigor against the American position. The London *Times* failed to

see why there should be any repugnance to allowing England and France to join in a guarantee, . . . The neutralizing of the canal would be for the benefit of all the states in the world, and we fail to gather from this communication any solid objection to allowing European powers to join in a work universally desirable. Every additional guarantor would strengthen the guarantee. . . . It seems, to say the least, to be an unhappy use of language to describe the sincere cooperation of the European governments in a common object as of the nature of an alliance against the United States.[29]

The London *Daily News* said that

. . . as a piece of logic the circular can hardly be considered by his best friends to be very powerful. . . . Their [the powers] signature to the guarantee will be absolutely necessary, unless the United States are prepared to take upon themselves an enormous responsibility.[30]

During the summer of 1881, while Mr. Blaine was awaiting some answer to his enunciation of the policy of the United States in regard to the canal question, there occurred an incident which considerably altered the situation. In 1859 Great Britain had negotiated a treaty with Nicaragua, which was designed to settle the question of British claims and influence along the

[29] Quoted in the *Annual Cyclopedia*, 1881, 717.
[30] *Ibid.*, 719.

Mosquito coast and thus to satisfy the United States, which had protested that influence in the name of the Clayton-Bulwer Treaty. This treaty of 1859 had not been satisfactory, and there was much friction in the Mosquito district. Great Britain maintained the independence of the Mosquito Indians against the pretensions to sovereignty made by Nicaragua, and British capital and enterprise became interested in the region. When the friction became intolerable, the two powers submitted their disputes to the Emperor of Austria as umpire, and in July, 1881, he delivered the award of the arbitration. His decision practically gave Great Britain control over the Mosquito coast, which meant control of the eastern outlet of any Nicaragua canal. The interest of Great Britain in the whole question of an interoceanic canal was now much greater, and it was absurd to expect her to relinquish any advantage which the Clayton-Bulwer Treaty might give. Blaine appears to have been unaware of the significance of this episode, or of how untenable it made his position.[31]

Lord Granville made no effort to return an immediate response to the circular note which Mr. Lowell had read him. The Gladstone Government was endeavoring to stem the tide of British imperialism and did not look with favor upon what appeared to be similar enterprises elsewhere. The summer and fall of 1881 had passed before his reply, dated November 10, was dispatched. It was a very brief and pointed reminder that "the matter in question had already been settled by

---

[31] Keasbey, *Nicaragua Canal and the Monroe Doctrine*, 377-378.

the engagements of the Clayton-Bulwer Treaty and that Her Majesty's government relied with confidence upon the observation of all the obligations of that treaty."[32]

This note of Granville's crossed on its way a dispatch from Blaine to Lowell, dated November 19. The circular note of June 24 had been addressed to all the European powers. That may have been the reason why Mr. Blaine had not mentioned the Clayton-Bulwer Treaty. In this second note to London alone, he remedied the deficiency in the earlier communication. This note of November 19 dealt exclusively and at length with the Treaty of 1850 and ended with the instruction that the matter be taken up with Lord Granville and the treaty modified to meet the American demands. Blaine insisted that the treaty was made under exceptional circumstances that had long ago ceased to exist, and that the remarkable growth of the Pacific coast had greatly changed the duties and necessities of the United States. The provisions forbidding the fortification of a canal would give the British Navy a position out of all proportion to the interests of the United States, which desired to be pacific and friendly, but "at the same time, this government, with respect to European States, will not consent to perpetuate any treaty that impeaches our rightful and long established claim to priority on the American continent." The United States wished the same control that England insisted

[32] Granville to Hoppin, November 10, 1881, *Sen. Exec. Doc.* No. 194, 47 Cong., 1st Session.

upon for her connections with India and offered abso-
lute neutralization, for, Blaine maintained, the United
States was the nation least likely to be engaged in war.
The Nicaragua canal project of 1850 had not been
taken up and completed by Great Britain, and the
United States was now ready to furnish capital for an
American canal.

For all of these reasons Blaine asked that the treaty
be modified to give the United States political and military control over the canal.   The United States would
make no acquisitions of territory and would make the
terminals of the canal into free ports if England wished
it.   There should be some sort of international regulation as to the distance from the canal for capture on
the high seas, and the clause extending the principle of
the treaty to other routes might well be dropped.   Finally, "It is the fixed purpose of the United States to
consider it strictly and solely as an American question,
to be dealt with and decided by American Powers." If
these modifications were accepted Blaine would be satisfied with the treaty.[33] He proposed, in short, an entire
reconstruction of the convention of 1850.

Upon receiving Granville's note of November 10th,
Blaine wrote a third dispatch dated the twenty-ninth of
the same month. This dispatch was a summary of the
history of the Clayton-Bulwer Treaty in an attempt to
prove that it had always been a cause for friction and

[33] Blaine to Lowell, December 19, 1881, *Sen. Exec. Doc.* No. 194,
47 Cong., 1st Session. These dispatches are printed also in *U. S. Foreign Relations*, 1881.

dissatisfaction to the United States.[34] This paper is a little misleading, for Blaine failed to note that the friction was not because of the neutralization or joint guarantee clauses and that the British adjustments of territorial rights in Central America had made the situation "entirely satisfactory" to Buchanan. Blaine stopped his historical objections with 1859 and thereby laid himself open to attack.[35]

In general, it is safe to say that Blaine's three notes were plausible and well written, and that they presented existing American feeling and the developing American position with considerable accuracy, but that at nearly every point his argument was weak. In the first place he was undoubtedly mistaken in holding that a joint guarantee of the neutrality of the isthmus and the canal was a violation of the Monroe Doctrine. At least, this was an extension of the Monroe Doctrine that had never been heard of before 1860-1870. Ira D. Travis in his monograph on the history of the Clayton-Bulwer Treaty says that Blaine must have confounded the new policy regarding the canal with the United States' attitude toward the extension of European dominion in this hemisphere.[36] That does not mean that public opinion in this country was not ready and willing for the State Department to make a new extension of the

[34] *Loc. cit.*

[35] Rodrigues, *Panama Canal*, 218. "As Mr. Blaine stopped his extracts from the correspondence in December, 1858, his whole dispatch becomes of no more importance than any story that falls through before the end is reached," i. e., before Buchanan's estoppel.

[36] Travis, "The History of the Clayton-Bulwer Treaty," 214.

Monroe Doctrine that would fit this new policy but only that the Doctrine could not well be used as argument, especially since the Monroe Doctrine had never been recognized by European countries nor accepted as international law. The argument that the United States had predominant interests in any canal which might be constructed was a further extension of the Monroe Doctrine and one which was destined to be adopted by later administrations.

Blaine's argument in regard to the Pacific coast development was invalid, for British interests in the Pacific were as great as those of the United States, and the relative position had not changed since 1850. Furthermore, the doctrine that changed conditions gave cause for the abrogation of treaties was a dangerous one, unknown to international law. It was a forerunner of the day when treaties were to be "scraps of paper." His analogy of the British control of the Suez Canal zone was fallacious because that canal had been neutralized by the Treaty of Constantinople. All of these points, as well as others, were brought out by Granville's two notes (January 7 and 14, 1882).[37] The British still held firmly to the treaty and maintained that an invitation should be extended to all maritime states to accede to the guarantee. The claims put forth for the modification of the treaty because of a non-fulfillment of the implication that a canal would be built across Nicaragua by British capital were quietly disposed of by pointing to the eighth clause, which explic-

[37] *Sen. Exec. Doc.* No. 194, 47 Cong., 1st Session.

itly extended the principle of the treaty to any other route that might be chosen.

The controversy was continued under Frelinghuysen during 1882 and 1883 with few new arguments on the American side. There were more pointed discussions of the Monroe Doctrine and accusations that Great Britain had violated the treaty in extending her position in Honduras, but Granville closed the dispute at the end of 1883 with no change in the treaty status.[38] Great Britain had had the best of the argument all the way through because she had behind her the firm wall of the treaty, which had been accepted for thirty years. There was no way out except by abrogation, and that step the United States was not willing to take.[39]

The Arthur administration attempted to accomplish its purpose and carry out the policy which, it felt, American interest demanded, by an act which practically repudiated the treaty without any announcement of its abrogation. Secretary Frelinghuysen negotiated a treaty with Nicaragua, which gave the United States the most liberal concessions for the construction of a canal to be built, owned, and exclusively controlled by the Government of the United States.[40] This was in

[38] *Sen. Exec. Doc.* No. 26, 48 Cong., 1st Session, contains all the correspondence to November 22, 1883. All the correspondence is collected in *Sen. Exec. Documents* Nos. 161 and 237, 56 Cong., 1st Session, Serial No. 3853.

[39] The discussion of the argument on both sides of the question is very detailed in Lawrence, *Essays on Some Disputed Questions in Modern International Law.*

[40] Frelinghuysen-Zavala Treaty, communicated to the Senate, De-

effect the establishment of a protectorate over Nicaragua and was a step far in advance of any which Mr. Blaine had given any evidence of willingness or desire to take.   The treaty was still before a Senate which, however much the policy appealed to that body, was concerned with the view which would be held by Great Britain, when the Arthur administration went out of office.   President Cleveland withdrew the treaty from the Senate and in his annual message in December, 1885, stated that he disapproved the policy, which was one of "entangling alliances" as well as one in contravention of our existing obligations.[41]

The policy which Secretary Blaine had advocated, the dissolution of the Clayton-Bulwer Treaty by mutual agreement and the construction of a canal under American control, was not to be vindicated and carried out until the beginning of the new century when the negotiation of the Hay-Pauncefote Treaty cleared the way.[42]

cember 10, 1884, and published in the New York papers, December 18. Arthur's message is in Richardson, VIII, 256 and the text of the treaty may be found in *The Interoceanic Canal of Nicaragua*, Appendix 5.

[41] Richardson, *Messages and Papers*, VIII, 327.

[42] Whether or not Secretary Blaine would have been able to secure the mutual abrogation of the treaty with Great Britain had he used a different method of approach and other arguments is a question which cannot, of course, be solved.   There is evidence, however, that while Lord Granville expressed the sentiments of the Prime Minister and of many Englishmen, there were prominent members of the Liberal party and of the Government who did not share that point of view.   Sir Charles Dilke (Gwynn and Tuckwell, *Life of Sir Charles Dilke*, 409) quotes from a letter from Mr. Gladstone, "I am glad Gambetta says that he is in the same boat with us in Panama. Our safety there will be in acting as if charged with the interests of the world minus Amer-

Mr. Blaine had not been able to accomplish the result he desired.   His arguments and tactics had at times been faulty, but he had prevented the abrogation of the Treaty of 1846 by Colombia and had stopped any

ica." Sir Charles comments: "This was a curious example of the world of illusions in which Mr. Gladstone lives. The Americans had informed us that they did not intend to be any longer bound by the Clayton-Bulwer treaty, and that in the event of the completion of the Panama canal they intended virtually to keep it in their own hands. Mr. Gladstone called in France in joint protest with us against this view, although he might have foreseen the utter impossibility in the long run of resisting American pretensions on such a point, and although he himself would have been the first, when the Americans threatened war (as they would have done later on), to yield to argument. It amused Harcourt, however, to concoct with the chancellor and Foreign Office portentous dispatches to Mr. Blaine, in which he lectured the Americans on the permanency of their obligation. How childish it all was! Moreover, the Monroe doctrine suits our interests."

Some time later (*Forum*, January, 1899), Dilke stated that in the discussions of 1881 Mr. Blaine disclaimed, on behalf of the United States, exclusive privilege in the passage and asserted his desire to secure its free and unrestricted benefit, both in peace and in war, to the commerce of the whole world. "That being so, there is not, and never has been, any real principle at stake." In a second article in the *Forum* (June, 1900), Sir Charles again referred to the discussion of 1881 with the statement that the attempt of Mr. Blaine in the direction of the unilateral denunciation of the treaty was dropped in consequence of joint representations by Great Britain and France in 1883. I have been unable to find any such joint note, either in printed documents or in the Archives in Washington, or any references to it in secondary accounts. It may be said, however, that Sir Charles Dilke was always well-informed and conversant with the policies and actions of his party. It is possible that the joint representation may have been informal and oral. In 1881 and 1882 Dilke was under-secretary of state for foreign affairs and, although not entirely in Gladstone's confidence, was intimately connected with the Foreign Office.

schemes for a joint guarantee in Central America. In the end his policy was to be the one adopted by an administration that was destined to meet with greater success.

CHAPTER III

CENTRAL AMERICA AND THE CARIBBEAN IN 1881

THE Garfield administration early set itself to make some definite achievement in accordance with its avowed purpose of bringing about peace and preventing future wars in this hemisphere. For many years Mr. Blaine had been interested in the trade relations of North and South America and in American shipping in general. He felt that the cultivation of friendly commercial relations with Latin America and the building up of our commercial connections with the south depended upon the existence and continuance of peaceful relations of the several Latin American States with each other.[1] This view was shared by President Garfield, and the State Department in 1881 endeavored in every way possible to induce the Spanish American States to adopt peaceful modes of adjusting their disputes.

One scheme which appealed to Blaine, as it has to many others, as conducive to such a state of peace and quiet prosperity was that of a Central American Union.

[1] Blaine, "Foreign Policy of the Garfield Administration," in *Political Discussions*, 411. For Blaine's interest in shipping and the merchant marine see Hamilton, *Blaine*, 439 ff.

The little States of Honduras, Guatemala, Nicaragua, Salvador, and Costa Rica were engaged in almost endless quarrels and petty warfare; no one of them had a stable government; and any of them would be quick prey to the depredation of any stronger power. There was, moreover, the interoceanic canal question to make the region more interesting and of more vital importance to the United States.

During the Hayes administration Mr. C. A. Logan had been sent as minister of the United States to Central America with instructions to visit all the states to which he was accredited and to endeavor to persuade them to desist from their constant quarrels and to form a confederacy such as had existed in the past. He was to promise them the aid and the encouragement of the United States in any such endeavor. His reports had been received by the State Department when Blaine came into office and gave the new Secretary an early opportunity to express himself on the subject.[2] He wrote to Mr. Logan on May 7, 1881:

It would have been a matter of great gratification if your dispatches had indicated the prospect of an early consummation

[2] Logan to Evarts, February 6, 1880, Manuscript Dispatches, Central America, Vol. 16. "He (Barrios) informed me that the States of Guatemala, Honduras and Salvador being a practical unit in government, it was the purpose to proclaim a confederation, and to take Nicaragua, *nolens volens*, into it; that he was to be the head of the federation of the four states which Costa Rica might join if she saw fit; that while he was a strong friend of the United States and would make every reasonable concession to promote the construction of a canal by an American company, he could not and would not recognize the right of a single state to decide upon a project which concerned

of such a confederation, or if you had been able to suggest some directly practical method by which the United States could aid in the establishment of a strong and settled union between the independent republics of Central America.

There is nothing which this government more earnestly desires than the prosperity of these states and our own experience has taught us that nothing will so surely develop and guarantee such prosperity as their association under one common government, combining their great resources, utilizing, in a spirit of broad patriotism, their local power and placing them before the world in the position of a strong, united, and constitutionally governed nation.

Logan was instructed to impress upon Central America the importance which the United States attached to this idea of a confederation, but he was warned to be tactful and told that it would be premature for the Government of the United States to do more than express its conviction of the wisdom of a union until it was ascertained whether the public opinion of Central America was ready to adopt the idea. Such a confederacy would stimulate such projects as the canal and would avoid the danger of international or European interference in Central America.[3]

Logan had studied the situation carefully and was

the vital interests of all in their separate capacities and greatly more so, in the character of a federation."

Logan to Evarts, April 14, 1880, Manuscript Dispatches, Central America, Vol. 16, No. 73. "My observations, thus far, lead me to believe that the time will soon arise if, indeed, it has not already come, when the United States must abandon all interest in Central America or assume an open and direct interference in their affairs."

[3] *U. S. Foreign Relations*, 1881, 102.

pessimistic over the possibility of any success. He reported that nothing except an absolute monarchy with great resources could unite these small but very particularistic states, and that lack of railroads and telegraph lines operated against any union as effectively as greater size and distances could. At present, only by coming under the protection of a powerful country would such a union be possible.[4]

There was a favorable response in but one quarter to this move toward a consolidation of Central America. President Barrios of Guatemala cherished ambitions, as president of the largest and most populous of the Central American States, to become president of such a confederation.[5] In June, 1881, Señor Ubico, the minister from Guatemala to the United States, wrote to Mr. Blaine, stating that there was much feeling in Central America on the subject of a union, that it was an accepted principle with patriots, and that when work was begun there would be cordial cooperation. He stated that the help of a foreign government was needed to accomplish the desired result without much bloodshed, and that that government could be no other than the United States. Guatemala was the only Central American State fitted to lead the undertaking, but Salvador and Honduras were friendly toward the project. He offered to negotiate a treaty with the United States in preparation for such a confederation in Cen-

[4] Logan to Blaine, May 24, 1881, *ibid.*, 105.
[5] He was in 1885 to attempt such a union unaided by any outside power. See also letters in note 2.

tral America and urged speedy action.[6] Needless to say, the rôle of promoter of the ambitions of President Barrios did not appeal to the State Department, and the idea of a confederation of Central American States was allowed to drop, although Secretary Blaine referred to it at various times as a cherished plan.[7]

If this attempt at some constructive policy which would insure peace was a failure, there were several episodes in the relations of the United States to the various Latin American States in 1881 which gave Blaine ample opportunity to express his views as to the relations of such states to each other and of the position to be taken by the United States toward any difficulties into which they might fall. Boundary disputes have always been favorite fields for discussion and causes for war among the Latin American States. Having, for the most part, been at one time provinces of one country, Spain, the inter-province boundaries were never clear or constant factors, and after independence was secured, these uncertain boundaries became fruitful sources for protracted disputes.

[6] Señor Ubico to Blaine, June 22, 1881, *ibid.*, 600.

[7] See Blaine's dispatch to Morgan, November 28, 1881, *U. S. Foreign Relations*, 1881, 816. For an excellent secondary account of this plan and of the Mexico-Guatemala boundary question see Matios Romero, "Blaine and the Boundary Question between Mexico and Guatemala," *American Geographical Society Journal*, XXIX (1897), 281-330. Romero inclines to the belief that Blaine was much more seriously influenced by Barrios' schemes than the evidence seems to show. It seems impossible to credit either Logan or Blaine with being convinced of the practicality of Barrios' plots.

The Republics of Argentine and Chile had been disturbed for years by just such a dispute over the Patagonian boundary, which became so agitated in 1880-1881 that war was threatened. In January, 1881, the United States minister to Argentine wrote his colleague in Chile proposing that they use their good offices in an attempt at settlement of the dispute. He thought that Argentine would give him a boundary line which would be accepted without war or arbitration and suggested that, if Chile would do the same, the two United States ministers might be allowed to attempt to settle the dispute. He felt sure that they could avoid a war. Some further correspondence was carried on, and an acceptable basis was reached early in June.[8]

With the initiation of this mediation, Secretary Blaine had nothing to do, but he gave it his hearty approval and took every opportunity to express the consistent attitude of the United States in favor of arbitration and the eagerness with which he welcomed the prospect of amicable settlement of such disputes. He instructed the minister to the Argentine Republic to

take especial care to create the trusting conviction on its part that the United States, whether as counseling peaceful arbitration or in the possible resort of being chosen as arbitrator would approach the question with absolute impartiality, having no bias toward either phase of the contention, and no desire for aught save the ascertainment of the right and the manifestation of justice. You should let it be distinctly seen that we do not

[8] *U. S. Foreign Relations*, 1881, 6-18.

seek the position of arbitrator, but if the offer were made, our duty to our sister republics of the distant South would forbid our declining it.[9]

Blaine received, as a result of the negotiation, one of the few marks of appreciation which came to him for his South American policy in the note of gratitude from Señor Carrié, the Argentine minister in Washington, who wrote:

. . . I deem it a high honor to inform your excellency of the grateful sentiments which are entertained by the Argentine people towards this great republic, and its worthy representatives, who have just furnished palpable evidence of the feeling of genuine friendship which is cherished by the United States for the South American republics, and of their desire for the existence among these republics of the cordial relations which should ever exist among nations having a common origin.[10]

A dispute between Guatemala and Mexico, which reached fever heat in the Garfield administration, was another case of the same sort. The origin of the dispute lay back in the days of the Spanish régime. The state of Chiapas in Mexico and Guatemala had both been parts of an old captain-generalcy. After the Spanish yoke was thrown off, Chiapas became one of the federal states of Mexico. Guatemala afterward claimed that the plebiscite which decided the matter was unfairly taken and that at least the southern province of

[9] Blaine to Osborn, June 13, 1881, *ibid.*, 6.

[10] Carrié to Blaine, July 28, 1881, *ibid.*, 15. Besides *Foreign Relations* there is correspondence in *Sen. Exec. Doc.* No. 156, 47 Cong., 1st Session, and in *House Exec. Doc.* No. 154, 48 Cong., 1st Session.

Chiapas, Soconusco, should belong to her and not to Mexico. The real bone of contention, the cause for the persistency of both sides, was the presence in Soconusco of a river which almost traversed the isthmus, with a fair harbor on the Pacific. The Guatemalan claim was extremely weak, for Mexico had been in possession for many years and had no intention of yielding any territory.[11]

Mr. Logan, the American minister to Central America, reported in May of 1881, that Mexico was apparently ready to come to an open rupture with Guatemala. President Barrios of the latter state was very unpopular outside his army and immediate circle of officials, and his government would probably collapse if a war kept him on the frontier. The new administration in Mexico hated Barrios, feared his strength, and distrusted his activity in working for a Central American confederation. Logan thought that Mexico might be planning to extend her southern boundary beyond the disputed territory, perhaps even to the extent of a protectorate over all Central America. He felt that any such attempt would be unsuccessful ultimately for the same reasons that prevented a confederation of Central American States, particularism and lack of railroads and of economic bonds of union.[12]

[11] See the long and painstakingly judicial article of Matias Romero on "Mr. Blaine and the Boundary Question between Mexico and Guatemala," *American Geographical Society Journal*, XXIX, 281 ff.
[12] Logan to Blaine, May 24, 1881. *U. S. Foreign Relations*, 1881, 104.

A few days later Mr. Logan reported that Guatemala was anxious for the aid of the United States against Mexican aggression. In the absence of instructions Logan had given evasive answers and had not encouraged too definite suggestions from Guatemala.[13] He felt that Guatemala would like to cede her claims to the disputed region to the United States to insure protection against Mexico. Pride would prevent her yielding the rather dubious claims to Mexico but would not prevent calling in a third power to share the responsibility and the dispute. Logan ended with the warning which has never failed, often as it has been repeated, to reach the attention of and stir to action any and every Secretary of State to whom it has been addressed. "All this amounts to nothing, however," he wrote, "except that when hope of assistance from the United States is abandoned, Guatemala will undoubtedly make this proposition to one of the European powers." [14] A month later he reiterated his warning in stronger terms, stating that Guatemala was determined to cede Soconusco to some third power in an attempt to stop the aggressions of Mexico.[15] He did not think that the idea had been communicated to any

[13] Romero thought that Logan was an earnest and firm friend of General Barrios. He had aided Barrios while entertaining no great hope for the success of his schemes. *American Geographical Society Journal*, XXIX, 292.

[14] Logan to Blaine, May 27, 1881, *U. S. Foreign Relations*, 1881, 106.

[15] Romero attempts at great length to prove that Mexico had no aggressive designs. If she had not, the effect was the same, for Logan and Blaine believed she had.

other power but felt that if the United States refused to help in any way that the proposition would be made elsewhere.[16]

A new administration, that of General Gonzales, had come into office in 1881 in Mexico. On June 1, before Secretary Blaine had received Mr. Logan's reports on the boundary dispute, a cordial letter had been sent to Mr. Morgan, the minister to Mexico, stating the friendly policy of the United States and expressing the desire of the Secretary of State for the furtherance of commerce and amicable relations between the two countries. The American capitalist was even then venturing into Mexico, and Mr. Blaine wished his path made smooth.[17]

[16] Logan to Blaine, June 28, 1881, *ibid.*, 109. The Manuscript Dispatches, Central America, Vol. 17, contains several additional letters dated June and July, 1881, to the same effect.

[17] Blaine to Morgan, June 1, 1881, *U. S. Foreign Relations*, 1881, 761. On June 16, Blaine sent a very long, confidential note to Morgan on the questions of trade with Mexico and the investment of capital in Mexico (Manuscript Instructions, Mexico, 1881, Blaine to Morgan, June 16, 1881). Blaine was desirous of improving relations with Mexico and of removing suspicion, and he expressed a desire that Mexico should develop the proper courts. "The result of such an assurance would not only be to give confidence to capital but would take away all occasion for that appeal to the protection of its own government which often makes foreign capital an embarrassment rather than a help to the government that encourages its investment. A sense of the vexatious nature of such embarrassments may at times lead to the adoption of measures for averting them which defeat their own ends." Blaine deplored Mexican limitations on capital and commerce and gave a long discussion of the restrictions:

"I have assumed, and taken unqualified pleasure in assuming, that the government of Mexico has acquired a stability hitherto unknown.

Later in the same month, however, came the news from Guatemala which brought a shadow over those relations with Mexico, which were to have been made so amicable. Señor Ubico, the Guatemalan minister to the United States, appealed to the United States for aid, stating that "all peaceful means of conciliation appearing to be exhausted, my government sees no resource left but to appeal to that of the United States as the natural protector of the integrity of the Central American territory." [18]

This appeal gave to Mr. Blaine an excellent opportunity for the expression of his policy in respect to the relation of Latin American States to each other and of the United States to them all. He used practically the same words in a dispatch written on the same day and sent to Morgan for transmission to the Mexican Foreign Office. The note to Ubico showed in Blaine's own

My object is that you should be able, from full knowledge of the views of this government, to impress upon the statesmen of Mexico that, above all things the United States desires to see its sister Republic still further develop into a well ordered & prosperous state. Believing that this growth will be aided by the investment of American capital and enterprise in railroads, mines and industrial undertakings in Mexico, and by the enlargement of its commerce with the United States, we desire, without undue interference with the domestic legislation of Mexico, to place the relations of the two countries upon such a footing as will most certainly foster this exchange of wealth and industry." Morgan was instructed to persuade Mexico that the United States had no desire to annex Mexican territory and no desire to acquire or extend influence for ulterior purposes. Blaine was sure Mexico would "reap a rich harvest" if the capitalists of the United States were encouraged.

[18] Ubico to Blaine, June 15, 1881, *U. S. Foreign Relations*, 1881, 598.

words precisely what he felt those relations should be:

   . . . Few subjects can more cordially commend themselves to the good judgment and sympathy of the President than the preservation of peace and friendship between the republics of Spanish America in their common interest no less than in our own.

The President does not understand that your presentation of the causes and course of the long pending disagreement with Mexico as to the respective rights or territorial limits of the two countries in the districts of Soconusco and Chiapas calls upon him for any expression of opinion as to the extent of the just jurisdiction of either. It is not the policy or the desire of this government to constitute itself the arbiter of the destinies in whole or in part, of its sister republics. It is its single aim to be the impartial friend of each and all, and to be always ready to tender frank and earnest counsel touching anything which may menace the peace and prosperity of its neighbors, and in this it conceives that it responds to its simple and natural duty as the founder and principal upholder of the true principles of liberty and a republican form of government upon the American continent.[19]

He mentioned the desire of the United States for a close union of good will among the Latin American States and stated that the responsibility for the maintenance of such an attitude rested upon all, upon strong states and weak states alike.

In the dispatch to Morgan, Mr. Blaine gave instructions that Mexico should be reminded of the danger of acts of aggression in the disputed territory before all

[19] Blaine to Ubico, June 16, 1881, *U. S. Foreign Relations*, 1881, 599.

peaceful measures had been exhausted and warned that the United States would consider it an unfriendly act toward her cherished plans for the furtherance of peace in the two Americas.[20]

Secretary Blaine, a few days later, supplemented these instructions by another dispatch caused by apprehension lest Mexico might be contemplating the eventual absorption of Central American States into the Mexican federal system.[21] This note adds one point to his Spanish American policy and bears quoting on that account. The United States, he believed, did not like to see any state depart from the American policy of the fixity of boundaries. "This is a matter touching which the now established policy of the government of the United States to refrain from territorial acquisition gives it the right to use its friendly offices in discouragement of any movement on the part of neighboring states which may tend to disturb the balance of power between them." The United States felt it a duty to exert her influence to protect the integrity of the sister republics whether the hostile movement might come from abroad or from another American State.[22]

[20] Blaine to Morgan, June 16, 1881, *ibid.*, 766. Señor Romero in the article in *American Geographical Society Journal*, XXIX, 306-307, gives a long analysis of this dispatch. He states that Blaine had accepted in entirety the views of Señor Ubico and that the dispatch was favorable to Guatemala in every way and that this partiality in Blaine's offer of arbitration was enough to cause Mexico to refuse it.

[21] The two dispatches from Logan of May 24 and 27 were received June 17.

[22] Blaine to Morgan, June 21, 1881, *U. S. Foreign Relations*, 1881, 768.

These instructions were duly followed by Mr. Morgan, and the good offices of the United States were tendered. Señor Mariscal, the Mexican foreign minister, felt that there was no need for arbitration, that the very request of Guatemala that the United States come to her aid was an act of bad faith and an insult to Mexico. He flatly refused to submit the vital question of the title to Chiapas and Soconusco to arbitration or to withdraw the Mexican troops from the disputed territory. Mexico hated Barrios and feared the plans which, it was rumored, the United States was furthering for a Central American confederation which would come under Guatemala's control.[23] In the meantime Señor Herrera, the Guatemalan minister to Mexico, was negotiating, on the side, with Mariscal, who told him that there could be no arbitration, that Mexico would go to war first, and that the United States had too strong financial interests in Mexico for her to give effective aid to Guatemala. Herrera asked if Mexico would pay an indemnity if Guatemala surrendered her claim to the disputed territory. Mariscal returned an evasive answer. Morgan wrote that Mexico had no money to buy a settlement and no intention of agreeing to an indemnity, and that she was furious with Guatemala and the United States.[24]

In September Morgan reported that a war between Mexico and Guatemala seemed imminent, that the an-

[23] Morgan to Blaine, July 12, July 19, August 11, 1881, *ibid.*, 773-791.
[24] Morgan to Blaine, August 25, 1881, *ibid.*, 801.

nual message of the Mexican president was threatening, and that Mexican troops had reached the frontier. He did not, apparently, quite approve of the policy of protecting Guatemala, for he ended his note with the statement that a long conversation with Mariscal had left him

more than ever convinced that nothing would prevent a war between the two countries unless a positive position is taken by the United States and I venture to suggest that unless the government is prepared to announce to the Mexican government that it will actively if necessary preserve the peace, it would be the part of wisdom on our side to leave the matter where it is. Negotiations on the subject will not benefit Guatemala, and you may depend upon it that what we have already done in this direction has not tended to the increasing of the cordial relations which I know it is so much your desire to cultivate with this nation.[25]

This note from Morgan, added to the repeated appeals from Guatemala, called forth an unusually forceful reply from Secretary Blaine:

"To leave the matter where it is," you must perceive, is simply impossible, for it will not remain there. The friendly relations of the United States and Mexico would certainly not be promoted by the refusal of the good offices of this government tendered in a spirit of the most cordial regard both for the interests and honor of Mexico, and suggested only by the earnest desire to prevent a war useless in its purpose, deplorable in its means, and dangerous to the best interests of all the Central American republics in its consequences.

[25] Morgan to Blaine, September 22, 1881, *ibid.*, 806.

He considered the Mexican attitude of reluctance and distrust a reflection upon the disinterestedness of the United States. He felt that a war with Mexico would be a war of annihilation for Guatemala, and that the friendly relations of the American Republics would be disturbed and the growth of "that community of purpose, and that unity of interest, upon the development of which depends the future prosperity of these countries," would be postponed. Morgan must once more assure Mexico of our impartiality and friendship and offer once more our good offices. An arbitration need not include the title to Chiapas but merely the boundary. Mexico was, of course, free to refuse, but the

government of the United States will consider a hostile demonstration against Guatemala for the avowed purpose, or with the certain result of weakening her power in such an effort, as an act not in consonance with the position and character of Mexico, not in harmony with the friendly relations existing between us, and injurious to the best interests of all the republics of this continent.[26]

This dispatch, heated in its tone, forceful in its wording, probably expressed the sincere opinion of its author on the question of the maintenance of peace in the Western Hemisphere. There may have been a selfish motive, a feeling that the United States would profit immensely by that peace, but what modern statesman has not had in the background a *tendenz*, due to the best interests of his own homeland and mistress? It

[26] Blaine to Morgan, November 28, 1881, *ibid.*, 816.

seems impossible in the face of the mass of diplomatic dispatches to various ministers of the United States abroad to doubt that Secretary Blaine was very sincere, almost painfully in earnest, in his desire that the nations of the Western Hemisphere should live together in peace and harmony, and that they should somehow manage to form a closer union and a greater community of interest.[27]

The withdrawal of Secretary Blaine from office soon after his last impassioned note to Mr. Morgan prevented him from having anything more to do with the affair, but the lines along which it was settled in the next year were probably not far from what they would have been, had there been no change in the office of Secretary of State. Mr. Frelinghuysen offered to act as umpire on the only question, the actual drawing of the boundary, which Mexico would submit to arbitration.[28] Guatemala finally consented to eliminate the difficulty over Chiapas and Soconusco by relinquishing without indemnity all claims to that region.[29] Such being the case, it was found that there was no need for arbitration, and a preliminary treaty was drawn up, which stated that Chiapas and Soconusco were to be

[27] Romero, while disapproving Mr. Blaine's course in this affair, states that the "only explanation I can find for a man of Mr. Blaine's great ability making so serious a mistake, is his very earnest desire to have arbitration take the place of war to end international disputes." *American Geographical Society Journal*, XXIX, 308.

[28] Frelinghuysen to Montúfar, June 27, 1882, *U. S. Foreign Relations*, 1882, 330.

[29] Montúfar to Frelinghuysen, July 21, 1882, *ibid.*, 330.

considered as an integral part of Mexico, and Guatemala was to claim no indemnity for them. A commission was to draw the boundary between Mexico and Guatemala. In case of disagreement over the line drawn, the President of the United States was to act as sole arbitrator.[30] In 1883 the final treaty was signed and ratified without necessity for recourse to arbitration.[31]

There is no reason for believing that Secretary Blaine would have forced any vital concessions from Mexico in behalf of Guatemala. He had no inclination to pull President Barrios' chestnuts out of the fire and was in no way blinded by the fulsome compliments and ardent appeals of the representatives of Guatemala. He was anxious for peace in Central America and for a confederation of South American States but had no intention, in the first place, of securing for Barrios a province the Guatemalan claim to which was, to say the least, very shaky, nor, in the second case, to further schemes for a confederation which would place the other Central American States, in some cases unwillingly, under the domination of Barrios and Guatemala.[32] If Guatemala had, at any time, had the intention of offering any territory, or claims to territory, to

[30] Señor Cruz to Frelinghuysen, October 14, 1882, *ibid.*, 332.

[31] *U. S. Foreign Relations*, 1883, 649 ff. (text of treaty).

[32] Before his resignation, Blaine had become convinced that Guatemala must give up all claim to title to the disputed area and that the arbitration, if arbitration there was, must be confined to the boundary question. He had, so far as can be discovered, never listened to Barrios' appeals as to the confederation.

a European power, that undesirable consummation also had been prevented.

On the other hand, if Mexico had been planning to assume an aggressive attitude in Central America with the intention of acquiring new territory to the south, of absorbing one or more of the weak Central American States, any such plans were frustrated, and she was given by the treaty only that to which she had as good, if not a better claim, than Guatemala. The rage of Mariscal and the Mexican Government generally, toward Barrios and the United States might indicate that there was some truth in the rumors that Central America was in danger. The prestige and influence of the United States, however, were not materially aided by the episode. Neither Mexico nor Guatemala was satisfied with the settlement and neither felt a deepened trust or affection for the United States.

One other boundary dispute, that of Colombia and Costa Rica, showed a slightly different phase of Mr. Blaine's policy toward Spanish America. The Chilean-Argentine settlement was probably of the variety that fitted in best with his policy and preference — both parties amicably agreeing to use the good offices of the United States to effect a quick settlement acceptable to both, with mutual good feeling throughout and sentiments of gratitude toward the United States for the services rendered. The affair of Mexico and Guatemala was not so satisfactory, for no such mutual satisfaction resulted from it, but Guatemala, at least, had appealed to the United States and asked her services as arbitrator. In the affair of Costa Rica and Colombia, however, an entirely different situation presented itself. Colombia was not friendly toward the United States because she wished the abrogation of the Treaty of 1846 and the building of the canal by De Lesseps without any interference from the United States. Intrigues against the United States carried on by the De Lesseps interests were rumored if not proved, and the anti-United States sentiments were fanned by all malcontents. Costa Rica was the most Spanish of the Central American States and the proudest. She had always looked to Europe for her trade and cultural interests and cared little for the big republic of the north. When the protracted dispute of these two states neared settlement and a treaty providing for arbitration was signed, it was not to the United States that they looked for their umpire.

In January of 1881 Logan, United States minister to Central America, reported to Secretary Evarts that he had received information that the boundary dispute between Costa Rica and Colombia was to be settled by arbitration. A treaty had been signed in December, 1880, which provided that the king of Belgium should be requested to act as arbitrator. In case he refused the trust, it should be offered to the king of Spain and in case he, also, declined, the president of the Argentine Republic was to be requested to act. Mr. Logan ended his dispatch with the words, "the selection of the arbitrator does not indicate a very favorable feeling toward the United States by the plenipotentiary of Colombia, at whose instance, as I am informed, the nominations were made." [33]

It was not until May 26, while the treaty was still awaiting acceptance by the Colombian Congress, that Secretary Blaine found time to take action upon the question. He had read the diplomatic correspondence from Central America carefully and had formulated a very definite opinion on the subject of any increase of European influence in the neighborhood of a possible interoceanic canal. His attitude is most clearly to be found in his own words. In a note to Dichman at Bogotá he wrote:

If I have rightly understood you, therefore, this contention involves the question as to whether certain portions of the littoral on both oceans, lying in the neighborhood of some of the projected interoceanic communications, belong to the State of Panama, the neutrality of which the United States of America have guaranteed by the 35th article of the Treaty of 1846 or to Costa Rica with whom our treaty relations are different.

Under these circumstances, while the Government of United States of America does not expect or claim the position of necessary arbitrator in differences between those two republics it cannot but seem strange that Colombia has not communicated to this government its intention to submit to arbitration the boundaries of the State of Panama, the territorial integrity of

[33] Logan to Evarts, January 25, 1881, *U. S. Foreign Relations*, 1881, 99. Dichman, in reporting to Blaine April 16, 1881, *ibid.*, 359, stated that ". . . it cannot be otherwise than gratifying to learn that, by the proposed treaty, . . . the danger of a breach of peace in Central America has been averted, and the anxiety in the public mind connected with that subject has been allayed."

which the United States of America have guaranteed by a treaty, the provisions of which they have been more than once called upon to execute. . . . The Government of the United States . . . thinks that its opinion both as to the character of the submission and the choice of arbitrator, should have been consulted and considered, and that it will not hold itself bound, where its rights, obligations, or interests may be concerned, by the decision of any arbitrator in whose appointment it has not been consulted, and in whose selection it has not concurred.[34]

On the same day Mr. Blaine wrote to Mr. Logan in Central America instructing him to say to the Government of Costa Rica that while the United States recognized the wisdom of settling disputes by arbitration, and while it did not pretend to be considered the only arbitrator to be chosen by Central and South American Governments, it felt that in the present case the Treaty of 1846 had given it especial interests in Colombia which entitled it to be considered when any changes were to be made in the boundaries of the State of Panama, the neutrality of which had been guaranteed by Article 35 of the treaty. He added that Costa Rica was to be informed that the United States would not hold itself bound by any decision the arbitrator might make.[35]

Costa Rica bitterly resented the interference of the United States, and the Minister of Foreign Affairs,

[34] Blaine to Dichman, May 26, 1881, *ibid.*, 356.
[35] Blaine to Logan, May 26, 1881, *ibid.*, 106.

Señor Castro, responded to Logan's unofficial [36] communication of SecretaryBlaine's viewpoint in a note, which,
though couched in language of Spanish courtliness, was,
nevertheless, a very real and direct snub. He reminded
Logan that Costa Rica was not a party to the Treaty
of 1846 between the United States and New Granada
and had never been notified of its ratification, and he
refused to discuss the arbitration treaty between Colombia and Costa Rica until Logan communicated with him
officially under definite instructions from Washington.
The correspondence was published, and the Costa
Rican newspapers at once expressed the sentiments of
the public. *El Mensajoro* of August 4, 1881, stated
that Costa Rica had been insulted by the United States,
that the Treaty of 1846 had not been signed by Costa
Rica and did not in any way apply to her. The "pre-
ponderant interests" of the United States in the region
of an interoceanic canal "could never serve as a crite-
rion in a matter of international right," and in this case
of the treaty between Colombia and Costa Rica, the
United States was not qualified, by reason of those
same interests, to act as arbiter.[37]

In the meantime, however, Mr. Blaine had taken
steps to block the carrying out of the arbitration treaty
which was about to be ratified. On May 31 he wrote
to Mr. Putnam, United States minister to Belgium,

[36] Unofficial because the United States had had no notification of the
ratification of the treaty.

[37] Titus to Blaine, August 22, 1881, with enclosures, *U. S. Foreign
Relations*, 1881, 111 ff.

mentioning that he understood that the King of Belgium was to be asked to act as umpire. He recalled Clause 35 of the Treaty of 1846 and stated that the Panama canal project had made our interest in the coaling stations off the coast important, and that the limits of Panama were a matter of direct interest to the United States. He stated that while the Government of the United States did not "claim or desire that the Republic of Costa Rica and the United States of Colombia should on all questions of difference which may arise between them seek either the advice or the arbitration of this government," still he felt that in a matter so directly touching the interests of the United States, there should have been consultation at least. Mr. Putnam was instructed to inform Belgium that the Government of the United States had interests in the region, had not been consulted in regard to the treaty, and would not hold itself bound by any decisions resulting from the arbitration.[38] In July Mr. Putnam reported that His Majesty, the King of Belgium, when officially informed of his selection as arbitrator under the treaty would decline to serve.[39] In short, Belgium had been warned off from any semblance of influence in American affairs and had quietly accepted the hint.

Mr. Blaine next proceeded to use the same tactics for the elimination of Spain as a possible arbitrator. A note similar to that sent to our representative in Brus-

[38] Blaine to Putnam, May 31, 1881, *ibid.*, 70.
[39] Putnam to Blaine, July 18, 1881, *ibid.*, 75.

sels was dispatched to Mr. Fairchild, who was to avoid anything in the nature of a protest but was to communicate to the Spanish Government the view taken by the United States whenever he learned that the King of Spain had been asked to serve as arbitrator.[40]   Mr. Fairchild found that the Spanish Government had not, as yet, been approached and knew nothing of the treaty but received assurances that, in case anything came of it, the views of the United States would be given careful consideration.[41]   He wrote again in November that in the course of a conversation with Señor Peralta, the minister of Costa Rica in Madrid, he asked if the arrangements for arbitration had been perfected.   Peralta replied that the position of the United States was a "cloud upon the project," but that he thought that a fair and friendly presentation of the whole question to the Department of State at Washington would make satisfactory arrangements possible.   Mr. Fairchild inferred that the King of Spain would hardly be pressed to act until after the arrangement with the United States had been made.[42]   The President of Costa Rica was visiting in Madrid in the fall of 1881, and undoubtedly the whole matter was gone over at the time and the Central American statesmen became convinced that no European power was inclined to serve them in any capacity in the face of the opposition of the United States.   This whole episode could not have furthered

[40] Blaine to Fairchild, June 25, 1881, *ibid.*, 1057.
[41] Fairchild to Blaine, July 22, 1881, *ibid.*, 1061.
[42] Fairchild to Blaine, November 23, 1881, *ibid.*, 1067.

Blaine's desires for amicable relations with Latin America, but he may have been comforted by the thought that neither Colombia nor Costa Rica were in a mood friendly to the United States anyway, and that, at least, he had prevented any European action.

In 1881 there occurred, also, an episode of some interest with respect to the claims of foreign nations against Venezuela. In the first half of the nineteenth century Venezuela, like many other Spanish American States, had incurred a large debt composed of various claims, loans, and all other varieties of obligations.[43] From 1860 on, the foreign nations to whom these debts were owed had made treaties with Venezuela arranging for the acknowledgment and gradual payment of the claims. France had made the first of these treaties in 1864 and by it had secured a pledge that 10 per cent of the total amount of the customs duties at four ports should be henceforth hypothecated to the reduction of the French debt. By the early seventies all the creditor nations had treaties making some sort of arrangements. In 1872 and 1873 the creditors protested because of the lack of payments, and new arrangements were made by which certain sums were allocated to each of them monthly in accordance with their respective treaty arrangements. By this agreement, France, whose share of the debt was less than half that held by Spain and not much more than half that of the United States,

[43] Called "the diplomatic debt" because the arrangements for payments were made by treaties.

received twice as much per month as either of the others.[44]

By 1879 Venezuela was failing in the payments pledged by this schedule and was anxious to make a new arrangement. She endeavored to persuade her creditors to accept 3 per cent Venezuela notes in lieu of the monthly payments derived from the customs receipts. The powers concerned refused to agree to this proposition, and on May 1, 1880, Venezuela resumed payments on a monthly basis from a certain fixed proportion of the customs receipts. By the new arrangement, however, the allocation of the money was to be made on the basis of monthly payments in proportion to the share of the total diplomatic debt held by the respective creditors. This reduced the French share from 28,275 francs to 11,637.55 francs, and greatly increased the share going to Spain, Holland, and the United States.[45] The total amount to be paid

[44] Foreign debt of Venezuela. From note of Blaine to Noyes, July 23, 1881, *U. S. Foreign Relations*, 1881, 1216.

Creditor	Total debt held (in francs)	Date of treaty	Monthly payment scheme, 1873-1880	Monthly payment scheme, May, 1880
Spain	7,704,457.64	1874	13,980	29,449.54
United States	5,847,163.32	1866	13,980	19,694.25
Holland	4,190,906.56	1866	7,220	14,115.70
France	3,455,155.60	1864	28,275	11,637.25
England	2,192,835.24	1878	10,020	7,385.84
Germany	200,000.00	1877	4,000	673.63
Denmark	161,241.16	1866	881.25	543.09

[45] See table in note 44.

by Venezuela was not materially changed by the new arrangement.[46]

France at once protested against the pro rata payments and the reduction of her monthly allotment, basing her protest upon the Treaty of 1864. She accused Venezuela of bad faith in the whole affair. In February, 1881, Secretary Evarts was requested to agree that a representative in Caracas should act as distributor of the amounts which Venezuela was to pay monthly to the foreign diplomatic creditors, the presumption being that friction would thus be avoided. He agreed so to act if an amicable arrangement could be made with the other powers, but in March, 1881, France decided to

[46] The Manuscript Dispatches of Jehu Baker, American minister to Venezuela, throw no light on the reasons for this change in allocation, which precipitated the trouble with France. The United States gained some 6,000 francs a month by the proceeding, but it appears to have been quite without any pressure put forth by Baker. He reported December 25, 1879, that he had been approached by the Venezuelan foreign minister on the question of this new scheme and had been asked if the United States would take charge of the distribution of the money. He apparently gave no reply and on January 8 wrote that the plan had been given up, due to the protests of creditor nations whose share would be reduced. For several months his dispatches were filled with complaints of the insults offered him by the Venezuelan minister, and his advice was evidently not asked on financial matters. In May he reported the initiation of the scheme but stated that he did not understand it, and Secretary Evarts wrote him on July 3, that the Department would be glad to have definite information as neither it nor Baker seemed to understand the scheme. Manuscript Dispatches, Venezuela, 1879, 1880, Nos. 187, 198, 231, 237.

There were, however, other foreign creditors who gained by the arrangement, notably Spain, who stood to make about 16,000 francs monthly by the change.

withdraw her diplomatic representative in Venezuela, "in consequence of the twenty years of bad faith observed by that government toward its creditors." France declared that she could not accept the present pro rata scheme of monthly payments, and that if Venezuela did not increase the French share, the French Government would take further steps.[47]

The Venezuela Government, through its minister of foreign affairs, at once appealed to Mr. Baker, requesting that the United States use its good offices to prevent aggressive action on the part of France.[48] Early in April, Baker sent to Blaine a statement of what, in his opinion, would be the best settlement of the matter. He thought that Venezuela ought to pay the full amount set apart by her own laws for the payment of the foreign debt, "13 per cent of 40 unities of her custom-house revenue." In the existing financial condition of Venezuela, she could do no more. The money thus paid should be distributed pro rata as by the law of May 1, 1880. He recommended that the United States should use all influence to harmonize Venezuela and France and apprehended no protest from any other of the creditor nations.[49]

France suspended all diplomatic relations with Venezuela, and the Venezuelan minister to France called upon Mr. Noyes, the American minister, to assume

[47] Señor Comacho to Blaine, March 22, 1881, *U. S. Foreign Relations*, 1881, 1202.

[48] Baker to Blaine, March 23, 1881, *ibid.*, 1202.

[49] Baker to Blaine, April 6, 1881, *U. S. Foreign Relations*, 1881, 1206.

protection of the Venezuelan subjects in France.[50] Secretary Blaine's acceptance of this obligation was undoubtedly a mere formality, but it was followed by a telegram which meant much more in the way of aid to poor, trembling Venezuela.[51] It stated that Venezuela had requested the United States to receive and disburse as trustees the sums designed for the payments on her debt, and that if the United States should consent, it would be without any guarantee of any part of the Venezuelan debt. The United States requested France to delay action in regard to her debt controversy while the former Government had this proposition under consideration. Mr. Noyes was to state that the United States offered its good offices in the French-Venezuelan dispute.[52] This telegram was followed by a long note to Mr. Noyes for communication to the French Government, containing much information about the Venezuela debt. After a long discussion of the history of the Venezuelan claims, he stated that he could not see that the fact that France had a prior settlement gave her any better claim upon the Venezuelan customs, and that the United States must insist upon the pro rata settlement. He ended with the suggestion that the United States

place an agent in Caracas authorized to receive said amount pro rata to the several creditor nations. Should the Venezuelan government default for more than three months in the regular

[50] Manuscript Dispatches, France, Vol. 88, No. 469.
[51] Manuscript Instructions, 1881, France. Blaine to Noyes, May 6.
[52] Blaine to Noyes, May 5, 1881, *U. S. Foreign Relations*, 1881, 1211.

installments, then the agent placed there by the United States and acting as the trustee for the creditor nations should be authorized to take charge of the customs houses at Laguayra and Puerto Cabello, and reserve from the monthly receipts a sufficient sum to pay the stipulated amounts, with a 10% additional, handing over to the authorized agents of the Venezuelan government all the remainder collected.[53]

In the meantime, there were rumors in Venezuela that France was planning by September or October to blockade the Venezuelan ports and take possession of the customs houses. The Venezuelan Government complained to Blaine that that would be "naught else but an *occupation of American territory* by a European state." [54]   Baker wrote hoping that the negotiations with France would speedily reach a satisfactory conclusion.   If, however, they should not, he felt that the United States should take occasion to cause the French Government to understand that any aggressive action on her part would be viewed with concern by the United States.[55] He reported, also, that he had learned through the English chargé d'affaires that on May 10 the English Government proposed to the French that a conference be called of representatives of Venezuela, Great Britain, and France to make a new settlement of the claims.   This proposal was refused by the French Government.[56]

[53] Blaine to Noyes, July 23, 1881, *ibid.,* 1216.

[54] Señor Seijas to Señor Comacho, June 27, 1881, *ibid.,* 1213, presented July 14.

[55] Baker to Blaine, July 13, 1881, *ibid.,* 1215.

[56] *Ibid.,* Great Britain's share of the proceeds of the customs had been cut in 1880 about 3,000 francs monthly. See note 44, p. 72.

France received the propositions of the United States in a noncommittal manner, expressed interest, appreciation of the position of the United States, and kind regards for the Government, but did not accept the tender of good offices.[57] In answer to Secretary Blaine's dispatch of July 23, M. Saint Hilaire stated that France based her claim to peculiar treatment not upon priority of settlement but upon the clause of that settlement which hypothecated to her 10 per cent of the customs receipts of four ports. He wrote that the practice of the Venezuelan Government in disregarding its treaty obligations was the real cause of the French attitude, and that until Venezuela changed that purpose, France could not resume diplomatic relations. "We are, however, none the less sensible to the evidences of good will shown to us by the government of the United States, in endeavoring to devise the bases of an acceptable arrangement and we have never had an idea of forestalling the effect of its good offices by any premature action." [58]

The last note of Mr. Blaine's on the subject was dated December 16 and was a dispatch to Morton. In it Blaine protested against the refusal of the French Government to resume relations with Venezuela as long as the treaty of 1864 was disregarded. He stated that the observance of that treaty would work an injustice to the other creditor nations, and that in private law one debt was as valid as another, and no debtor had a right

[57] Morton to Blaine, August 23, 1881, *U. S. Foreign Relations*, 1881, 1223.

[58] St. Hilaire to Morton, September 15, 1881, *ibid.*, 1225.

to make special arrangements with one creditor to the disadvantage of other creditors.[59] The note ended with this statement:

> Beyond and above the pecuniary interest involved, either for France or the United States, in the matter of the Venezuela claims, there lies a consideration which appeals with equal force to the two leading republics — France and the United States. That consideration is the fraternity of feeling and the harmony of relations which should be maintained between all the republics of the world.[60]

It was not, he said, a question of debt repudiation on the part of Venezuela but merely of the payment of all nations at the same ratio. The anxiety of the United States was not because of its pecuniary interests, but because of a desire to avoid hostilities between France and Venezuela. It is, however, difficult to forget that the United States was the gainer by the new financial arrangement and France the loser.[61]

Secretary Blaine's resignation prevented his carrying through this little episode in Venezuelan history, but he had prevented the proposed aggressive action of

[59] When the question of Venezuelan debts came up before the Hague Tribunal in 1903 the Tribunal's award gave a priority of treatment to the blockading powers. It was conceded that the law of nations afforded no clear rule on the subject and the decision has been looked upon by many critics as an unwise one. See the Venezuelan Arbitration of 1903, the final report of W. L. Penfield, *Sen. Exec. Doc.* No. 119, 58 Cong., 3rd Session, Serial No. 4769.

[60] Blaine to Morton, December 16, 1881, *U. S. Foreign Relations*, 1881, 1228.

[61] The United States advanced from 13,980 to 19,694 francs monthly while France went back from 28,275 to 11,637 francs.

France. He had substituted for the principle of European self-help in Latin American relations, the new principle of the intervention of the United States to see that the weaker sister republics lived up to their financial obligations in return for protection from the United States to prevent action from abroad. His plan for the control of Venezuelan customs by the United States and the payment of the creditors by the customs receipts was little short of prophetic. Here again was the Monroe Doctrine extended and an example shown, to be followed in later years by other executive officers of the United States. In this and in other incidents Secretary Blaine initiated a policy in the Caribbean which anticipated the establishment of protectorates of the United States in that region. Economic penetration and its resultant political action are clearly foreseen as early as 1881.

CHAPTER IV

CENTRAL AMERICA AND THE CARIBBEAN, 1889-1892

THE second period when James G. Blaine was Secretary of State was much longer than the first but, strangely enough, seemed far less productive of opportunity for him to give definite expression to his American policy. In 1881 there had been four boundary disputes between various Latin American powers in attempting the settlement of which Mr. Blaine had found occasion to explain his position in regard to the relations of the American States to each other and, individually and collectively, to European States. The period from 1889-1892 contains but one episode of any importance to indicate that the Blaine interpretation of the Monroe Doctrine had not changed in the intervening ten years, and that his American policy had, if anything, advanced.

It is not necessary here to enter into the long and complicated history of the dispute between Great Britain and Venezuela over the boundary line between British Guiana and Venezuela. The dispute started in 1814 when Great Britain acquired the old Dutch claims in the disputed area. From then on, both parties at times made extravagant claims, and neither for many years was willing to make a compromise or moderate settlement. In 1881, after slumbering for many years, the dispute was revived, and Venezuela's proposal of arbitration opened a new phase of the question. This proposal was ignored by Great Britain and, when renewed in 1884, was met by a refusal to submit the difficulty to arbitration. In the meantime, by peaceful penetration, British subjects were advancing into the disputed territory and settling there under the jurisdiction of the colony of Guiana. The discovery of valuable ores and other products made the region of more importance, and in accordance with British traditional policy, it was apparent that time was working with the Empire in the acquisition of territory. Great Britain was not at all anxious to hurry the settlement of the dispute. There were some slight efforts made toward settlement in the years immediately following the refusal to arbitrate, and in 1887 the Venezuelan secretary of state distinctly demanded the evacuation of the disputed territory and stated that unless such evacuation should be made and accompanied by an acceptance of arbitration by February, 1887, all diplomatic relations between the two countries would cease. Great Britain paid little attention to these demands, and on February 20 the Venezuelan minister was recalled from London.[1] This diplomatic rupture continued until the final settlement of the dispute in 1897.

[1] There is a mass of material upon the Venezuelan dispute. For this brief sketch of the situation to 1887 see Grover Cleveland's *Presidential Problems*, "The Venezuelan Boundary Controversy," and

The United States had for many years paid little attention to the controversy. Venezuela was so torn by internal disputes, poverty, and revolutions that her affairs seemed hopelessly tangled. The British advance was slow and quiet and into a region in which the United States had few interests. In the eighties some interest was aroused, and in 1887 Secretary Bayard made a formal offer of mediation and arbitration. Salisbury declined this offer on the ground that the attitude of Venezuela was such that Great Britain was prevented from entering any arbitration agreement.

So the matter stood when Blaine came into office in 1889. In November of that year Venezuela solicited the good offices of the United States to the end that diplomatic relations between Great Britain and Venezuela be restored and the disputed boundary be settled by arbitration.[2] General Guzman Blanco, with whom Great Britain had persistently refused to deal, was no longer in office, and Venezuela wished the aid of the United States in securing the reception in England of a special agent of Venezuela. The colonial governor of British Guiana in December, 1889, took possession of the principal mouth of the Orinoco River, and the Venezuela Government protested and appealed again for the good offices of the United States.[3] Secretary Blaine

Henry James, *Richard Olney and His Public Services*. For a very fair statement of the factors influencing British action see James, *Olney*, 98-99.

[2] Scruggs to Blaine, November 12 and November 16, 1889. Manuscript Dispatches, Venezuela, Vol. 39.

[3] Scruggs to Blaine, December 21, 1889, *U. S. Foreign Relations*, 1891, 776.

responded by a telegram instructing Mr. White, chargé of the United States in Great Britain, to confer with Lord Salisbury concerning the re-establishment of diplomatic relations between Great Britain and Venezuela upon the basis of a temporary restoration of the *status quo*.[4]

No immediate reply was received to this tender of good offices, and Venezuela made repeated appeals to Blaine for aid in preventing further advances on the part of Great Britain and in bringing about a settlement of the existing dispute. Señor Peraza, the Venezuelan minister to the United States, wrote Blaine that:

The government of Venezuela is unwilling to abandon the hope which it bases upon the sincere friendship of the United States, that the latter will request Great Britain to consent to submit its dispute with Venezuela to arbitration and it has consequently instructed me with a view to bringing about this result, to beg your Excellency with redoubled earnestness to lend the good offices of the United States government which is now more than ever the only source from which Venezuela can hope for assistance since the nations of Europe, feeling irritated at the attitude which has been taken by the republics of South and Central America with the design of drawing closer their commercial relations with the United States, will not be willing to give any support to Venezuela . . . in consequence of the commercial and fraternal union with this Republic which is now being established through the International American Conference.[5]

[4] Blaine to White, December 30, 1889, *ibid.*, 322.
[5] Peraza to Blaine, February 17, 1890, *U. S. Foreign Relations*, 1891, 782 ff.

In April Señor Peraza informed Mr. Blaine that
Señor Urbaneja, the minister of Venezuela to France,
had gone to London to endeavor to secure the restoration of diplomatic intercourse. His efforts were blocked
because of the fact that Mr. Lincoln had received no
instructions to aid him. Peraza reminded Blaine of
the promise made to him that when the International
American Conference should adopt the plan of arbitration for the settlement of disputes, the United States
would make representations to Great Britain in behalf
of Venezuela. Peraza hoped that the United States
would now tender its good offices.[6]

Moved by this and other appeals, Mr. Blaine telegraphed to Lincoln on May 1 to use his good offices
with Lord Salisbury to bring about the resumption of
diplomatic intercourse as a preliminary step toward the
settlement of the boundary dispute by arbitration. Lincoln was also instructed to propose to Lord Salisbury
that an informal conference be held in Washington or
in London by the representatives of the three powers.
In such a conference the position of the United States
would be solely one of "impartial friendship to both
litigants." [7] Lord Salisbury, in answering Lincoln's
note, embodying the Secretary of State's instructions,
stated that the termination of diplomatic relations had
been an act of the Venezuelan Government, and he
intimated that Venezuelan Governments were often
unstable and difficult to deal with. He asserted, how-

[6] Peraza to Blaine, April 24, 1890, *ibid.*, 784.
[7] Blaine to Lincoln, May 1, 1890, *ibid.*, 337.

ever, that Great Britain was ready for friendly intercourse and was ready to abandon some claims to territory and would arbitrate others but would not arbitrate
where she believed the rights claimed admitted no reasonable doubt.[8]

Mr. Scruggs, the United States minister to Venezuela, was, in the meantime, collecting much material
on the dispute, which he forwarded to Blaine. All of
Scruggs's reports were sent to Lincoln, and vice versa.
Secretary Blaine may have formed some opinion as to
the merits of the case, but officially his conduct was
impartial and irreproachable. He wrote to Lincoln on
May 6 that it was desired that

you shall do all that you can consistently with an attitude
of impartial friendliness to induce some accord between the
contestants by which the merits of the controversy may be fairly
ascertained and the rights of each party justly confirmed. The
neutral position of this government does not comport with any
expression of opinion on the part of this department as to what
these rights are, but it is evident that the shifting footing on
which the British boundary question has rested for several years
is an obstacle to such a correct appreciation of the nature and
grounds of her claims as would alone warrant the formation of
any opinion.[9]

In a later note he stated that, "as the essential elements
of the determination of the problems are matters of
record, there should be no difficulty in reaching a just
conclusion on the merits, and, in the expectation of such

[8] Salisbury to Lincoln, May 26, 1890, *ibid.*, 340-341.
[9] Blaine to Lincoln, May 6, 1890, *ibid.*, 339.

a result, it is proper to refrain from any pre-judgment of opinion on the merits of the British contention." [10]

In June Señor Pulido reached London as the Venezuelan confidential agent, and Lincoln presented him to Lord Salisbury. Nothing came of whatever negotiations were thereupon set in progress, and Salisbury made no response to Blaine's suggestion of a conference upon Venezuelan affairs. Great Britain obviously was in no hurry and made no effort to advance the settlement of the dispute. Each additional year saw more extensive British settlement, and the unsettled political condition of Venezuela made negotiation seem futile. Furthermore, in much of the territory, Great Britain felt that its claims were not disputable.

Secretary Blaine had gained nothing by his first move in behalf of Venezuela. He was, moreover, engaged in a more pressing diplomatic controversy with Lord Salisbury on the question of the protection of the Alaskan seal herd, but he did not forget the cause of Venezuela nor neglect an opportunity to further it. In a long confidential note to Mr. Scruggs, dated more than a year later, he went into the subject in detail and expressed himself fully. It is well worth quoting in full:

In addition to the official instructions which you have received, there is one subject upon which I desire to communicate to you in a confidential manner the views and wishes of the President. As you are aware from your knowledge of the correspondence of the Department of State the government of the

[10] Blaine to Lincoln, May 26, 1890, *ibid.*, 340.

United States has been neither a disinterested nor a passive spectator of the continuous, and persistent advances of Great Britain upon the territory of Venezuela bordering on the British colony of Guiana. At the inception of the controversy it was deemed the wiser policy of the United States, concurred in by Venezuela, to maintain such an attitude as would not disqualify this government from accepting the functions of an arbitrator between Great Britain and Venezuela. As time progressed and events developed, it became apparent that the United States could no longer maintain that attitude and its position was changed to one of direct interposition between the disputant powers with a view to bring them to a friendly accord and settlement of the boundary question. It was with this object that our Minister to London, Mr. Lincoln, was instructed to cooperate with Señor Pulido and other representatives or agents of Venezuela, in seeking by impartial friendship to both parties to bring about arbitration upon an equitable basis with Great Britain.

But it is now apparent that all such efforts in the future, as they have been in the past, are likely to prove unavailing. Meanwhile the reports which you and the Minister of Venezuela in Washington have communicated to the Department go to show that Great Britain continues to enlarge its pretensions and extend its occupation within the domain of Venezuela.

In the presence of these facts, the President has reached the conclusion, that, by reason of the appeals which Venezuela has made to the United States and of the latter's interest in sustaining republican institutions on the American continents, unembarrassed by the encroachments and menace of European monarchies, this government should at an early day take an advanced and decisive step in support of the claims of Venezuela to the territory which Great Britain has, in spite of repeated remonstrances and protest, entered upon, appropriated and fortified.

He, therefore, desires that you should put yourself in confidential communication with the Minister of Foreign Affairs on this subject, and assure him of the readiness of the United States to enter with his government upon joint or concurrent diplomatic action towards Great Britain with a view to reaching a just and honorable settlement of the boundary dispute with as much promptness as the gravity of the question will permit.

In order to make this action effective it is regarded as essential that the government of Venezuela should agree to take no step in the negotiations or in its political relations towards Great Britain and the colony of British Guiana affecting this subject, without the previous knowledge and concurrence of the United States. It will be evident to the Minister of Foreign Affairs that only by harmony of views and unity of action on the part of the two Republics can they hope for success and it is not doubted that he will readily give you this assurance. Should you find the Minister in accord with the policy initiated in this letter, you can say to him that I hold myself in readiness to consider with him, either through you or the Venezuelan Minister in this city, the time and method of negotiations best adapted to secure satisfactory action on the part of Great Britain.[11]

Nothing seems to have been done on either side to follow up this very frank and illuminating letter from Mr. Blaine. He was, apparently, willing to go as far in furthering the Venezuelan cause as Secretary Olney did some four years later and might well have made the same extension of the Monroe Doctrine, by applying its prohibition to the aggrandizement of European col-

[11] Blaine to Scruggs, October 28, 1891. Manuscript Instructions, Venezuela, 1891. After this note there was no other instruction sent Scruggs until August, 1892.

onies in the Western Hemisphere whose founding ante-dated the Doctrine itself. President Harrison's message of December 9, 1891, contained a reference to the matter, expressing regret that friendly efforts had thus far proved unavailing. He stated that "this government will continue to express its concern at any appearance of foreign encroachment on territories long under the administrative control of American States," and hoped for a settlement of the dispute.[12]

It is not difficult to ascertain why Mr. Blaine did not follow up his note of October 28. He remained in office only seven months longer, and those months were filled with other matters of more immediate interest to the United States. In February of 1892 the treaty was signed which committed the long disputed question of the fur seals to arbitration, and it may have been that Blaine did not wish to disturb the amicable relations with Great Britain which were thus obtained. His own health was steadily failing, and he had determined upon his retirement from office. He may, therefore, have refrained from initiating a controversy which would devolve upon his successor to carry on. The relations between Secretary Blaine and President Harrison became very strained in the spring of 1892, and the presidential nominating convention and the campaign were

[12] *U. S. Foreign Relations*, 1891, IV. It may well have been that Mr. Blaine's willingness to bring pressure to bear upon Great Britain in this matter was due, in part, to a desire to use a convenient weapon to force concessions in the fur seals controversy. It is true, however, that Mr. Blaine's constant interest in Latin America would doubtless have proved sufficient cause for action.

matters of supreme importance. Blaine may well have felt that 1892 was, for any or all of these reasons, not the suitable year for the opening of such an important diplomatic question with Great Britain.

The interest of Secretary Blaine in the Caribbean was not confined to Venezuela. His American policy contemplated, from the beginning, the possibility of acquiring one or more coaling stations in the Caribbean or on the Central or South American coast. During his first term as Secretary of State no definite steps were taken in that direction, but there is evidence that only the brevity of his tenure of office prevented such action. General Hurlbut, sent as United States minister to Peru in 1881, made an attempt to obtain a harbor and a nearby coal mine from Peru, then prostrate because of defeats in the war with Chile. Mr. Blaine immediately and quite correctly repudiated this concession as being, under the circumstances, too much in the nature of a grant, if not forced, at least made in hope of aid which might be given Peru in return by the powerful recipient of the concession. In the same year Blaine sent George Earle Church on a special mission to Ecuador to investigate and report upon the condition of men and affairs in that little state.[13] Other such investigators may have been sent out. Whether their reports would have led Mr. Blaine to negotiate for coaling stations or other concessions is not, of course, ascertainable, but they

[13] Manuscript Report of George Earle Church, in the Archives of the Department of State. See note, p. 121. It was not possible to find other reports in the Archives of the Department of State.

serve to illustrate the keenness of his interest in all aspects of the American situation.

When Blaine became Secretary once more in 1889 an opportunity was at hand for a decisive move toward the acquisition, by lease or cession, of the desired Caribbean harbor and coaling station. The opportunity with all of its rather unsavory implications was created by the preceding administration. Mr. Blaine cannot be considered responsible for the policy of interference in the confused tangle of interests which were concerned in the Haitian Revolution of 1888-1889, but there is no denying the fact that he took all possible advantage of the work of his predecessor in his attempt in 1891 to secure a lease of the harbor of the Môle St. Nicholas.

In August of 1888 the government of President Salomon was overthrown as a result of his attempt to modify the constitution and obtain his own reëlection for a second seven-year term. President Salomon resigned and anarchy ensued. One faction of revolutionists held the northern half of the island republic and another the southern. A provisional government under General Légitime was set up in the south. The northern faction in opposition to the provisional government apparently had the support of the United States minister, Mr. Thompson, and the United States refused to recognize the government of Légitime even though France, England, Italy, and Portugal had done so. There was a rumor that Légitime had promised the Môle St. Nicholas to France, which may or may not have influenced Secretary Bayard. At any rate the non-recognition of Légitime was considered one cause of the prolongation of the struggle.   Since the provisional government had not been recognized, the United States courts held that the neutrality laws could not apply, and New York became an actual base for the northern faction from which arms and supplies were shipped to Haiti.   The United States Navy sent several war ships to Haitian waters to secure free access and egress for American ships, for non-recognition meant that the blockade announced by the Légitime faction had no legal existence.   Under cover of this protection by the United States Navy, aid for the insurgents undoubtedly entered Haiti.[14] The whole imbroglio ended in December of 1889 when Hyppolite, the leader of the northern faction, came into power after subduing the other faction and going through the farce of a free election. He was at once recognized by the Harrison administration, and his representative, Mr. Hannibal Price, was received by Mr. Blaine. The sequel to this affair was the attempt on the part of the United States to secure a lease of the harbor of the Môle St. Nicholas.[15]

[14] The case of the "Haitian Republic" is a case in point. See *Sen. Exec. Doc.* No. 69, 5ᴏ Cong., 2nd Session. Also *U. S. Foreign Relations*, 1888, 932 ff., and 1889, 487 ff. This vessel landed men and supplies.

[15] It has been very difficult to arrive at any definite conclusion as to the extent of the aid given Hyppolite by the United States and as to the pledges given by Hyppolite as payment for that aid. The fact of such a bargain, however, seems obvious. The above account is based upon a study of the Manuscript Notes from the Haitian Embassy in Washington, Vol. 5, for the years 1888-1889, especially one entitled "A Statement as to the Diplomatic Relations of the United States with

The Hyppolite Government was allowed to establish itself in office, and time was given for Haitian affairs to settle down before Mr. Blaine made any move to seek concessions. Frederick Douglass, a negro of considerable culture and ability, was sent to Haiti as United States minister. His oral instructions had, apparently, contained reference to a coaling station, for early in January, 1891, he wrote to Blaine a confidential report of an interview in which he had sounded Mr. Firmin, the Haitian secretary of foreign affairs, upon the subject. Firmin, it seemed, had brought the subject up himself in making a denial of the statement in the New York *Sun* that President Hyppolite had promised to cede the Môle St. Nicholas to the United States. Douglass had been noncommittal on that point but had stated that he felt authorized to say that the Government of the United States would be very willing to acquire by lease, rent, or purchase such a coaling station at the Môle. Douglass reported that he did not feel at all sanguine that the project would be favorably received since "there is perhaps no one point upon which the people of Haiti are more sensitive, superstitious and excited than upon any question touching the cession of any part of their territory to any foreign power." [16] Douglass himself was apparently honestly

the Republic of Haiti from August, 1888, to March, 1889," drawn up by Stephen Preston, the Haitian minister to the United States. The best secondary account of the revolution is a brief statement in G. H. Stuart's *Latin America and the United States*, 216-217.

[16] Douglass to Blaine, January 5, 1891, Manuscript Dispatches, Haiti, Vol. 25, No. 104.

convinced that the coaling station would be of mutual benefit and was willing and anxious to work for it.

Secretary Blaine had, a few days prior to this interview, initiated the movement toward the acquisition of the coaling station by appointing Admiral Gherardi special envoy to Haiti with instructions to cooperate with Douglass for the purpose of acquiring a coaling station for the United States in West Indian waters. Since the Haitian constitution prohibited the alienation of territory, Gherardi was to ask for a lease of the Môle St. Nicholas. He was to stress the advantages to both parties in such a lease:

> The President assumes that the government of Haiti must at once recognize the advantage and the great protection which the presence of a part of the navy of the United States will afford to the Haytian Republic. It will be equivalent to a guaranty of the autonomy and independence of the Haytian government without any treaty relations which might appear as a subordination of the one Republic to the other.

Gherardi was to insist that, in case Haiti consented to the lease, there should be a clause stating that similar ports and privileges should not be granted to any other "power, state or government." [17]

Admiral Gherardi arrived at Port au Prince on January 25 and negotiations were at once set in motion. It is a significant fact that it was Admiral Gherardi who had been in charge of the war ships in Haitian waters in 1888-1889 when the aid, whatever it may have been,

[17] Blaine to Gherardi, January 1, 1891, Manuscript Instructions, Haiti.

which was accorded the Hyppolite faction was given. Minister Douglass and Admiral Gherardi met President Hyppolite and his foreign minister on January 28. Douglass emphasized the advantages to Haiti of such a lease and the fact that the traditional prejudice of Haiti toward the outside world no longer had a reasonable basis for existence.[18] In this first interview Gherardi laid emphasis upon the terms offered by the Hypolite faction to the United States early in 1889 when the lease had been pledged in return for aid which the United States subsequently gave. Gherardi stated that the United States now looked to Haiti to fulfill her part of the agreement.[19] Firmin asked if Gherardi demanded the lease as a fulfillment of a treaty or requested it as a concession from a friendly nation. Gherardi stated that the United States was willing to look upon it as a concession but did not surrender its right to

[18] Douglass to Blaine, January 29, 1891, Manuscript Dispatches, Haiti, Vol. 25, No. 123. Douglass' view of the whole affair may be obtained also from his article entitled, "Haiti and the United States: Inside History of the Negotiations for the Môle St. Nicholas," which appeared in the *North American Review*, September, 1891. This article is the only account in print of the episode which I have been able to discover. The very brief account in Stuart, *Latin America and the United States*, is based on the Douglass article.

[19] Gherardi to Blaine, January 31, 1891, Manuscript Dispatches, Haiti, Vol. 25. Gherardi was perfectly outspoken and specific in respect to this "bargain." It was made by Mr. Élie, an accredited agent of the Hyppolite faction in the United States in 1889. Gherardi referred to a *Résumé* drawn up by Élie and the State Department which I have been unable to find. Preston's notes of 1888-9 refer to the presence of Élie in the United States, and it may well be that some such document existed.

demand it in fulfillment of conditions under which services had been rendered.[20] Mr. Firmin said that the
granting of the lease would cause the fall of the Hyppolite Government or of any Government. He admitted that if the Môle were seized by the United States,
the Haitian Government and people would probably do
nothing, but he did not expect the United States to act
in so high-handed a way. Gherardi reported that the
interview was cordial, but that he did not expect successful results. The President and Mr. Firmin were
not disposed to accept the proposition nor to show any
feeling of obligation to the United States.[21]

Admiral Gherardi had another interview with Mr.
Firmin on February 2 in which Firmin referred to his
fear lest any such lease cause his Government to fall.
Gherardi told him that he would pledge the strong
support of the United States if necessary to keep the
Government of Hyppolite seated. He also suggested
to Blaine that in case of final refusal, he be authorized
to seize the Môle. Such an act, Gherardi believed,
would relieve the Haitian Government of responsibility
and render easy negotiations based on a *fait accompli*.[22]

The Haitian Government thereupon played for time.
On February 16 Mr. Firmin found some fault with

[20] *Loc. cit.*
[21] *Ibid.*
[22] Gherardi to Blaine, February 9, 1891, Manuscript Dispatches,
Haiti, Vol. 25. It is a pretty proposal indeed — that the United States
use force to maintain in power a government which she had assisted
into office in return for a promise to grant concessions known to be
looked upon askance by the Haitian people, and second, if that were

Gherardi's credentials, and the latter cabled for full powers to treat. Blaine telegraphed that full authority would be sent him at once. When the formal credentials arrived, Gherardi on April 18 had an interview with Firmin, making a formal offer for the Môle; and a few days later Haiti returned a formal refusal of that offer. Hyppolite had apparently spent the interval in feeling the public pulse and had decided that the pledge made as leader of an insurgent faction should not be allowed to cause the fall of the president of the Republic of Haiti. He flatly denied that the lease of the Môle had ever been promised and stated that it could not now be granted because it would cause the Government to appear to be yielding to pressure.[23] That Hyppolite was correct in his diagnosis of the public opinion in Haiti was shown by the burst of excitement when rumors of the negotiation were bruited about the capital. He then announced the refusal to lease the Môle and publicly denied ever having promised to do so.[24]

So the episode closed. Secretary Blaine's first effort to obtain a coaling station in the Caribbean was a failure. Attention was then turned toward the Dominican Republic, where a lease of Samana Bay would have

refused, a forcible seizure of the harbor to "relieve the Haitian government of responsibility and embarrassment"! There is no comment from the Secretary of State on this request but when the refusal came Gherardi's suggestion was not followed up.

[23] Douglass to Blaine, April 23, 1891, Manuscript Dispatches, Haiti, Vol. 25, No. 156.

[24] Douglass to Blaine, May 7, 1891, Manuscript Dispatches, Haiti, Vol. 25, No. 165.

been desirable. But at the mere rumor of such a proposal General Gonzales, the Dominican secretary of state, was forced to flee into exile from an outraged public.[25] Once again the pride of the little republics and apprehensions as to the designs of the United States prevented the granting of a concession which might well have been of mutual advantage. No West Indian coaling station was obtained in Harrison's administration.

When Mr. Blaine had been Secretary of State in 1881, there had been a series of boundary disputes in Central and South America which had given him an opportunity to put into definite, written form his political theories in regard to the relations of the several states of this hemisphere to each other and that of the United States toward all the others. His second period in office did not afford such wide opportunities, but there were a few episodes which indicated that the ten years' interval had brought no change in his attitude toward Latin America.

The revolution which took place in Salvador in 1890 is a case in point.[26] On June 25, 1890, Mr. Mizner,

[25] Stuart, *Latin America and the United States*, 217.

[26] Although not in a Central American or Caribbean State, it might be well to mention the revolution in Brazil in November, 1889. The Portuguese dynasty was overthrown, and a republic with a constitution similar to that of the United States was established. The revolution was complete and peaceful and unattended by riots. Mr. Blaine at once ordered the recognition of the republic, an act quite in accord with precedent since the provisional government was undoubtedly *de facto*. Two years later when there seemed danger that the monarchy

United States minister to Central America, reported that a provisional government under General Ezeta had been set up in Salvador. Guatemala held that the fact that the three States of Salvador, Honduras, and Guatemala had agreed to a union compact gave them a mutual interest in each others' governments. For that reason the President of Guatemala refused to recognize the new Salvadoran Government in any way and moved troops to the frontier, where they were at once faced by an equal number from Salvador.[27] Both countries prepared for war as quickly as possible. They were quite evenly matched in military strength although Guatemala had a larger population and greater resources in case a struggle should be prolonged. Mr. Mizner asked that United States war vessels be sent to Central American waters for the protection of American interests.[28]

During the days when war seemed imminent but had not yet been declared, the Pacific Mail Company's steamer "Colima" arrived in a Guatemalan port with a cargo of arms ordered by agents of Salvador. The

might be restored, Mr. Blaine telegraphed "his fervent hope that the free political institutions so recently established might not be impaired." This, also, was in accordance with precedent, for the United States has ever been glad to welcome new states into the sisterhood of republics, and it had been a source of gratification to Mr. Blaine to feel that with the overthrow of the Brazilian Empire the last vestige of monarchial government had disappeared from Latin America. For the correspondence see *U. S. Foreign Relations*, 1889 and 1891, Brazil.

[27] Mizner to Blaine, June 25, 1890, *U. S. Foreign Relations*, 1890, 28.
[28] Mizner to Blaine, July 9, 1890, *ibid.*, 31-32.

arms were seized by Guatemala in contravention of her agreement with the steamship company, but in accordance with the right of self-protection granted by the law of nations. This episode was the subject of a long triangular correspondence between the United States, the Pacific Mail Company, and Guatemala. The United States claimed that such belligerent rights were granted only after war had been declared or was in progress. In the end, practically at the end of the war, the arms were surrendered by Guatemala, and Mr. Blaine's demand for an apology was complied with.[29] Guatemala yielded to the physical rather than the legal superiority of the position of the United States.

In the beginning of the dispute between Salvador and Guatemala, Mr. Mizner had tendered the good offices of the United States in an effort to maintain peace, emphasizing the fact that as he was accredited to both parties in the dispute, the absolute impartiality of his position must be recognized.[30] The entire diplomatic corps under Mr. Mizner's leadership worked industriously for peace. The Governments of Guatemala, Honduras, Nicaragua, and Costa Rica signed a treaty recognizing the legal, pre-revolution Government of Salvador, demanding the withdrawal of General Ezeta, and pledging territorial integrity and an amnesty to all participants if Salvador complied. The signatory powers then asked for the good offices and moral support of the United States. Failing a response

[29] Blaine to Kimberly, December 22, 1890, *ibid.*, 142.
[30] Mizner to Blaine, July 16, 1890, *ibid.*, 33.

from Salvador, war was declared by Guatemala, and martial law was decreed.[31]

Mr. Blaine instructed Mizner to tender the good offices of the United States, but the Guatemalan terms of an unconditional restoration of the overturned Government and an assumption of all war costs was entirely unacceptable to Salvador. Nicaragua and Costa Rica sent special peace missions to the belligerent states, but their efforts were viewed askance by Salvador because of the treaty with Guatemala, which they had signed but a few days before. Mexico, too, was interested in the outcome of the disturbance to the south and, on July 30, offered to join the United States in mediation between the two belligerents.[32] The cooperation of Mexico was cordially received, but the United States considered it best to make simultaneous rather than joint representations.[33] In the meantime General Ezeta followed the example of Guatemala and asked for the mediation of the United States on the basis of non-intervention and the autonomy and independence of Salvador.[34] Early in August some slight successes upon the battlefield encouraged General Ezeta, and he refused the good offices of the United States stating that

[31] Mizner to Blaine, July 22 and 23, 1890, with enclosures, *ibid.*, 35-39.

[32] Ryan to Blaine, July 30, 1890, *ibid.*, 648.

[33] Wharton to Ryan, August 15, 1890, *ibid.*, 652.

[34] Ryan to Blaine, July 30, 1890, *ibid.*, 650. Owing to the fact that telegraphic correspondence between the United States and Central America was interfered with by both Guatemala and Salvador, much of the negotiations was carried on by way of Mexico.

he intended to hoist his flag in Guatemala City.[35] Mediation and peace were forced to wait until military reverses should cool the truculence of the opposing leaders.

Events moved rapidly and it became evident that neither side could win a complete victory. On August 18, therefore, Mr. Mizner was able to report that the good offices of the United States had been accepted by both belligerents.[36] There was some difficulty over the terms of peace, and the diplomatic corps made strenuous efforts to bring the two parties together. It was at last agreed that Salvador should hold an election for president with the understanding that if elected Ezeta might retain power. There were to be no territorial cessions. On August 26, the preliminary agreement was signed and a truce declared until a definite treaty could be drawn up. The armies were to be disbanded and peace was declared.[37]

Secretary Blaine and President Harrison expressed themselves as well pleased with the action of Mr. Mizner, who had been untiring in his efforts to bring about peace. Mr. Blaine had authorized the tender of the good offices of the United States and had been willing in every way to further the cause of peace. He had expressed himself as willing to cooperate with Mexico or to aid in the submission of the difficulty to the decision of American arbitrators. Mr. Mizner's efforts

[35] Mizner to Blaine, August 5, 1890, *ibid.*, 59.
[36] Mizner to Blaine, August 18, 1890, *ibid.*, 75.
[37] Mizner to Blaine, August 27, 1890, *ibid.*, 81.

met with the approval of both Salvador and Guatemala, and he and the Department of State had cause for self-congratulation.

Two days after the preliminary treaty of peace was signed there occurred an incident which was destined to turn Mr. Mizner's rejoicing into sorrow. Its primary interest is in the field of international law, but it deserves mention because of the evidence it gives as to the attitude of Mr. Blaine toward the Central American Republics and toward a more or less undetermined legal question. On August 28, General Barrundia, a citizen of Guatemala en route to Salvador, was arrested by Guatemalan authorities on board the Pacific Mail steamer "Acapulco" in the Guatemalan port of San José. General Barrundia was accused of treason and other high crimes and was called an enemy of the state. His arrest was demanded on various grounds, but it was evident that Guatemala considered him a political offender. His career had been notorious, and common crimes might well have been the cause for his arrest.

The arrest was quite in keeping with present day views of international law. The "Acapulco" was a merchant vessel and as such was subject to the jurisdiction of the port. Since the end of the nineteenth century there has been no question as to the right of authorities of the port to arrest on a merchant vessel within the harbor any offender against the laws of the country in which the port was located, whether his offenses had been criminal or political. At the time of the Barrundia affair there existed some doubt as to whether excep-

tion might not be made in the case of the political offenders against Latin American States. The ever-recur-
ring revolutions and the tendency toward mob violence
and retaliatory measures in those States had caused this
feeling that exception should be made. Secretary Bayard had refused to accept the idea that distinction
should be made, and Secretary Gresham was to settle
the question finally by stating that merchant vessels in
any port were subject to the jurisdiction of that port,
and that offenders of every kind might be taken from
them by the authorities of the port. Secretary Blaine,
between these two administrations, preferred to sub-
scribe to the earlier doctrine.

Mr. Mizner became involved in the affair, most dis-
astrously for himself, by advising the captain of the
"Acapulco" to surrender his passenger to the authorities. Both the Guatemalan minister of foreign affairs
and the captain of the vessel had applied to Mizner,
the first for permission to arrest and the second for
advice as to yielding. Mizner asked and obtained the
pledge of Guatemala that the prisoner would be safeguarded and given a fair trial and then, to the best of
his legal knowledge and following the precedent of
Bayard's decision a few years earlier, he stated that he
felt the captain should surrender Barrundia.

Mr. Blaine disavowed Mizner's action, reprimanded
him for having exceeded his authority in having advised
the captain to submit to the Guatemalan authorities,
and recalled him from his post.[38]   Commander Reiter

[38] There seems to have been a confusion of issues in this case.
Mr. Blaine appears to have regarded it as a matter of the abuse of

of the U.S.S. "Ranger" stationed off San José received punishment for what the Navy Department held was his sin of omission in not having offered Barrundia asylum upon the "Ranger," which would have effectually prevented his arrest. Reiter had been conversant with the situation and had corresponded with Mizner prior to the arrival of the "Acapulco" at San José. In a most scathing letter the Secretary of the Navy, Tracy, relieved him of his command and ordered him to return to the United States. It must be admitted that in the case of Reiter as in that of Mizner, the weight of the law lay with those who received chastisement.

It is rather an inconsistency in Mr. Blaine's policy toward the Latin American Republics that he should have been so insistent upon the right of asylum, so nearly obsolete in law and little practiced except in semi-civilized countries. It seems strange that the man who had as his major thesis the betterment of the relations between the United States and Latin America should have been the one Secretary of State in the latter part of the century to inflict upon those States the humiliation of the old doctrine of the right of asylum as applying to political offenders, be they found upon merchant vessels or men of war. It is significant that both Blaine and Tracy were to take the same view a year later in regard to the more important cases arising from the Chilean revolution.[39]

the right of asylum, whereas Mizner, quite correctly, considered it a case of the jurisdiction over a merchant ship in a Guatemalan harbor.

[39] The correspondence from the State Department for the Barrundia

affair may be found in *Sen. Exec. Doc.* No. 51, 51 Cong., 2nd Session, and from the Navy Department in *House Exec. Doc.* No. 50, 51 Cong., 2nd Session. The legal aspects of the affair are discussed in Charles C. Hyde, *International Law: Chiefly as Applied by the United States*, I, 401-402. See also John Bassett Moore, "The Chilean Affair," *Political Science Quarterly*, VIII (September, 1893).

CHAPTER V

THE WAR BETWEEN CHILE AND PERU, 1879-1883

AS HAS been seen, boundary disputes between the Central and South American States were sources of trouble to the Department of State in 1881 and, at the same time, offered excellent opportunity for the enunciation of Blaine's policy. In one case only did the dispute flare into war which could not be prevented nor terminated by the action of the United States. The war began in February, 1879, and was occasioned by the alleged violation on the part of Bolivia of a treaty between Bolivia and Chile. This treaty, drawn up in 1874, made a division of the Pacific coast territory, claimed by both States, and decreed that for twenty-five years neither country should, within that territory, tax the citizens, industries, or capital of the other in excess of the rate then fixed by law.[1]

The development by Chilean capital of great nitrate beds in the heart of the Atacama Desert in a region alloted to Bolivia made the self-denying ordinance irk-

[1] *Sen. Exec. Doc.* No. 79, 47 Cong., 1st Session, p. 73. Osborn to Evarts, February 28, 1879. This document (700 pp.) contains practically all the correspondence for the years 1879-1882. *Sen. Exec. Doc.* No. 181, 47 Cong., 1st Session, continues it for the Trescot Mission.

some to that State, and in 1878 the Bolivian Congress passed a law that each quintal of nitrate exported should pay ten cents into the Bolivian treasury. Chile protested, Bolivia refused to rescind the law, and Chile, thereupon, declared the treaty abrogated. Chilean war vessels landed troops at Antofagasta, and the nitrate works were soon in Chilean control. Bolivia alone could not expect to have any success in a war against the much more powerful adversary, but she had an ally, Peru, bound by the treaty of 1873, the secret clauses of which were reputed to provide for an offensive-defensive alliance.[2]

From the first the success of the war was almost entirely with Chile. Bolivia was very weak and soon became a negligible quantity, and Peru could not hold back the victorious Chileans. There was much discussion in South America from 1879 on, of mediation or even intervention on the part of the United States. Judge Pettis, minister to Bolivia, on his return from the United States in the summer of 1879, stopped in Valparaiso to make an effort, unofficially, to secure peace and to ascertain whether mediation would be acceptable.[3] Nothing came of this move nor of the

[2] Gibbs, U. S. minister to Peru, to Evarts, February 19, 1879, *Sen. Exec. Doc.* No. 79, 47 Cong., 1st Session, 195.

[3] Hunter to Pettis, U. S. minister to Bolivia, October 1, 1879, *ibid.* "Unauthorized and even rash as your experiment might appear, it may at least have led the contestants to the healthy consideration of the terms on which the strife might be ended. Should the knowledge of the views of each other thus gained, induce to an eventual settlement, this government could not but rejoice at the result. It is not,

effort at mediation in the same summer on the part of Colombia.[4] The mediation of European powers was also a possibility looked at with distaste by the United States and with disdain by the Governments of the belligerent powers.[5] Osborn, the United States minister in Chile, reported to Secretary Evarts that Chile was sure of success and did not wish the United States to mediate. He felt sure that the guano and nitrate beds of Bolivia and Peru were the causes of contention, and that Chile would most certainly refuse to give them back.[6]

In the summer of 1880 Italy, England, and France offered mediation. Chile accepted on the condition that Tarapaca be ceded, but the other belligerents preferred the good offices of the United States.[7] After much negotiation all three powers consented to accept the mediation of the United States and sent representatives to Arica to join with the ministers of the United States to the belligerent states in an attempt to arrive

however, disposed to dictate a peace, or to take any steps leading to arbitration or intervention in disparagement of belligerent rights or even to urge the condition under which they might be reached. Its good offices have not been officially tendered but, if sought, on a practicable basis of arbitration, submitted to the several parties, the President would not hesitate to use them in the interest of peace."

[4] Evarts to Christiancy, U. S. minister to Peru, August 8, 1879, *ibid.*, 255.

[5] Evarts to Christiancy, October 1, 1879, and Evarts to Christiancy, March 9, 1880, MS. Instructions, Peru, 1879.

[6] Osborn to Evarts, June 5, 1879, *Sen. Exec. Doc.* No. 79, 47 Cong., 1st Session, 87.

[7] Osborn to Evarts, September 14, 1881, *ibid.*, 39.

at terms of peace. The conference was held on a United States cruiser in the last days of October, 1880, and was a complete failure. Chile was not in the mood to make concessions, refused arbitration, and tried to break up the Bolivia-Peru alliance.[8] The United States Government was thanked for its good offices, expressed its willingness to act as arbitrator at any time, and the war went on.

This was the situation when Mr. Blaine came into office. All that had been done by Evarts was in accord with the Blaine policy of using every means to preserve or secure peace for the Western Hemisphere. There was no reason to expect from the new Secretary of State any change in the attitude of the United States toward the war. He was informed that there was little prospect of an early peace. Chile was victorious and felt that time would bring her the coveted territories, which she did not even yet quite dare to demand too loudly.[9] There was almost immediately the added complication

[8] Adams (Bolivia) to Evarts, November 6, 1880, *ibid.*, 51.

[9] Chile had begun the war with a disclaimer of any intent to enlarge her domain at the expense of Peru. The nitrate beds of Peru had been the main resource of the Peruvian Government, which exploited the nitrates. The nitrate bonds of Peru, as they were called, were held extensively in Europe, especially in France, Holland, and Italy. The foreign creditors of Peru were, therefore, much interested that nothing be done to affect the value of the guarantees which Peru had given them. Chile was apprehensive lest this interest might lead to intervention. It was perhaps one cause of the attempt at mediation. England was deeply interested, commercially, in Chile because the largest commercial houses were English, and was equally interested in the securing of peace. William Henry Hurlburt, *Meddling and Muddling: Mr. Blaine's Foreign Policy.*

of a revolution in Peru. At the beginning of the war there had been a shift in government in Peru, and an old revolutionary leader, Pierola, returned and was made president. In 1881 his Government fell in its turn, and he fled to the mountains, where, refusing to resign, he maintained a pseudo-government for some time. After a period of almost no government at all Señor Calderon formed a provisional government with the consent of victorious Chile. On April 9, Blaine authorized the recognition of Calderon.[10]

Regardless of difficulties Blaine started out optimistically to do all in his power to secure a workable peace treaty. The United States ministers to Chile and Peru, Mr. Thomas A. Osborn and Mr. I. P. Christiancy, had become too ardent partisans of the countries to which they were respectively accredited, so they were replaced in June, 1881, by new appointees. The new administration found posts for several officers of the Civil War. General James Kilpatrick went to Chile and General S. A. Hurlburt to Peru, and within a few months they were as violently partisan as their predecessors. Kilpatrick had married a Chilean lady, the niece of a high dignitary in the church, and his interests were entirely with the country to which he had been sent. The two

[10] Blaine was severely criticized in the press for this recognition of Calderon when there was far from a *de facto* government in Peru. See the *Nation*, XXXIX, 172, and other newspaper and periodical accounts. Accusation was made that he was financially interested in Peru. The correspondence seems to show that he was influenced only by the fact that Chile's support of Calderon indicated a possibility of peace if he were established.

ministers soon quarrelled merrily with each other and committed various indiscretions in their relations with the two Governments. Secretary Blaine had secured no more satisfactory representatives than those he dismissed.

The instructions to Kilpatrick and to Hurlburt are both dated June 15, 1881, and contain a very clear statement of Blaine's ideas in regard to a peace.[11] Hurlburt was instructed to "do all you properly can to encourage the Peruvians to accept any reasonable conditions and limitations" necessary to secure peace. He was told that it was vitally important that Peru be allowed to resume the functions of an orderly government and was instructed to use all influence he might have with the Peruvian authorities to obtain a just and reasonable settlement. Blaine did not deny that Chile had acquired rights by the successes of the war but hoped that a cession of territory would not be made a preliminary of negotiations although such a cession might be an ultimate necessity.[12] The United States did

[11] Blaine to Kilpatrick, June 15, 1881, *Senate Executive Document* No. 79, 47 Congress, 1st Session, 157. Blaine to Hurlburt, *ibid.*, 500. Hurlburt's brother states (*Meddling and Muddling*, 55) that after the general had conferred with Blaine he visited him in New York before going to Peru and "he gave me distinctly to understand that he was going out to Peru commissioned to support the Calderon Government, if he found it possible in any efforts to bring about peace on the basis of a war indemnity for Chile. The *Crédit Industriel* was to provide the money. He was instructed to support Peru against Chile who relied upon England."

[12] Throughout the war the desire of the United States in regard to a peace settlement seems to have remained the same. Peru should be

not deem the time opportune to mediate but if Peru could work out a program of concession that had any prospect of satisfying Chile, the United States would tender her good offices. Hurlburt was warned that England would support Chile. Blaine seems to have been possessed by the idea that the Chilean cause was an English one, for he stated in his testimony before the Congressional committee in 1882 that, "It is an English war on Peru with Chile as the instrument, and I take the responsibility for that statement." He evidently felt that the coveted nitrate beds were the bait offered by Chile to English capital. It was never difficult to arouse in Blaine's mind suspicions against Great Britain and apprehensions of undue influence on her part.[13]

To Kilpatrick instructions of a similar nature were sent. He was to urge moderation on Chile. The United States Government did not "pretend to express an opinion" as to whether any annexation of territory was necessary but held that all such forced territorial changes should be avoided whenever possible. Chile should be advised to give all possible aid to the restoration of stable government in Peru and to postpone discussion of territorial acquisition until Peru could treat with her. The instructions ended with the significant statement that the United States sought only to perform

left strong enough to carry on governmental functions. If possible an indemnity was to be substituted for cession of territory. The United States did not object to foreign capital guaranteeing the indemnity.

[13] See note 36, p. 126.

the part of a friend and hoped that no complication of European aid or intervention would lead to a change in the feeling of friendliness.

During the course of the correspondence between Chile and Peru, there is the constant reference to the possibility of European offers of mediation or attempts at intervention. Blaine followed Evarts in looking with disfavor upon any such complication and so instructed both Hurlburt and Kilpatrick in June, 1881. In August, 1881, Morton, the United States minister to France, reported an interview with President Grévy in which the French president tried to discover what measures might be jointly adopted by France, Great Britain, and the United States to reach a satisfactory solution of the Chile-Peru difficulty.[14] Blaine replied:

The United States has not belonged to that system of states, of which France and Great Britain are such important members, and has never participated in the adjustment of their conventions. Neither interest nor inclination leads this country to wish to have a voice in the discussion of those questions; but our relations to the states of the American continent are widely different and the situation is so nearly reversed that this government, while appreciating the high and disinterested motive that inspired the suggestion is constrained to gravely doubt the expedience of uniting with European powers to intervene, in the affairs of American states.[15]

President Grévy immediately told Morton that France

[14] Morton to Blaine, August 11, 1881, *Sen. Exec. Doc.* No. 79, 47 Cong., 1st Session, 596.
[15] Blaine to Morton, September 5, 1881, *ibid.*, 597-599.

was satisfied and was willing to act with the United States or to permit the United States to act alone.[16]

The whole duty of the envoys to Peru and Chile, therefore, was to do all that they could to bring about a peace on terms as advantageous to Peru as possible. Secretary Blaine felt that a liberal war indemnity should be substituted for a cession of territory. Early in 1881 a movement of which the State Department was cognizant had been initiated to give Peru financial assistance in paying for her peace.[17] Foreign capital, chiefly French, was to be used to organize the *Société Générale de Crédit industriel et commercial*, which was to facilitate the payment of war expenses and indemnity. From the beginning the State Department refused to have anything officially to do with this or any other scheme. Any plan which would aid the reconstruction of Peru was looked upon with favor, but the United States was to further none of them. This position was taken by Mr. Evarts in February,[18] and by Mr. Blaine in the fall of 1881.[19] It is possible that General Hurl-

[16] Morton to Blaine, *ibid.*

[17] Evarts to Christiancy, February 17, 1881, *Sen. Exec. Doc.* No. 79, 47 Cong., 1st Session. Evarts gives an account of an interview with Mr. Montferrand, one of the French backers of the scheme.

[18] *Ibid.*

[19] Telegram, Blaine to Hurlburt, October 27, 1881, *ibid.*, 545. In a letter dated November 19, 1881 (*ibid.*, 564) Blaine referred to the telegram forbidding Hurlburt to lend his influence to the *Crédit Industriel* and stated that it had been caused by rumors that Hurlburt was furthering the scheme. Blaine's views were clearly expressed as follows: "However trustworthy the *Crédit Industriel* may be, I did not consider it proper for the Department to have anything whatever to

burt may have given a certain amount of aid to the corporation, but his action was not in any way authorized by the Department of State.

Aside from the question of the restoration of peace the representatives of the United States in Chile and Peru were, of course, to be concerned with the interests of citizens of the United States in the belligerent countries. In Peru this question became of interest, for two companies, organized to exploit the nitrate beds in territory which had been captured during the war by Chile, claimed to be controlled by citizens of the United States. Secretary Blaine was severely criticized for the support given these claimants, and a Congressional committee was appointed in 1882 to investigate the charges against the United States minister to Peru and the Department of State. The committee completely exonerated Blaine and found no evidence of dishonesty on the part of Hurlburt, whose death in 1882 prevented his appearing to give evidence in his own behalf. Neither the printed correspondence nor the archives of the Department contain any material which was not used by the investigation committee.

With the Cochet or Peruvian Company claim, Blaine

do with it. It is a foreign corporation, responsible to French law, and must seek its patronage and protection from France. At the same time it is no part of your duty to interfere with its negotiations with the Peruvian Government. If it can be made an effective instrumentality to aid that unhappy country in its prostrate and helpless condition, it would be ungenerous and unjust to obstruct its operation. Your duty is negative and you have fully complied with your instructions by simply abstaining from all connection with the association."

never had anything to do. From the beginning he distrusted its promoter and felt that the United States had no interest involved in it.[20] The other great claim against Peru, the Landreau claim, Blaine felt was better founded. Landreau was an American citizen and his contract with Peru was a bona fide one by which he was entitled to a definite payment for each quintal of nitrate taken out by the company he organized. Hurlburt was instructed to investigate what Peru was doing to live up to its obligations, to use his good offices in seeing that Landreau had a hearing before an impartial tribunal, or that the case be referred to arbitration. If the treaty of peace gave the guano beds, which were discovered by Landreau, to Chile, then the Peruvian Government should stipulate that the royalties guaranteed to Landreau, provided the claim was adjudicated in his favor, should be a prior lien upon the property.[21]

There seems nothing improper in thus attempting to obtain fair treatment for the claims of an American citizen.[22] Blaine's instructions in this case go no further than those of many other Secretaries of State in respect to claims against other Latin American States. General Hurlburt was again instructed a few months later that there were all sorts of rumors abroad as to Peruvian finances, and that he was to take no important steps

[20] Blaine to Hurlburt, November 17, 1881, *ibid.*
[21] Blaine to Hurlburt, August 4, 1881, *ibid.*, 508.
[22] The State Department had been pressing the claim since 1874, and each Secretary thereafter had written dispatches urging its adjudication.

without orders. Blaine may have felt that his appointee had been somewhat over-zealous, for he wrote:

To extend all proper protection to American citizens and to secure for them, in any interests they may have, a respectful hearing before the tribunals of the country to which you are accredited and generally to aid them with information and advice are among the imperative and grateful duties of a Minister — duties which increase his usefulness and add to his respect. To go beyond and assume the tone of advocacy with its inevitable inference of personal interest and its possible suspicion of improper interest will at once impair if it does not utterly destroy the acceptability and efficiency of a diplomatic representative.[23]

This matter of the Landreau claim was not the only occasion for concern in our relations with Peru. When the contest between Chile and Peru grew critical again in the fall of 1881, when Chile withdrew her support of the Calderon Government, Hurlburt constantly appealed to the United States for intervention to save Peru.[24] There were three occasions when he exceeded his instructions and caused difficulty for the State Department. His partisanship led him to give the impression that the United States was ready to intervene actively in behalf of Peru. In a letter to Admiral Lynch, Chilean naval commander, he stated that the United States would "regard with disfavor" the annex-

[23] Blaine to Hurlburt, November 19, 1881, *ibid.*

[24] Hurlburt's brother was convinced that had Blaine listened to these pleas and used strong measures, a satisfactory peace might have been obtained. There seems little substantiation for such a theory, and furthermore Blaine had lost confidence in Hurlburt.

ation of Peruvian territory and in general gave the impression that the United States was the supporter of Peru. In a letter to the secretary of the deposed President Pierola, he practically announced that the United States recognized the Calderon Government because it was pledged to refuse the cession of territory. In the third place, he had negotiated, without the knowledge of the State Department, with Peru for the cession to the United States of a coaling station in the Bay of Chimbote and had arranged for a railroad concession from the harbor to coal mines in the back country with himself as agent or trustee until the road could be turned over to an American company. Blaine reproved in no uncertain terms the conduct of the minister, reminding him that as envoy accredited to the Calderon Government, he should have held no intercourse with either Lynch or Pierola. In regard to the last incident he ordered all negotiations dropped and expressed his astonishment that Hurlburt should ever have so forgotten his position and "every rule of prudence and propriety that should govern the conduct of a representative of this country." The letter ended with the announcement of a special mission from the United States to visit both Chile and Peru and take over all matters connected with the question of peace.[25]

Kilpatrick in Chile also caused trouble for the State

[25] Blaine to Hurlburt, November 22 and December 3, 1881, *Sen. Exec. Doc.* No. 79, 47 Cong., 1st Session, 565. Hurlburt's letters of explanation with enclosures are in the same document. The full account of the indiscretions is in the *Annual Cyclopedia*, 1881.

Department. He quarreled at long distance with Hurlburt and fomented the feeling against him in Chile. In November Blaine notified Kilpatrick that:

The present condition of affairs, the difficulty of communication with the legations of Peru and Chile and the unfortunate notoriety of the differences between yourself and your colleague in Peru, have, in the judgment of the President, rendered a special mission necessary.[26]

The special envoy chosen was William H. Trescot, former Assistant Secretary of State and a man of much diplomatic experience. He was accompanied by Walker Blaine, the son of the Secretary of State. The instructions given the envoy were minute and expressed Blaine's policy in regard to Latin American disputes very clearly. Trescot was to use his influence to persuade Chile to permit the formation of a government in Peru. Although the right of Chile to indemnity was not questioned, the United States hoped that territory would not be forcibly retained unless an indemnity could not be paid. He was to urge that the indemnity be reasonable and not so large that the demand would make cession of territory necessary. The instructions ended with the statement, "The single and simple desire of this government is to see a just and honorable peace at the earliest day practicable." The United States was willing to act as umpire if invited but if not, was willing to aid and work with any other American Government in obtaining peace.[27]

[26] Blaine to Kilpatrick, *Sen. Exec. Doc.* No. 79, 47 Cong., 1st Session, 168.

[27] Blaine to Trescot, December 1, 1881, *ibid.*, 174-179. Blaine may

Before the mission reached its destination, Blaine's resignation was accepted, and Frederick Frelinghuysen was Secretary of State. The policy of Secretary Blaine in regard to Chile was changed in nearly every detail with as much effort as possible to discredit it. The entire correspondence was sent to the Senate on January 26, including not only Blaine's instructions to Trescot but also the instructions which Frelinghuysen had

have been influenced by the interesting Manuscript Report of a Special Mission of George Earl Church to Ecuador, 1881. The following letter was enclosed from Santiago, Chile, October 2, to Blaine:

"About two weeks ago, I had a long conversation with President Garcia Calderon in Lima. He assured me, firmly, that under no circumstances would he sign a treaty of peace with Chile ceding territory, but is ready to conclude peace on the basis of a war indemnity which he believes will not exceed sixty millions of dollars. This amount he pretends that he is in a position to pay to Chile, but I cannot understand from what source unless it is through a pledge to capitalists of the nitrate deposits of Tarapaca.

"In confidence, I may say that it is the opinion of the President of Chile and his most valued advisors that the previous Government made a stupid and almost unpardonable blunder at the Arica conference in laying down as an ultimatum, the cession of Tarapaca and a part of Bolivia. It greatly complicated the results of the war and prolonged the struggle more to the advantage of Chile than that of the allies. And yet, I have the strongest reasons to believe that this administration is as hotly bent on acquiring possession of Atacama and Tarapaca as was the previous government but in a different way. Their plan now is to conclude a treaty of peace with the allies, leaving the drained provinces in the hands of Chile and under its civil and military administration as a pledge for the war indemnity they propose to exact. This indemnity they propose to make payable over a series of from twenty-five to thirty years, the longer the term the better. . . . During the term of occupation, the policy will be to crowd into Atacama and Tarapaca as many Chilean settlers as possible, put all enterprise under Chilean capital. This is already the condition of affairs there now to a considerable extent, there being

drawn up on January 9, modifying them and practically withdrawing the mission. The news of the publication of the documents and the substance of the new instructions were telegraphed the Chilean Government by its representative in Washington some time before Trescot received the dispatch of January 9. The envoy of the United States was placed in the humiliating position of receiving his instructions through the secretary of state of the Government to which he was accredited.

about 20,000 Chilean settlers there and even during the war, many more pouring in.

"The Chileans have made careful studies of the mineral wealth of the district they desire to hold and have found it vast, beyond what the world generally supposes. They already have in prospect, under government guarantee, lines of railway to penetrate Bolivia from the coast across Atacama and Tarapaca but this is as yet a secret.

"I have no doubt that the development of the coveted territory would be rapid and advantageous to the commerce of the world under the energetic and intelligent management of Chile much more than under the characteristic bad faith of Bolivia or the unfortunate corruption of Peru. . . .

"I find the Chilean government sorely troubled by the letter of Minister Hurlburt to Admiral Lynch, despite the letter of General Kilpatrick. They have even gone to considerable expense for war stores and armament to provide against contingencies; fearing that there may be truth in General Hurlburt's letter, and that it might result in a contest with the United States, which, however great the odds, they are now proud enough to think they could, at least for a time, make head against. The conflicting correspondence of the two ministers has not added to the comfort of either contestant and leaves the views of the United States so undefined that it adds to the perplexities and prolongation of the war. If General Hurlburt be right, Peru will struggle for good terms; if General Kilpatrick's official letter to the Chilean Government be endorsed at Washington, then Peru will resign hope and Atacama and Tarapaca will hereafter float the Chilean flag."

Trescot arrived in Chile early in January and had some hope of being able to assist in negotiating a satisfactory peace. He felt that Chile needed peace, and the Government would be glad to find a solution permitting them to withdraw from Peru.[28] When he was informed of the Chilean terms he judged them too high. Chile, he felt, could, unless the United States intervened, compel Peru to accept any terms she chose to impose. The Chilean demand was for the cession of Tarapaca and Arica and an indemnity of twenty million dollars. Trescot desired to offer the good offices of the United States on the basis of the cession of Tarapaca alone or of an indemnity alone, not both, and he felt that he had some prospect of success.[29]

The special mission had been entrusted with the delivering of the invitation to the proposed peace conference to be held in Washington in 1882.[30] Trescot felt that this should be done at the conclusion of the negotiation but, upon hearing that Hurlburt had presented the invitation to Peru, he found it necessary to present it to Chile. Accordingly he asked for an audience with Señor Balmaceda for himself and Mr. Walker Blaine, who was acting as minister in the vacancy resulting from the death of Mr. Kilpatrick. As soon as Balmaceda knew the purpose of the interview, he informed them that it was useless, as the United

[28] Trescot to Frelinghuysen, January 13, 1882, *Sen. Exec. Doc.* No. 181, 47 Cong., 1st Session.

[29] *Ibid.*, Trescot to Frelinghuysen, January 27, 1882.

[30] See Chapter VII.

States Government had withdrawn the invitation, and that the instructions of Trescot himself had been changed in very important particulars, that the whole correspondence was published, and that new instructions were on their way. Mr. Trescot's account of this embarrassing interview ended with this justifiable complaint:

> I could not suppose that such an instruction would be made public while I was endeavoring to secure, and not without some hope of success, the amicable solution of this delicate and difficult question. Still less could I believe that if my original instructions had been seriously modified any communication of such a change would have been made public or even confidentially to the Chilean government, before I could possibly have received it. I could not admit, what the Secretary (Balmaceda) clearly implied, that I did not represent the wishes or intention of my government and that he was better instructed than myself as to the progress of my mission.[31]

It was perfectly obvious that after this episode there could be no hope of success from the Trescot mission. Peru was to be abandoned to her fate. When the instructions of January 9 finally arrived, Trescot received orders to refrain from dictating in any way whatsoever to Chile and was forbidden to make any suggestions as to terms of peace. The invitation to a peace conference was postponed and practically withdrawn.[32] Under the circumstances Balmaceda refused to make any modifi-

[31] Trescot to Frelinghuysen, February 3, 1882, *Sen. Exec. Doc.* No. 181, 47 Cong., 1st Session.
[32] See Chapter VII.

cation of his demands and Trescot withdrew the good offices of the United States and left Chile.[33] Walker Blaine wrote to his father that he did not believe that

. . . in my time the United States will ever get back influence worth considering with anyone of these South American countries, and if the Department had stood firm, we could, I honestly believe, have settled the question to the satisfaction of all and to our own (the country's) advancement.[34]

He was quite right in at least the first part of the statement, for both Chile and Peru resented the intervention of the United States. The treaty made in 1883 by the two powers was not a final settlement of the difficulties, and the question of the final ownership of the disputed territories has not yet been determined. The action taken by the State Department in recent years has been productive of no more success than the original negotiations.

In this matter of the mission to Chile and Peru and in the withdrawal of the invitations to the peace conference, neither President Arthur nor Secretary Frelinghuysen appear in a favorable light. It had seemed to the political enemies of Blaine, and they were not few, that the situation offered an opportunity for attack, and the obvious intention was to ruin his official career with charges of inefficiency, rashness, over-reaching policy and, even of dishonesty in the advocacy of claims and hope of financial gain in the protection of

[33] *Sen. Exec. Doc.* No. 181, 47 Cong., 1st Session, Trescot to Frelinghuysen, March 4, 1882.

[34] Hamilton, *Life of James G. Blaine*, 554.

Peru. Mr. Blaine met the attack with dignified silence, broken only to express his views on the withdrawal of the invitations to the peace conference.[35] He appeared, when called upon, before the committee of the House of Representatives to give testimony on the conduct of Mr. Hurlburt and on other questions. The committee completely exonerated both the State Department and its representatives from any blame for the conduct of the Chile-Peru negotiations[36] but the imputation of corrupt dealing was difficult to efface, and the campaign of

[35] See Chapter VII.

[36] *Letters of Mrs. James G. Blaine*, II, 9-10, note quoting from *House Reports*, 47 Cong., 1st Session, Vol. 6.

"The principal inquiries with which the Committee (Foreign Relations of the House of Representatives) is charged is whether one or more ministers plenipotentiary of the United States were personally interested in the business transactions in which the intervention of this government was requested or expected in the affairs of Chile and Peru. The discussion may be divided under 3 heads. 'First: The condition of affairs in Chile and Peru. . . . Second: The history and claims of the parties who requested the intervention of the United States. Third: Investigation as to the connection between ministers plenipotentiary of the United States and these parties.' The parties mentioned were the Cochet or Peruvian Company claimants, the Landreau claimant and the Crédit Industriel, a French company, organized in Paris in 1839, and the investigation was made necessary by the charges of the agent of the Peruvian Company, Jacob R. Shepherd of New York, to the effect that our minister to Peru, Mr. Stephen A. Hurlburt, was in the pay of the Crédit Industriel. The proceedings were complicated and saddened by the sudden death of Mr. Hurlburt as he was embarking for this country, so that, in the words of the Report, 'the lips of the most important and interested witness were closed forever.'

"It was also charged that the Honorable Levi P. Morton, our Minister to France, after his appointment as Minister, became interested

1884 was filled with repetitions of the slurs and insulting charges made in the attack upon Blaine.[37]

in a contract with the Crédit Industriel for the sale of Peruvian product in the United States. . . . As it has been impossible actually to separate these ministers from the home State Department, whose representatives they were, and under whose instructions they are bound to act, it is proper to state that there has not been the slightest intimation or even hinted suspicion that any officer in the Department of State has at any time had any personal or pecuniary interest, real or contingent, attained or sought, in any of these transactions.

"The investigation resulted in the most entire vindication of both the gentlemen named, and in the complete discrediting of Mr. Shepherd.

"If Shepherd had any grounds for this accusation beyond the jealousy and suspicion engendered by his own nature . . . they were but the vagrant hearsay scandals which he has been unable even approximately to substantiate. . . . There is no evidence that he (Mr. Hurlburt) did anything regarding either of these claims beyond instructions which from time to time he received, and nothing in the remotest degree casting suspicion upon his absolute integrity. . . . The Committee are clearly of the opinion that Mr. Morton has done nothing and at no time had he the remotest intention of doing anything which could compromise the honorable discharge of his official duties.

"During the course of the investigation, Mr. Blaine was called upon to testify as a witness for Mr. Hurlburt and incidentally was questioned as to the proceedings of the State Department in connection with the Landreau and Crédit Industriel claims and other South American interests. He was subjected to a degree of discourtesy which even the manifest ignorance of the gentlemen conducting the examination in regard to the questions involved could not excuse."

[37] The effect upon Mr. Blaine and his family is best seen in *Letters of Mrs. James G. Blaine*, I, 293 ff., and II, 39, note.

CHAPTER VI

THE CHILEAN REVOLUTION IN ITS RELATION TO THE UNITED STATES

THE position taken by Blaine in 1881 during the War of the Pacific resulted in a strong feeling in Chile against the Government of the United States and especially against its Secretary of State, who had formulated and outlined that position. Victorious Chile bitterly resented any attempt to deprive her of the full fruits of her victory and looked upon the Trescot mission and its implication of possible intervention as an insult to Chilean sovereignty. Mr. Blaine had instructed Trescot to threaten suspension of diplomatic intercourse in certain contingencies[1] and to state:

If our good offices are rejected and this policy of the absorption of an independent state be persisted in, this government . . . will hold itself free to appeal to the other republics of this continent to join it in an effort to avert consequences which cannot be confined to Chile and Peru, but which threaten with extremest danger the political institutions, the peaceful progress and the liberal civilization of all America.[2]

Mr. Blaine's policy was reversed, as has been seen, and the mission recalled. Chile imposed a humiliating

[1] See above, p. 120.
[2] *Sen. Exec. Doc.* No. 79, 47 Cong., 1st Session, 178.

and disastrous peace upon Peru and acquired control over the coveted nitrate beds, but she did not forget the blow to her pride. Mr. Blaine's remarks during the Congressional investigation in regard to the relations of Chile and England and the publicity given to all sorts of fantastic rumors about the former Secretary during the presidential campaign of 1884 were not calculated to reduce the animosity of Chile. These rumors even went so far as to accuse Blaine of so strong a desire to retain office in 1881 that he contemplated a war with Chile in order to force President Arthur to keep him on.[3] The military success of Chile gave her an aggressive exuberance and overconfidence, which led her to feel that she could undertake any conflict which might offer, and various jingoistic designs were entertained by certain elements there. A rumor that Chile had designs upon the Panama canal zone seemed of sufficient importance to cause Frelinghuysen to send instructions providing for investigation and prevention to all representatives of the United States in the Latin American countries.[4]

As the years went by and no new causes for friction arose, this feeling of animosity and suspicion seemed to disappear. Chile became peaceful and extremely pros-

[3] Repeated and countenanced in Hurlburt, *Meddling and Muddling*, 68.

[4] Frelinghuysen to Logan, August 7, 1882. Manuscript Instructions, Chile, 1882. The design was said to be the occupation of the State of Panama with the support of England, Brazil, and Ecuador. There is no evidence that the minister discovered any such design to be seriously contemplated.

perous. The United States was, however, excluded from any share in that prosperity, for the exploitation of the nitrate beds and the resultant increase in commerce fell to English capital, and the bonds between England and Chile grew constantly closer.[5] In 1886 the election of Balmaceda as president of Chile inaugurated a period in which the United States was to receive more consideration. Under Balmaceda's administration prompt and energetic steps were always taken to see that the persons and property of citizens of the United States were protected. Cordial feelings existed between the two Governments and the feeling of citizens of the United States, resident in Chile, was most friendly toward Balmaceda.[6]

Balmaceda became, however, more and more unpopular in Chile. He was an enthusiastic liberal and an honest administrator, but he incurred for one reason or another the opposition of each of the influential classes in Chile. Chile had been for generations republican in form but oligarchic in nature, and the aristocracy opposed Balmaceda's democratic schemes for the elevation of the lower classes. He antagonized the clergy by anti-clerical legislation and the English element and the capitalists by his opposition to the foreign control of Chilean economic life.[7] By 1890 practically

[5] William E. Curtis, *From the Andes to the Ocean*, 408-409. "This national prejudice against the United States was stimulated in a considerable degree by the jealousy of British tradesmen who were enjoying a monopoly of the foreign trade of Chile."

[6] Anson Uriel Hancock, *A History of Chile*, 367.

[7] G. F. Scott Elliott, *Chile: Its History and Development, Natural Features, Products, Commerce and Present Conditions*, 229.

all groups in Chile opposed him and he followed the
dangerous expedient of attempting a dictatorship in
order to prevent failure of his efforts. A special session
of the Chilean Congress summoned in December, 1890,
refused to pass Balmaceda's measures or to agree to
his budget, and he exercised his constitutional power of
proroguing it. On January 6, 1891, he issued a proclamation declaring that he would continue under the old
estimates until a new election should provide an acqui-
escent legislature. The Congressionalists immediately
revolted and civil war began. The army remained loyal
to Balmaceda, but the navy was in the control of the
revolutionists, who were thus able to acquire the northern provinces of Chile from which came most of the
revenue. Owing to the topography of the region, the
nitrate-bearing provinces could be held only by the faction controlling the sea forces, so Balmaceda found
himself in a dangerous situation. By May, 1891, the
Congressionalists had all the northern provinces. Balmaceda could not move without ships, and the revolutionists could not advance without arms. After a few
weeks' deadlock the opponents met in the battle of Pla-
cillas, in which the revolutionists were victorious. Balmaceda committed suicide in September. Elections were
held, and the revolution came to an end with the establishment of the new Government under President Jorge
Montt in September, 1891.[8]

Diplomatic relations with a country which is torn by
revolution and civil war must always present difficult

[8] The details of the civil war may be found in either of the histories
of Chile mentioned above.

problems. The revolution in Chile was the cause for occurrences of so serious a nature that the United States and Chile were very nearly involved in war. It is the purpose of this study to examine the part played in these episodes, and in the diplomatic crisis resulting from them, by the Secretary of State, his minister in Chile, and by other branches of the Government of the United States.[9]

The minister of the United States in Chile in 1891 was Mr. Patrick Egan, who had been appointed by President Harrison at the request of Secretary Blaine. Mr. Egan was an Irish American of the group known in political circles as "Blaine Irishmen." He had been treasurer of the Irish Land League in Ireland and had left Ireland hastily in 1882 to escape arrest during one of the periods of difficulty between the British Government and Ireland. He was in 1889 a newly naturalized American citizen. He was a man of ability and honor,[10]

[9] The correspondence for the period has been published practically *in toto* in *House Exec. Doc.* No. 91, 52 Cong., 1st Session (Serial 2954), about 700 pages. This correspondence includes the dispatches to and from the minister to Chile, to and from the Chilean minister in Washington, and the correspondence of the Department of the Navy on the subject. With it was published President Harrison's message of January 25, 1892, which summarized the events of the preceding year. The best secondary accounts of the Chilean controversy are "The Itata Incident" by Osgood Hardy in the *Hispanic American Historical Review*, V, 195-226, and Albert Bushnell Hart, "The Chilean Controversy," in *Practical Essays in American Government*, 98-132. Admiral Robley D. Evans, *A Sailor's Log; Recollections of Forty Years of Naval Life*, gives much light on the naval aspects of the question.

[10] H. T. Peck, "A Spirited Foreign Policy," *The Bookman*, XXI (June, 1905), 370.

and those who knew him spoke highly of his business experience and of his character.[11] His appointment as minister to Chile, however, invited much criticism. Not only had he had no diplomatic experience but of all Latin American States, Chile was the last to be chosen for him because of the close commercial connections between Chile and England.[12]

It is interesting but perhaps profitless to conjecture Mr. Blaine's motives in the appointment of Egan. The Republican party was openly endeavoring to break the ranks of the Irish Democrats and was willing to advance the interests of the Irish Republicans. Was this merely an attempt to find a berth for a political adherent of an influential group, or did the fact that the Irish Egan would be *persona non grata* to the English in Chile, whose influence Blaine had always resented, add just a bit to the attractiveness of the appointment? Did President Balmaceda's well-known antipathy for the English in Chile influence the appointment and did Blaine expect Egan to advance the interests of the anti-English capitalists and concessionaires? It is impossible to answer these questions but equally impossible to prevent their rising and absurd to presume that Blaine did not realize all the effects of such an appointment.[13]

Mr. Egan was favorably received by the Balmaceda

[11] Hart, "Chilean Controversy," 79.

[12] Egan's appointment was hotly criticized by the English element in Chile. See Curtis, *Between the Andes and the Ocean*, p. 409.

[13] It would be necessary to know Mr. Blaine's reasons for the appointment before agreeing with Mr. Hart that it was "upon its face unsuitable and impolitic." "Chilean Controversy," 107.

Government and cordial relations existed between that Government and the United States citizens in Chile. It was natural, therefore, that, when the revolution began, they should feel considerable sympathy for the Balmacedists. The United States Government was formally correct in refusing to recognize the revolutionist provisional government and was acting in accordance with the tradition of the United States, which held that a government to be recognized must be a *de facto* government and in actual control. When the success of the revolution became apparent in September, 1891, recognition was immediately accorded.[14] The Congressionalists, however, had for a long time had the support of the English element and bitterly resented the attitude of the United States, which, if officially correct, had an undercurrent of support for Balmaceda. In addition to this failure to recognize the government of the Congressionalists, it was known that Balmaceda had attempted to buy ships from the United States and although he had been promptly refused,[15] the fact that Egan had forwarded the request increased his unpopularity in Chile. The appointment of Egan's son as agent for a railroad company which had a large claim against the Chilean Government also created a bad impression in Chile.[16] In June of 1891 Mr. Egan made an unsuccessful attempt to use the good offices of the

[14] *House Exec. Doc.* No. 91, 52 Cong., 1st Session, 71. Egan recognized the government of the Congressionalists on September 5, 1891, at Blaine's orders.

[15] Wharton to Egan, July 12, 1891, *ibid.*, 55.

[16] Hart, "Chilean Controversy," 115.

United States in securing negotiations between the two factions for the restoration of peace.[17]

In the period of the revolution itself, that is from January to September, 1891, Mr. Egan and the Department of State made only this slight contribution to the situation. The slowness with which recognition was given was officially correct and in accordance with tradition. Mr. Egan's indiscretions were of a minor character, and there had been no departmental seal of approval for his slight efforts made in behalf of Balmaceda. Mr. Blaine and the Department of State could not be held accountable for other events of the period which caused trouble between the United States and Chile but with which the minister of the United States had nothing to do. The cause for the ill will against the United States which led to the "Baltimore" affair, which nearly provoked a war between the two countries in the winter of 1891-1892, must be sought elsewhere.

In May, 1891, occurred the "Itata" incident, which was in large measure responsible for much of the feeling in Chile against the United States. The Congressionalists had been victorious in the northern provinces and had set up their provisional government at Iquique. They had ships and money but only a small supply of arms and ammunition. The Balmacedists were daily expecting vessels being built abroad, and it became a race between the opposing forces to remedy these deficiencies.[18] Early in March, 1891, the Balmacedan Gov-

[17] *House Exec. Doc.* No. 91, 52 Cong., 1st Session, 51-54.
[18] Ricardo Trumbull, a graduate of Yale and a descendant of

ernment passed a decree prohibiting the importation of arms into Chile, and Señor Lazcano, Chilean minister to the United States, requested Mr. Blaine to communicate this decree to the customs houses of the United States in order to prevent the shipment to Chile of arms and munitions of war.[19] Mr. Blaine at once, and quite correctly, answered that by the laws of the United States, which were understood to be in conformity with the law of nations, traffic in arms and munitions was permitted. He stated also that the laws on the subject of neutrality were put in force upon application to the courts, and that the laws not only forbade the infringement of neutrality but also provided penalties for their infraction.[20] This appears to have been the only contact between the Department of State and the "Itata" incident.

This incident may be summarized, in brief, as follows:[21] Ricardo Trumbull reached New York in March, 1891, and through the W. R. Grace Company, which had extensive interests in Chile, he purchased arms to be shipped to San Francisco whence they were

Jonathan Trumbull, was sent by Montt to the United States as the agent of the revolutionists. (Montt to Blaine, May 6, 1891, *House Exec. Doc.* No. 91, 52 Cong., 1st Session, 199.) He said, "If we had 5000 arms we could wipe Balmaceda's army off the face of the earth." (Quoted in Hardy, "Itata Incident," 221.)

[19] Lazcano to Blaine, March 10, 1891, *House Exec. Doc.* No. 91, 52 Cong., 1st Session, 197.

[20] Blaine to Lazcano, March 13, 1891, *ibid.*, 197.

[21] The account follows Hardy, "Itata Incident," *Hispanic American Historical Review*, which is a work representing much research into manuscript and newspaper material not easily accessible.

to be delivered to the "Itata," sent from Chile at Trumbull's request. It reached San Diego harbor on May 3 and put in ostensibly for provisions and coal, claiming to be bound for San Francisco with passengers and cargo of merchandise. On May 5 the vessel was visited by Major George R. Gard, United States marshal, who arrested the captain and vessel and placed a deputy on board.

The detention of the "Itata" was ordered by the United States Attorney General W. H. Miller because of the appeal of Minister Lazcano on the ground that she was about to violate the neutrality laws of the United States.[22] Señor Lazcano had, after his rebuff by Blaine, taken his own measures to prevent the exportation of arms to the revolutionists. He employed detectives to watch Mr. Trumbull, and retained Mr. John W. Foster as counsel for the Balmaceda Government.[23] The detectives supplied Lazcano with information as to the sale of the munitions and the plans for their disposal. He went to the State Department to ask that the coasting schooner "Robert and Minnie" upon which they had been loaded be detained. The United States customs officials visited the schooner but found no reason for the detention of the cargo.[24] No aid being forthcoming from the State Department, Lazcano apparently applied to the Attorney General and to the Treasury Department, for on May 4-6 orders were

[22] Hardy, "Itata Incident," 205.
[23] Foster, *Diplomatic Memoirs*, 289.
[24] Hardy, "Itata Incident," 206.

sent out from both departments to detain both the "Itata" and the "Robert and Minnie." Mr. Foster appeared openly as director of Lazcano's campaign in a telegram to Judge Brunson requesting his aid in the detention of the vessel and arms by "legal proceedings even if eventually defeated. The attorney general will not object." [25] The "Robert and Minnie" had, however, already left the harbor at Wilmington, and upon being pursued, at once went into Mexican waters where she could not be taken. The "Itata," seized May 5, was permitted to remain with steam up and on May 6, weighed anchor and left the harbor with the United States deputy on board. Somewhere on the high seas off the coast of Southern California it met the "Robert and Minnie," took off the arms, and made at once for Iquique, the headquarters of the revolutionists.

The escape of the "Itata" was considered a serious affront to the United States. President Harrison was indignant that the authority of the United States should be so flippantly treated, and the Secretary of the Navy dispatched the "Charleston" to take the "Itata" by force if necessary and bring it to San Diego with cargo intact. The "Charleston" did not sight the "Itata" in the long voyage down the coast. The two vessels reached the Chilean coast early in June just a day apart. Long before the ships reached Iquique, the Congressionalist leaders had come to the conclusion that they could not incur the results of an attempt to retain

[25] Quoted from the Manuscript Cole Papers, Hardy, "Itata Incident," 207.

either the "Itata" or the cargo. So on May 18 the minister of foreign affairs of the provisional government gave Rear-Admiral Brown, in command of the United States squadron in Chilean waters, written assurance that the vessel would be turned over to him upon arrival.[26] This was done and on June 13 the "Charleston" left Iquique with the "Itata" for the return trip to San Diego where it was libeled in the United States courts but was discharged on the ground that there had been no violation of the United States neutrality laws. The Government appealed the case but the decision of the lower court was upheld.

Mr. Foster stated long afterward that "our purpose was attained in preventing the military supplies from reaching the revolutionists, but our success proved of no substantial value as the revolutionists were victorious in the next battle with the the government forces. Balmaceda committed suicide and my client, his minister, left Washington." [27] The surrender of the "Itata" was felt by the revolutionists to have caused the prolongation of the struggle for some months and aroused much hard feeling, which was not lessened by the ultimate return of the vessel; and the fact that the Government of the United States was not upheld in its own courts rather added to, than diminished, the sense of injury.

The "Itata" incident can in no way be directly connected with the Department of State or with Secretary

[26] *House Exec. Doc.* No. 91, 52 Cong., 1st Session, 257.
[27] Foster, *Diplomatic Memoirs*, II, 290.

Blaine. There is no evidence that he had anything to do either with the detention or the chase of the "Itata," and there is some evidence that he disapproved of both. The episode created, of course, a great amount of newspaper excitement, and in several papers appeared reports that while Attorney General Miller and Secretary Tracy felt that the "Itata" should be recaptured the rest of the administration did not.[28] Mr. Foster wrote of President Harrison's "indignation" but made no mention of the attitude of his friend, Secretary Blaine. With the "Itata" affair, therefore, it seems safe to say, the Secretary and Mr. Egan had nothing to do.

The United States Navy was unpopular in Chile as a result of this incident, an unpopularity increased by subsequent events. The cable owned by the Central and South American Telegraph Company, incorporated in the United States, connected Chile with the outside world. It landed at Iquique, which was in the hands of the revolutionists, who thus controlled the connection and shut off the region to the south. At Mr. Egan's request the United States squadron gave protection to the cable company and a direct offshore connection was made.[29] In this case the right seems to have been with the company, but the revolutionists believed that they had one more evidence of the partiality of the United States,[30]

[28] Hardy, "Itata Incident," 214.
[29] *House Exec. Doc.* No. 91, 52 Cong., 1st Session, 275.
[30] Hart, "Chilean Controversy," 111.

Late in August occurred another irritating incident. The revolutionists, about to end the war by an attack upon Santiago, felt that secrecy was all-important. It was rumored that the attempt was to be made to land a force in Quintero Bay some twenty miles north of Valparaiso. Admiral Brown left the harbor of Valparaiso on the "San Francisco" at noon and returned about five o'clock. A port boat came out to the flag ship with the United States consul on board, and upon his return the news of the landing of the Congressionalist forces was announced.[31] Admiral Brown always insisted that he had given orders that no news should be given out, but he must be held responsible for the leak.[32] It is possible that some of the attacks upon Admiral Brown and the United States Navy were due to false reports spread by the Balmacedists, who were not anxious to preserve the reputation of the United States as a neutral.[33] Once again, for the cable affair and for the indiscretions of Admiral Brown, no blame can attach to the Secretary of State nor to Mr. Egan.

Notwithstanding these disturbing incidents, the new government of Chile started out in September, 1891, on very good terms with the United States minister. The life of this Government, of which Señor Matta was secretary of state for foreign affairs, may be considered as coincident with a second period in the relations of

[31] *Ibid.*

[32] *House Exec. Doc.* No. 91, 52 Cong., 1st Session, 74 ff.

[33] John Bassett Moore, "The Chilean Affair," *Political Science Quarterly*, VIII (September, 1893), 467 ff.

the United States and Chile.[34] In the first period it must be admitted that there were blunders made which gave the Chilean insurgents cause for irritation against the United States. In the second period the blunders were Chilean, while the conduct of the representative of the United States was irreproachable.

Mr. Egan reported on September 17:

Since the unfortunate episode of the "Itata," the young and unthinking element of those who were then in opposition to the government have had a bitter feeling against the United States, and the English element, as has always been their custom in this country, do all in their power, from motives of self interest, to promote and foster this feeling. The more reasonable men of the party in power, on the other hand, admit that a mistake was made on the part of some of those who, on their behalf, were responsible for that transaction, and that the United States could not consistently have taken any other course than the one she adopted. . . . The hostile element, however, has let no opportunity pass of misrepresenting and villifying everything pertaining to the United States.[35]

The attempt at mutual understanding was to be of short duration and in a few days suspicion against the United States was again rampant. Cheated of revenge upon their principal adversary by Balmaceda's death, the new Government determined to institute criminal proceedings against all the officials of the late Government, some twenty of whom had been refugees in the

[34] The first period, January, 1891-September, 1891; second period, September, 1891-January 1, 1892; and the third period, January, 1892-August, 1892.

[35] Egan to Blaine, September 17, 1891, *House Exec. Doc.* No. 91, 52 Cong., 1st Session, 74.

United States legation since the fall of Balmaceda. Mr. Egan was called upon, September 24, to terminate the asylum. He felt that to do so would be to sacrifice the lives of the refugees and asserted that he would permit them to leave the legation only under proper safe conduct to neutral territory. The legation was placed under police surveillance, and the movements of inmates and visitors spied upon and interfered with.[36]

Secretary Blaine, who had not been in good health during the summer, was still at Bar Harbor, and Mr. Wharton, who was acting Secretary of State until the end of October, 1891, approved Mr. Egan's conduct and instructed him to insist firmly that the respect and inviolability due to the minister of the United States and to the legation buildings should be observed. He wished to have information, also, as to whether the representatives of other countries were exercising the right of asylum, and whether Chile was according them the same treatment.[37] Mr. Egan replied that several other legations had received refugees, that the Spanish minister had asked for a safe conduct for those in his legation, but that it had been refused by Señor Matta.[38] The legations appeared to be receiving the same treatment. Mr. Egan stated that he was acting strictly in the spirit of the Barrundia affair, in which the United States had extended its views upon the granting of asylum.[39]

[36] Egan to Blaine, September 24, 1891, *ibid.*, 77.
[37] Wharton to Egan, September 26, 1891, *ibid.*, 78.
[38] Egan to Blaine, September 28, 1891, *ibid.*, 79.
[39] See above Chapter IV, p. 104. Mr. John Bassett Moore in his

On October 1 Mr. Wharton telegraphed Egan:

The President desires to establish and maintain the most friendly relations with Chile, but the right of asylum having been tacitly, if not expressly, allowed to other foreign legations, and having been exercised by our minister with the old government in the interest and for the safety of the adherents of the party now in power, the President cannot but regard the application of another rule accompanied by acts of disrespect to our legation, as the manifestation of a most unfriendly spirit.[40]

Mr. Egan was instructed to send a copy of this telegram to the minister of foreign affairs. Egan thus had the approval of the Department of State and of the President for his conduct thus far. The matter of asylum has ever been a delicate one and one upon which there has been much debate among students of international law.[41] It seems difficult to discover, however, just what Mr. Egan could have done except that which he did do in admitting and protecting the refugees, for they were indisputably in dire need of asylum. After the first few days there were but fifteen men being protected by the American flag, and they were all charged with political offenses. Mr. Egan pledged that there would be no abuse of the asylum and asked for the refugees a safe conduct out of the country. His conduct throughout this period seems to have been cool and circumspect. He confined himself almost

article in the *Political Science Quarterly* says that this was a bad precedent and that the demand for safe conduct had no standing in international law.

[40] Wharton to Egan, October 1, 1891, *ibid.*, 88.

[41] See Hyde, *International Law*, I, 400 ff.

entirely to a verbal transcript of his instructions and his entire attitude was moderate. He appears to have given full weight to the confused and difficult situation in Chile, and neither he nor the Department of State wished to exert any great pressure.[42]

So the situation stood when there occurred, on the night of October 16, an incident which nearly brought the United States into war with Chile. Captain Schley of the "Baltimore," then in Valparaiso harbor, gave shore leave to about one hundred sailors and petty officers. This extensive leave may have been unwise under the circumstances, for Valparaiso had been the scene of riotous proceedings in the preceding weeks, and it was known that there was great animosity toward the United States Navy because of the occurrences of the preceding summer. It seems quite natural, therefore, that there should have been difficulty between the United States seamen and the discharged longshoremen and Chilean sailors, who were frequenting the saloons and streets of the port.[43] This lack of foresight on the part of Captain Schley does not, of course, afford excuse for the riot which occurred on the night of October 16, when the American seamen were attacked

[42] Evans, *A Sailor's Log. Recollections of Forty Years of Naval Life*, 276. Evans's diary for December 27, 1891, states, "As to Egan, he has done only what he was instructed to do from Washington and he has done it capitally well. The Chilean Secretary of State has found himself outclassed every time he has tackled the little Irishman who really writes beautifully, clearly and forcibly and so far they have not scored one point against him." See also Hart, *Practical Essays*, 115.

[43] Hancock, *Chile*, 368-369.

by a mob, which killed two of them and wounded many others.[44] From the viewpoint of the United States the attack appeared to have been unprovoked and premeditated, against the uniform the men wore and not against them as individuals. There was evidence that the police had not taken prompt or effective measures to subdue the riot, if, indeed, they had not actually participated in it. The question of especial interest was, of course, what would be the attitude of the Chilean Government and, in case that attitude were unsatisfactory, what should be the position of the United States.

Captain Schley at once conducted an inquiry to determine just what had taken place and where, if at all, the blame lay. He sent a report to the Navy Department, which was at once transmitted to Mr. Wharton. The report showed that the "Baltimore" sailors were unarmed and gave no provocation, that the police did not give them protection, and that many were arrested and held for some time.[45] Mr. Wharton wrote to Mr.

[44] The details of the "Baltimore" affair may be found in all the secondary accounts and in the summary given by President Harrison in his message of January 25, *House Exec. Doc.* No. 91, 52 Cong., 1st Session.

[45] Schley to Tracy, October 23, 1891, *ibid.*, 293. Captain Schley took great pains to prove that his men were not even intoxicated, which called forth a characteristic comment from Commander Evans, who reached Valparaiso with the gunboat "Yorktown" shortly after the "Baltimore" affair. He says in *The Sailor's Log*, 259:

"He (Schley) was in the midst of a correspondence with the intendente, conducted in the most perfect Castilian, to show, or prove, that his men were all perfectly sober when they were assaulted on shore. I did not agree with him in this, for in the first place, I doubted the

Egan on October 23, telling him that there had been, in the week which had elapsed, no expression of regret on the part of Chile, nor any pledge of an inquiry or of punishment of the guilty. Egan was instructed to bring the facts as reported by Schley before the Government of Chile and to inquire whether

. . . there are any qualifying facts in the possession of that government or any explanation to be offered of an event that has very deeply pained the people of the United States, not only by reason of the resulting death of one of our sailors and the pitiless wounding of others, but even more as an apparent expression of an unfriendliness toward this government which might put in peril the maintenance of amicable relations between the two countries. If the facts are as reported by Capt. Schley, this government cannot doubt that the government of Chile will offer prompt and full reparation.[46]

The Chilean answer to Mr. Wharton's note was insolent in the extreme. Señor Matta stated that the

fact, and in the second, it was not an issue worth discussing. His men were probably drunk on shore, properly drunk, getting drunk which they did on Chilean rum paid for in good United States money. When in this condition they were more entitled to protection than if they had been sober. This was my view of it, at least, and the one I always held about men whom I commanded. Instead of protecting them, the Chileans foully murdered these men, and we believed with the connivance and assistance of armed policemen. That was the issue — not the question of whether they were drunk or sober."

[46] Wharton to Egan, October 23, 1891, *House Exec. Doc.* No. 91, 52 Cong., 1st Session, 107-108. It is this telegram which has been regarded as President Harrison's work and as committing Blaine to a forceful policy of which he did not approve. See Crawford, *Life of Blaine*, 617. On the other hand by some, in particular Secretary of Navy Tracy, the note was thought to be mild in the extreme. Curtis, *Between the Andes and the Ocean*, 411.

note "emits appreciations, formulates demands, and advances threats that, without being cast back with acrimony, are not acceptable nor could they be accepted in the present case, nor in another of a like nature." He said that Chilean authorities were investigating the matter, and that they had the sole power to deal with such cases. When they arrived at a decision, he would communicate it but he declined to accept the view that anything had happened at Valparaiso which could imperil the maintenance of friendly relations.[47] The issue was now joined. Whether peace or war was to result depended upon the conduct of affairs during the next two months. In Chile the critical questions were whether the irascible Señor Matta would remain in office, and what were to be the results of the judicial inquiry. In the United States the situation depended upon the respective attitudes of the President and his Secretaries of State and Navy. In how far was the conduct of affairs the policy of each? The published documents contained little for the months of November and December to indicate what the final policy and solution were to be.[48] Officially the Government of the United States waited patiently for the results of the Chilean inquiry. It is, however, possible to fill in the gaps in the documents to a certain extent.

Mr. Blaine returned to Washington before the first

[47] Egan to Blaine, October 28, 1891, *House Exec. Doc.* No. 91, 52 Cong., 1st Session, 120.

[48] They consist almost entirely of dispatches from Mr. Egan and Captain Schley relating to the conduct of the inquiry and the Chilean attitude toward the refugees in the legation.

of November and assumed the conduct of the negotiations with Chile. He was quite willing to give that tempest-torn state ample time to get on its feet and come to its senses. Latin judicial processes were, he recognized, quite different from the Anglo-Saxon, and he was willing to await their arrival at a decision. Chile, in November, conducted elections and did away with the provisional government. The old cabinet, however, was to hold over until the end of December when the newly-elected president, Señor Jorge Montt, would be inaugurated.[49] Mr. Egan reported that he hoped and expected more amicable relations under the new and more regular government. Mr. Blaine felt justified, therefore, in waiting until the new ministry should be in office, provided, of course, that no new source of friction should arise. His biographer, who was a close intimate of the family, states:

Mr. Blaine was disposed from every motive to take a moderate view of the situation. . . . Mr. Blaine would waive no hair's breadth of the right of asylum and the President refused even to consider the question whether asylum had been properly given until the privileges of the legation were restored, . . . but toward a country rent by internal wars, Mr. Blaine believed every consideration should be shown. He could not learn that there was any official wrong intent. He thought the affair was in the nature of a street scrimmage between sailors and landsmen aggravated by strong suspicion that the American flag had been used to shelter the foes of Chile, but without government instigation or countenance. He

[49] Egan to Blaine, November 10 to 14, 1891, *House Exec. Doc.* No. 91, 52 Cong., 1st Session, 137-140.

thought Chile was too small and our country too large to permit a fierce attitude toward a neighbor even when offending. There could be no glory in any victory by force; and he was exceedingly desirous to win the friendly cooperation and confidence of Chile, not to compel her submission. He demanded for the "Baltimore" sailors open trial and proper representation; but he could not magnify a brawl into a battle. . . . It was with difficulty that such a circumstance could take on continental dimensions. . . . Even in the earliest heat he found Chilean dispatches "temperate for Chile" and saw, some thought too readily, a disposition in Chile to apologize.[50]

This attitude of toleration may have been somewhat difficult to maintain, for the conduct of Señor Matta, the Chilean minister of foreign affairs, was indubitably most irritating. Mr. Egan's letters were filled with accounts of the molestation of the inmates of the legation, of drunken police spies, who broke windows and insulted servants, and of total lack of aid from the Chilean Foreign Office.[51] President Harrison's message to Congress of December 9, contained a long reference to the Chilean affair ending with the statement, almost a threat, that the Government was awaiting the result of the investigation conducted by the criminal court of Valparaiso and hoped for some "adequate and satisfactory response" to the note of October 23, which called the attention of the Chilean Government to the "Baltimore" incident.

If these just expectations should be disappointed or further

[50] Hamilton, *Blaine*, 675-676.

[51] For instance, Egan to Blaine, November 20, 1891, *House Exec. Doc.* No. 91, 52 Cong., 1st Session, 147-148.

needless delay intervene, I will by special message bring this matter again to the attention of Congress for such action as may be necessary.[52]

The President appears to have been less patient than his Secretary of State.[53]

Irritated by Harrison's message and by the report of the Secretary of the Navy which accompanied it, the easily angered Señor Matta again flew into print. He sent a telegram to the Chilean minister of the United States, which was at once read in the Chilean Senate and published in the Chilean papers. The Chilean minister to the United States, Señor Pedro Montt, was authorized to communicate its contents to the Department of State and to print it in the newspapers of the United States. It was sent also to all Chilean legations in Latin America and in Europe. The note was in the nature of a diplomatic atrocity, starting with the remark:

Having read the portion of the report of the Secretary of the

[52] Richardson, *Messages and Papers*, IX, 186. The original response from Señor Matta had been so offensive in tone that it had remained unanswered.

[53] Peck, *Twenty Years of the Republic*, 243. "At this time the opposition press in the United States very intemperately accused Mr. Blaine of seeking to stir up a war with Chile. Looking back upon all the evidence, it is impossible to hold this view. Mr. Blaine's attitude was a firm one, yet it is certain that all the while he was exerting his influence to hold back the President. Mr. Harrison was, perhaps unconsciously, influenced by the thought that a foreign war would almost certainly re-elect him; but whatever his motives, he seemed anxious to force matters to a point at which war would be inevitable. Mr. Blaine on the other hand, employed patience and refrained from any action which could be regarded as precipitate."

Navy and the message of the President of the United States, I think it proper to inform you that the statements on which both report and message are based are erroneous or deliberately incorrect.

Señor Matta went on to state that Egan's complaints of the molestation of the legation were lies, and that "with respect to the seamen of the 'Baltimore' there is, moreover, no exactness nor sincerity in what is said at Washington." Piling one innuendo upon another and imputing double dealing and untruthfulness to all officials of the United States in Chile, Señor Matta ended his note with the truculent instruction:

Deny in the meantime everything that does not agree with these statements, being assured of their exactness as we are of the right, the dignity, and the final success of Chile, notwithstanding the intrigues which proceed from so low [a source] and to threats which come from so high [a source].[54]

The publication of such a document was an act incendiary in a high degree. Patience and forbearance are qualities much to be commended, but they are apt to wear thin when repeated assaults are made upon them. Mr. Egan sent a sharp demand for an official copy of the note to the ministry of foreign affairs and upon its receipt suspended diplomatic relations.[55] The police interference to which the legation had been subjected, thereupon increased until it was practically in a state of seige. The situation became so strained that the Argentine minister, as dean of the diplomatic corps,

[54] *House Exec. Doc.* No. 91, 52 Cong., 1st Session, 179-180.
[55] Egan to Blaine, December 14, 1891, *ibid.*, 181-183.

protested to the Foreign Office and received a promise that the interference would cease.[56]

Evans, who was in command of the "Yorktown," the only United States vessel in Chilean waters, wrote in his diary, December 12:

I don't see how Mr. Harrison can help sending a fleet down here to teach these people manners. . . . I certainly would like to hear what Mr. Blaine has to say in reply.

And again on December 16:

The papers here grow more and more insolent, and I don't see how Mr. Harrison can avoid sending an ultimatum at a very early day. In the meantime the Chileans are working like beavers to get their ships ready, and in two weeks from now the whole fleet will be ready for service.[57]

A few days later Evans had orders to keep his ship filled with coal, and on December 28 he recorded that he had met the head of the commercial house of Grace and Company, who had showed him a telegram from W. R. Grace, an intimate friend of Blaine, who had been in Washington

for the past ten days trying to convince Secretary Blaine that we must not have war. He wires that Harrison is for war, that the Navy Department is making every preparation for war and that Blaine, while in favor of war under certain conditions only, cannot stem the tide, and that unless Chile makes ample apology at once nothing can prevent war. . . . Taking all things into consideration, the crew of the "Yorktown" will sleep at the loaded guns tonight and every night until I get some better news.[58]

[56] *Ibid.*, 184.
[57] Evans, *A Sailor's Log*, 265 ff.
[58] *Ibid.*, 277.

On January 5, he wrote that he had met Egan's son, who had just come from Washington with word that Harrison was wild over the "Baltimore" affair and that it was all Blaine could do to hold him back.[59]

In those turbulent weeks after the Matta note, there was not one dispatch from Blaine either to Señor Pedro Montt or to Minister Egan, beyond the barest formalities.[60] Mr. Egan was warned against letting any of the legation dispatches become public. No ships were sent to sustain the little "Yorktown." The State Department awaited the formation of the new Chilean Government. On January 1st Egan telegraphed that a new ministry had been formed, that two of the ministers were his personal friends, and that conciliation would mark the disposition of the new Government toward the United States. He said that at least two of the new cabinet had openly expressed disapproval of the Matta note and that, since it was also condemned by public opinion, he felt it would now be no difficult matter to have it withdrawn. He also thought that the safe conduct for the refugees and the question of the "Baltimore" assault and the disrespect to the legation could be settled.[61]

On January 4 Señor Montt sent Mr. Blaine a copy of a telegram received from Señor Pereira, the new

<hr>

[59] Evans, *op. cit.,* 285.

[60] All the correspondence seems to have been published. No additional material appeared in an examination of the archives of the State Department.

[61] Egan to Blaine, January 1, 1892, *House Exec. Doc.* No. 91, 52 Cong., 1st Session, 187-188.

Chilean minister for foreign affairs, which authorized him to inform Blaine that a summary of the judicial proceedings relative to the "Baltimore" affair, "which Chile had lamented and does so sincerely lament," would be sent at once.[62] On January 8 Señor Montt forwarded that summary, stating in addition that he had special instructions to state that the Government of Chile had felt regret for the unfortunate events of October 16, that Chile sincerely deplored the occurrence and would do all in its power to secure the trial and punishment of the guilty parties.[63]

Then and then only did Secretary Blaine move. The moment for which he had been waiting with such patience had arrived. He felt that the new Government of Chile was ready to make amends, and that a statement somewhat more definite than the communication of Señor Montt was due the United States and would be forthcoming. On January 8 he telegraphed Mr. Egan asking

whether all that is personally offensive to the President and other officers of the United States in the December circular of the late Minister of foreign affairs will be withdrawn by the new government, also whether a safe conduct will be granted to the refugees who are still in the legation, and finally whether all surveillance of the legation has been removed.[64]

Egan replied, January 12, that he had secured permission for the refugees to leave the country in lieu of

[62] *Ibid.*, 226.
[63] *Ibid.*, 228.
[64] *Ibid.*, 188.

a written safe conduct; that the legation was free from espionage; but, in regard to Mr. Blaine's first point, he must await the return to the city of President Montt.[65] When the President returned, he informed Egan that his Government had no objection to withdrawing all that was considered disagreeable to the United States. He likened the Matta note to a message to Congress of a President of the United States, which had ever been considered a document of which another government could not take diplomatic cognizance. Mr. Egan felt that an expression of regret for such parts of the document as were considered offensive to the President should supplement the withdrawal and obtained from Pereira assurance that Señor Montt had been authorized to express regret for all which had created unpleasantness.[66]

This rather equivocal withdrawal of Señor Matta's offensive note did not seem to Secretary Blaine sufficient response to his requirements, and he requested more definite and suitable terms. He stated that the note had been unprecedented and was not at all similar to a message from the President to the Congress of the United States. Chile did not, moreover, continue her tacit agreement as to the departure of the refugees. Angered by the salute which Commander Evans gave the Spanish minister who had accompanied the refugees on board the "Yorktown," Pereira flatly refused to guar-

[65] Egan to Blaine, Jaunary 12, 1892, *House Exec. Doc.* No. 91, 188.
[66] Egan to Blaine, January 16, 1892, *ibid.*, 190.

antee their security if they left the "Yorktown" for a passenger steamship.[67]   On January 20, Señor Montt asked Secretary Blaine for the withdrawal of Minister Egan on the grounds that he was *persona non grata* to the Government of Chile.[68]

This continuation of unconciliatory actions seemed somewhat less than Blaine felt was due in the way of reparation. On January 21 there was sent to Chile a dispatch, which was along the lines of Mr. Blaine's preceding instructions but was more peremptory, so that it bore the character of an ultimatum. Mr. Egan was to ask for a suitable apology and adequate reparation for the injury suffered by the Government of the United States in the "Baltimore" affair and for a withdrawal and suitable apology for the Matta note. In case these

[67] Commander Evans' response to this criticism was hardly calculated to calm Pereira. He had not been called "Fighting Bob" Evans without reason. The account in his *A Sailor's Log*, 288-294, of the arrival of the refugees on the "Yorktown" is very vividly told. In regard to the salute to the Spanish minister, Evans "promptly requested Mr. Egan to say to the minister of foreign affairs that I was responsible to my own government and not to that of Chile for my conduct, and I considered his remarks about my salute to the Spanish minister offensive and would not submit to them; also that I should cable the matter to my government, which I did, and, as they have not said a word about it, I assume that they aprove my action." p. 292. Evans may have had no reprimand from Secretary Tracy for the language used upon this occasion, but Mr. Blaine, when called to account by Señor Montt, admitted that the wording of the telegram was improper and objectionable. *House Exec. Doc.* No. 91 (Part 2), 51 Cong., 1st Session.

[68] *House Exec. Doc.* No. 91, 52 Cong., 1st Session, 229.

results were not forthcoming, diplomatic relations were to be severed. No response was to be made to the request for Mr. Egan's withdrawal until the Chilean reply to the ultimatum was received.[69]

It is just at this point that the Secretary of State has received much censure on the conduct of the negotiations. It has been said that from January 1 on, the Chilean Government had been making every effort, short of an abject apology, for the amicable settlement of all questions involved, and that there was no necessity for a demand for further humiliation of Chile; that she had expressed regret for the "Baltimore" affair and for the Matta note, and that the ill-treatment of the United States legation had ceased. Señor Montt and Mr. Blaine had discussed the possibility of an arbitration agreement to determine the indemnity, provided the Chilean criminal court found Chile responsible for the "Baltimore" episode.[70] Why then were further demands necessary? It has been said that the political situation in the United States was the deciding factor in the case: that President Harrison wished to take advantage of the war spirit to ensure his re-election, and that Secretary Blaine refused to be left behind, thinking to secure his own nomination by a similar bid for votes.[71]

[69] Blaine to Egan, January 21, 1891, *House Exec. Doc.* No. 91, 52 Cong., 1st Session, 173-174.

[70] Montt to Blaine, January 23, 1892, *House Exec. Doc.* No. 91 (Pt. 2), 52 Cong., 1st Session, 3. Montt had never actually offered arbitration.

[71] See Fish, *American Diplomacy*, 390.

It does not appear that there is ground for such conclusions after a careful study of the evidence. In the first place, the forbearance of the Secretary of State had been great, and his demands of January 8 were not exorbitant. Chile did not meet these demands squarely, nor did her subsequent conduct give much cause for further consideration. In the second place, it was well known that President Harrison and Secretary Tracy were anxious for war and it is doubtful whether they could have been satisfied with less than a direct apology. Mr. Blaine was, in the winter and spring of 1892, a sick man, a doomed man, and it is very doubtful whether he ever seriously entertained a thought or desire for a nomination which he had so flatly refused in 1888. It is possible, however, that the Chilean affair did estrange the President and the Secretary of State, and that the coolness which resulted in Mr. Blaine's resignation may have dated from these January days.

Regardless of the reasons and the responsibility for the note of January 21, there can be no doubt that the policy of the following days was that of President Harrison. Secretary Tracy stated much later that as soon as the ultimatum, which he attributes to President Harrison, was dispatched, preparations for war began.[72] Senate and House committees conferred with the Secretary of the Navy, coal was purchased, plans of action

[72] They probably began much earlier. Some were made at the time of the "Itata" incident. Commander Evans, sent to Valparaiso early in September, wrote in his diary at that time of the possibility of war and active service. The feeling of the Navy all along appears to have been bellicose and impatient of delay.

were mapped out, and commanding officers were designated.[73]

In addition to all this warlike preparation, President Harrison took a step which was quite as warlike in its way as Tracy's activity. On January 25, before there had been time to receive the Chilean reply to the so-called "ultimatum," he sent all the correspondence on the Chilean controversy to Congress with an accompanying message of most uncompromising character.[74] The message summarized at length the history of the controversy and ended with the following statement:

In submitting these papers to Congress for that grave and patriotic consideration which the questions involved demand, I desire to say that I am of the opinion that the demands made of Chile by this government should be adhered to and enforced. If the dignity as well as the prestige and influence of the United States are not to be wholly sacrificed we must protect those who, in foreign ports, display the flag and wear the colors of this government against insult, brutality and death inflicted in resentment of the acts of their government and not for any

[73] Curtis, *Between the Andes and the Pacific*, 411-413. Mr. Tracy concluded his account, made long after 1892, with the statement:

"According to the plan laid out, after the fleets had concentrated, they were to proceed to Chile, drive the Chilean men-of-war under the guns of the forts at Valparaiso, and then attack the whole coast line of Chile. The coal mines in the southern part of that country were to be seized, thus cutting off the coal supply for the warships of the enemy, and all other details were looked after. Then came Chile's note of apology and her offer of $75,000 indemnity, which was accepted." Even after so many years Mr. Tracy's tone seems regretful!

[74] *House Exec. Doc.* No. 91 (Pt. 1), 52 Cong., 1st Session, which has been used throughout this study. The correspondence seems to have been printed in entirety.

fault of their own. It has been my desire in every way to cultivate friendly and intimate relations with all the governments
of this hemisphere. We do not covet their territory; we desire
their peace and prosperity. We look for no advantage in our
relations with them, except the increased exchanges of commerce
upon a basis of mutual benefit. We regret every civil contest
that disturbs their peace and paralyzes their development, and
are always ready to give our good offices for the restoration of
peace. It must, however, be understood that this government
while exercising the utmost forbearance towards weaker powers
will extend its strong and adequate protection to its citizens, to
its officers, and to its humblest sailor when made the victims of
wantonness and cruelty in resentment, not of their personal misconduct, but of the official acts of their government.

.   .   .   .

I have as yet received no reply to our note of the 21st inst.
but in my opinion I ought not to delay longer to bring these
matters to the attention of Congress for such action as may be
decreed appropriate.[75]

It is difficult to understand the necessity for such
haste unless it was that the President expected Chile to
continue her policy of equivocation and delay, and that
a declaration of war would thus be a contingency for
which Congress must be prepared. As a matter of fact
the ultimatum, received in Chile January 23, was answered January 25 (received in Washington the following day) by a complete surrender on the part of
Chile on every point. The "Baltimore" incident was
sincerely lamented, and it was left to the Supreme Court
of the United States or to a court of arbitration to

[75] Harrison's Message, *ibid.*, pp. i-xiv.

decide what reparation Chile should make. The Matta note was absolutely withdrawn, and good relations with the United States were pledged. No further steps were to be taken in regard to the request for the recall of Mr. Egan.[76] Señor Pereira had conceded all, and more, that had been asked by Mr. Blaine. It must be said, however, that so complete a surrender and so full a concession could but leave an aftermath of hard feeling and unfriendliness. The immediate publication in the United States of this, as well as the earlier correspondence, did not lessen the resentment of Chile.

President Harrison sent the Chilean note to Congress on January 28, with the statement:

This turn in the affair is very gratifying to me, as I am sure it will be to the Congress and to our people. The general support of the efforts of the Executive to enforce the first rights of the nation in this matter has given an instructive and useful illustration of the unity and patriotism of our people.[77]

The Chilean controversy passed its crisis with the Pereira note of January 25. The agreement in the summer of 1892 whereby Chile later paid $75,000 indemnity for the men killed and wounded on October 16, 1891, gave a formal end to the affair.[78] Even in this

[76] Egan to Blaine, January 25, 1892, *House Exec. Doc.* No. 91 (Pt. 2), 52 Cong., 1st Session.

[77] *Ibid.* The gratification expressed by President Harrison was for a policy which had been in its last and more aggressive stages peculiarly his own. Whatever were his reasons for such aggressiveness, there can be no gainsaying his responsibility. The *Congressional Record* for this period contains little reference to Chile. Congress asked for correspondence but did not evidence great interest or excitement.

[78] In this as in other incidents President Cleveland reversed the

last negotiation the administration was much more exacting than Secretary Blaine had advised in the days before he retired from office. Miss Hamilton in her *Life of Blaine* quotes from a letter to Harrison in which Blaine wrote:

I herewith send you a draft of a note to Chile. It may seem to you too cordial, but I believe it to be in the highest sense expedient. I have relied on Chile's good sense for reparation, and I believe we will get it more easily that way than by arbitration.

When we made the settlement with the Spaniards in the "Virginius" affair in a very aggravated case — we took $2,500 apiece for the sailors, thus setting a price. We followed the same example when we made reparation for the Chinese who were murdered. You remember I proposed the same for the Italians who were murdered at New Orleans, so that the real money value we should recover would be small. We can afford to be very generous in our language and thus make a friend of Chile, if that is possible. At all events we can afford to venture $5,000 on it and that is all we will get for the two sailors.[79]

Blustering at times Mr. Blaine undoubtedly could be, but it was one of the main tenets of his diplomatic policy and one of his strongest desires as Secretary of State to preserve peaceful relations with the states of this hemisphere. He had been pledged through his

Harrison policy. The question of asylum came up again in 1893 when Egan once more received political refugees. He was reprimanded by the Secretary of State and instructed to terminate the asylum. See *U. S. Foreign Relations*, 1893, Vol. IV, Message of Cleveland, December 4.

[79] Blaine to Harrison, January 29, 1892, Hamilton, *Blaine*, 676.

entire career to the endeavor to improve and make closer those relations and he had ever been willing to sacrifice much for this end. It is difficult to discover in his conduct of the relations of the United States with Chile in 1891-1892 any desire to deviate from that policy, nor does it seem just to hold him responsible for ominous rumblings of war which could be heard in that period.

CHAPTER VII

THE INTERNATIONAL AMERICAN CONFERENCE

WHILE engaged in these numerous attempts at arranging settlements of Latin American difficulties which would be satisfactory not only to them but to the Government of the United States, Mr. Blaine never lost sight of his desire to encourage permanent and lasting peace as well as the growth of real friendship and more extensive commerce. President Garfield and his Secretary of State regarded such an attempt as one of the "most honorable and useful ends to which the diplomacy of the United States could contribute." They felt that no lasting or satisfactory result could be reached by a mere repetition of such settlements as that which ended the Chile-Argentine boundary dispute, for instance, but that some common agreement which should be permanent and of continental extent should be secured if at all possible. Before President Garfield was shot on July 2, it had been arranged to invite all the States of North and South America to meet in Washington in March of 1882 in a peace conference. The plan was postponed until President Arthur came into office, and the invitations were not issued until November 22, but the scheme then presented was upon the same basis as the plan formulated under President Garfield.[1]

This plan was not, however, entirely original with Blaine and Garfield. The ground for the issuance of such an invitation had been prepared in the preceding administration. In 1880 there was a House bill calling a conference for the promotion of commerce.[2] Nothing came of it, and it was merely the first of many moves toward closer commercial relations. In the midst of the acrimonious discussion of the canal project, a committee was delegated by the House to call for a convention of the South American States and to report on the Monroe Doctrine. This committee reported that it felt itself prevented by the Clayton-Bulwer Treaty from discussing the canal question in such a conference.[3] In December of 1880 Dichman, the United States minister to Colombia, sent word to Secretary Evarts that Colombia had issued a circular invitation to the Spanish American Republics for a meeting at Panama in 1881 to execute an international arbitration treaty under which the President of the United States was to be asked to serve as the permanent arbitrator. For that reason the United States was not invited to attend the Congress, but Dichman suggested the sending of representatives to express friendship and willing-

[1] Blaine, *Political Discussions*, "Foreign Policy of the Garfield Administration," 412.

[2] *International American Congress*, IV, Reports of Committees and Discussion thereon, Historical Appendix, 293.

[3] Keasbey, *Nicaragua Canal and the Monroe Doctrine*, 390.

ness to assist.[4] Thirteen Latin American States[5] accepted the invitation, but before the date set for the meeting of the Congress, war had broken out between Chile, Peru, and Bolivia, and it never convened.

In November, 1881, in the midst of the war between Chile and Peru, but when Blaine felt that there was a chance that his special mission to South America might make some settlement possible, President Arthur issued the invitations planned before Garfield's assassination. The letter of invitation was one of Mr. Blaine's most eloquent state papers and was the epitome of his attitude toward Latin America. He stated that the attitude of the United States was well known, that this Government had made many efforts to prevent wars or to end them with mediation or arbitration. He maintained that this attitude had been consistent, and that the United States had ever acted with fairness and impartiality. The position of the United States as the leading power of the Western Hemisphere might be considered as giving a claim to speak with authority in bringing about peace.

Nevertheless, the good offices of this government are not, and have not at any time, been tendered with a show of dictation or compulsion but only as exhibiting the solicitous good will of a common friend.

[4] Dichman to Evarts, December 6, 1881, *International American Congress*, IV, "Correspondence relating to the proposed Congress of Panama in 1881," 217.

[5] Chile, Peru, Santo Domingo, Costa Rica, Mexico, Nicaragua, Argentine, Guatemala, Salvador, Ecuador, Bolivia, Uraguay, Honduras.

The United States had noted with great appreciation the fact that there was a growing tendency of Spanish American countries to use arbitration and to appeal to the United States as an arbitrator. The President felt, therefore, that the time was ripe for a conference for peace. All the American States had a common interest in its object and the President expected cooperation and assistance from all of them. Invitation was, therefore, extended for a congress of North and South American States to meet on November 24, 1882, to consider and discuss methods of preventing war between the nations of America. The President wished the attention of the congress to be confined strictly to this one object.

Mr. Blaine went on to emphasize the fact that the United States did not assume a position of counseling any solution of existing questions. Such were not to come before the congress. Its work was to be for the future, and its mission was the higher one of seeking a permanent solution for such difficulties. The United States would not attempt nor desire to prejudge any issues to be presented to the congress and would be on the same footing in the congress as any other power. Each state was asked to send two representatives provided with powers to consider the great question contemplated by the invitation.[6]

[6] Blaine, *Political Discussions*, "The Proposed Peace Congress," 403-406, gives the invitation sent to the Argentine Republic dated Nov. 29, 1881. Similar invitations were sent to the other Latin American States.

The invitation was withdrawn by Secretary Freling-huysen, who succeeded Blaine in the State Department on December 19. In a letter to Mr. H. Trescot, the special envoy to Chile and Peru, he said:

The United States is at peace with all the nations of the earth, and the President wishes hereafter to determine whether it will conduce to that general peace, which he would cherish and promote, for this government to enter into negotiations and consultation for the promotion of peace with selected friendly nationalities without extending a like confidence to other peoples with whom the United States is on equally friendly terms. If such partial confidence would create jealousy and ill-will, peace, the object sought by such consultation, would not be promoted.

The dispatch ended with the statement that at any event the President wished time to consider the entire proposition.[7]

In April, 1882, President Arthur sent a message to Congress submitting the whole proposition and asking for authorization to proceed and for provision to be made for such a conference if Congress thought it expe-dient. No action was taken by Congress and none had been expected by the administration, which had thus for reasons connected with internal politics reversed Mr. Blaine's policy. In August, 1882, therefore, the invitation was formally withdrawn, not to be issued again for another half-dozen years.

Before knowledge of Secretary Frelinghuysen's dis-patch of January 9 had reached Latin America, more

[7] Frelinghuysen to Trescot, Jan. 9, 1882, *U. S. Foreign Relations,* 1882, 57.

than half of the Central and South American States had accepted the invitation with varying degrees of enthusiasm.[8] After the formal withdrawal, some half-dozen states sent their regrets that the project should thus be abandoned.[9]

Mr. Blaine bitterly resented the reversal of his policy, a step which he justly felt was taken with the intent to hurt him politically and diminish his influence in the party and in the country. At first he maintained a dignified silence, but when rumors were started that he had meant to plunge the country into war, and that President Arthur had not known of the invitation to a congress until after the invitations had been sent, he determined to make a public statement of the facts and of his position.[10] He wrote a letter to President Arthur

[8] Blaine, *Political Discussions*, 406. The letters of acceptance were printed in Volume IV of the *International American Congress*.

[9] *International American Congress*, IV, 272.

[10] The best source for the attitude of Mr. Blaine in this period is the *Letters of Mrs. James G. Blaine*, edited by Mrs. Harriet Blaine Beale, 293 ff. In a letter to her daughter, dated January 28, 1882, Mrs. Blaine wrote, "What he, the Pater, may do hereafter, I do not know, but at present he has decided on the patient dignity of perfect silence. But he says he never wrote papers of which a man or his children ought to be more proud." Again a few days later to the same daughter, "Undoubtedly the State Department intended the life of your Father, which they expected to take, with all due regard for the *convenances*, and with so much dignity on their own part that nobody would know that anybody was hurt, only, by and by, it would strike people that our dearest dear was forever silent. He faces round, and is not deterred from striking back, for fear of hurting the clothes or gentility of his assailant. So with your Father — what difference does it make to him that Frelinghuysen is a nice man who does a dirty thing? He knows the act and the man, and holds the latter to account

on February 3, which was also sent to the press because, as he said, the dispatch of Frelinghuysen, foreshadowing an abandonment of the peace congress, had been made public at the president's direction. The letter began with the statement that President Arthur had approved the plan for a peace congress and had authorized the issuance of the invitations. The policy had originated with Garfield but had been adopted and carried on by Arthur. The Frelinghuysen letter, which practically abandoned the project, had come as a surprise, and the reasons Secretary Frelinghuysen had given seemed entirely inadequate. Blaine quoted from the dispatch of January 9 and scoffed at the fear expressed for the displeasure of European powers which, he said, met in congresses of one sort or another at any time they pleased without notification to the United States. Two presidents in 1881 had

adjudged it expedient that American Powers should meet in

for the former. I verily believe the Secretary of State expected to silence Blaine. They revoked his instructions though they were Arthur's as well; they kept back his papers, they sent to Congress garbled despatches of Trescot's, they permitted private letters of Christiancy to be sent to Congress. . . . Your father will be vindicated in every particular. His policy is a patriotic one, and the people are going to so recognize it. Not a selfish thought is in it, but it is in all its ramifications American." And on February 8 to Walker in Chile, "There can be no doubt, however, that a strong feeling is growing for your Father's policy. It appeals to the *American* sentiment and the friends of the Administration have done the President incalculable harm by rushing to his defense with all sorts of wild assertions; such as, that he did not know of the Peace Conference, that Mr. Trescot had private instructions from the Secretary, etc., which, proved to be true, would condemn Arthur out & out."

Congress for the sole purpose of agreeing upon some basis of arbitration of differences that may arise between them, and for the prevention, as far as possible, of wars in the future. If that movement is now to be arrested for fear it may give offense in Europe, the voluntary humiliation of the United States could not be more complete, unless we should petition European Governments for the privilege of holding the Congress.

Mr. Blaine begged the President to consider the effect of withdrawing the invitation and if it had not yet been formally done, to hesitate before taking such a step. He ended the letter with a consideration of the material ends to be gained by such a conference in increase of commerce and industrial interests in Spanish America.[11]

In 1882, also, Mr. Blaine published his apologia, a pamphlet entitled *The Foreign Policy of the Garfield Administration*.[12] In it he justified the calling of the peace conference and declared that the objects of the administration had been to further the ends of peace and to promote better commercial relationships. The latter aim was dependent upon the first. Spanish America needed external aid in the maintenance of peace, and the Garfield policy would have supplied that aid had it been carried out as it was planned. He feared a European guarantee and guardianship of the inter-oceanic canal and deplored the fact that the Spanish American Republics were turning toward Europe for trade rather than toward the United States. After a

[11] Blaine, *Political Discussions*, Letter to President Arthur, February 3, 1882, pp. 407-410.

[12] *Ibid.*, pp. 411-419.

discussion of commercial conditions in Latin America, he came back to the idea of the peace conference in a final statement, which summed up his hope for his policy and his bitterness at its frustration:

In no event could harm have resulted from the assembling of the Peace Congress. Failure was next to impossible. Success might be regarded as certain. The subject to be discussed was Peace, and the meaures by which it can be permanantly served in North and South America. The labors of the Congress would probably have ended in a well-digested system of arbitration, under which all future troubles between American States could be promptly and satisfactorily adjusted. Such a consummation would have been worth a great struggle and a great sacrifice. It could have been reached without struggle and would involve no sacrifice. It was within our grasp. It was ours for the asking. It would have been a signal victory of philanthropy over the selfishness of human ambition; a complete triumph of Christian principles as applied to the affairs of nations. It would have reflected honor on our own country and would have imparted a new spirit and a new brotherhood to all America. Nor would its influence beyond the sea have been small. The example of seventeen independent nations solemnly agreeing to abolish the arbitrament of the sword, and to settle every dispute by peaceful adjudication, would have exerted an influence to the utmost confines of civilization, and upon generations of men yet to come.

The relations between the United States and Latin America were not forgotten in the interim between Mr. Blaine's two terms of office.[13] Each session of Congress

[13] The measures introduced in both Houses of Congress are given and discussed in *International American Conference*, IV, 293 ff. An

witnessed the introduction of bills dealing with some phase of the subject, and it became more and more apparent that the country was not satisfied with the existing conditions affecting the contact between Latin America and the United States. Commerce with Central and South America in some one of its ramifications was the subject dealt with in almost all of this proposed legislation. Mr. Blaine's great objective, a conference devoted to the consideration of measures to secure peace, was somewhat neglected, but his supplementary policy of furthering the increase of trade received much consideration. In brief, the subjects taken up in the various bills were as follows: commissions to visit South America to study commercial conditions and the attitude of the states toward the United States,[14] the attitude of Spanish America toward a North and South American railroad,[15] the establishment of an American customs union,[16] an arbitration conference,[17] a commercial congress which should decide on questions of "mutual interest and common welfare," [18] a silver trade coin.

excellent summary of Mr. Blaine's connection with the whole affair is given in A. Curtis Wilgus, "James G. Blaine and the Pan-American Movement," *Hispanic American Historical Review*, V, 662-708.

[14] February 8, 1883. Introduced in the Senate by Cockrell of Missouri.

[15] December 11, 1883. Introduced in the Senate by Sherman of Ohio.

[16] January 7, 1884. Introduced in the House by Townshend of Illinois.

[17] January 26, 1886. Introduced in the House by Worthington of Illinois.

[18] February 23, 1886. Introduced in the Senate by Frye of Maine.

These bills were introduced at intervals, reported on adversely, killed in committee, only to be resurrected and reintroduced. In 1884 one of them, that to provide for a committee to investigate commercial conditions in South America, was actually passed, and a commission of three was sent to South America. The commissioners were William E. Curtis, S. O. Thacker, and Thomas C. Reynolds. Their report was printed and widely circulated. Finally, on January 4, 1888, a bill was introduced in the House similar to that of Senator Frye of 1886.[19] It was designed "to promote the establishment of free commercial intercourse among nations of America and the Dominion of Canada by the creation of an American Customs Union or *Zollverein*." Before it was passed by both Houses, it was considerably modified, but its intent was the same. It provided for the calling of a conference to consider various economic and commercial problems and to formulate some scheme of arbitration. It was passed on May 10, 1888, and became a law without the signature of President Cleveland.[20]

On July 13, 1888, Secretary Bayard issued the invitation to a conference along the lines laid down by the law.[21] It was sent to the Governments of Mexico, of the Central and South American countries, Haiti, and San Domingo. The questions to be considered by the Conference were those provided in the Act of Con-

[19] See above, note 18.

[20] The administration had given no approval to any of the legislative attempts but at the same time had not opposed them.

[21] *International American Conference*, I, 9-11.

gress: first, measures to preserve and promote the prosperity of American States; second, an American customs union; third, transportation and communication; fourth, uniform customs and port regulations; fifth, uniform weights and measures and uniform laws of copyrights and patents and extradition of criminals; sixth, adoption of a common silver coin; seventh, a plan for the arbitration of all disputes; eighth, any other subjects relating to the welfare of the several States that might be presented. Secretary Bayard called attention to the fact that the Conference would be consultative and recommendatory only and would be without power to bind the States represented. The Conference was to convene in Washington, October 2, 1889, and each State might send the number of delegates it wished although having but one vote.

The invitation was accepted by every State to which it was sent except San Domingo where there was considerable hesitation because the United States had not ratified a reciprocity treaty negotiated in 1884. Haiti was so disturbed by revolution that its acceptance was not sent until October 4, 1889, but Haitian representatives reached the Conference before it had met for actual work.[22] Chile sent delegates instructed to discuss commercial and economic questions only. The other States did not limit their representatives. It was peculiarly fitting that the Conference should be greeted on

[22] All of the letters of acceptance have been printed in *International American Conference*, I, 12 ff.

October 2, 1889, by the man who had tried eight years before to bring about such a meeting.

Mr. Blaine must have felt considerable satisfaction as he gave the address of welcome, which was brief, eloquent, and very friendly.[23] He made little mention of the commercial objects of the Conference but confined himself to the idea of the importance of such a gathering for the purpose of promoting the general welfare of so vast a region. He emphasized the necessity for closer bonds between the nations of the Western Hemisphere, saying:

We believe that friendship, assured with candor and maintained with good faith, will remove from American States the necessity of guarding boundary lines between themselves with fortifications and military force.

We believe that standing armies, beyond those which are

[23] The New York *Tribune* (quoted in Wilgus, "Blaine and the Pan-American Movement," *Hispanic American Historical Review*, V, 693), in an editorial October 1, expressed the sentiments of the admirers of the Secretary of State: "It may be instructive to recall the acrid criticism and envenomed denunciations which the original proposition called forth in 1881. Mr. Blaine's enemies then condemned as incipient jingoism and a policy of diplomatic adventure this statesmanlike expedient for bringing the nations of the continent into closer and more harmonious relations with one another. They ridiculed it as a fantastic and 'viewy scheme.' . . . The Congress is now about to meet for the same objects as contemplated by Secretary Blaine in 1881, and there is neither criticism nor ridicule from any quarter. . . . Partisanship succeeded in temporarily discrediting it eight years ago, but enlightened public opinion now accepts and sanctions it as the embodiment of the best and oldest traditions of American diplomacy."

needful for public order and the safety of internal administration, should be unknown on both American continents.

We believe that friendship and not force, the spirit of just law and not the violence of the mob should be the recognized rule of administration between American nations and in American nations.

. . . It will be a great gain when we shall acquire the common confidence on which all international friendship must rest. It will be a greater gain when we shall be able to draw the people of all American nations into closer acquaintance with each other, an end to be facilitated by more frequent and rapid intercommunication. It will be the greatest gain when the personal and commercial relations of the American States, south and north, shall be so developed and so regulated that each shall acquire the highest possible advantage from the enlightened and enlarged intercourse of all.[24]

Mr. Blaine was at once elected president of the Conference. It was recognized that his duties as Secretary of State would prevent his constant attendance at the meetings, and arrangements were made for presiding officers in his absence. As a matter of fact, he did devote much more time to the Conference than had been anticipated, for his tact and judgment were often necessary to preserve the amicable relations upon which effective work depended. Mr. Mattias Romero, the Mexican minister to the United States and a delegate

[24] *International American Conference*, I, 41-43. This address and, in fact, the entire Conference, met with an entirely partisan response. Newspapers and periodicals which opposed Blaine for party or personal reasons scoffed at the work of the Conference; his following was enthusiastic.

to the Conference, published in 1890 two articles in the *North American Review*[25] upon the work of the Conference. In regard to the election of Mr. Blaine as president he wrote:

Subsequent events . . . showed in a very clear manner how wise was the election of Mr. Blaine, because he was invested with full powers to negotiate with the Latin American delegates — powers which were really much broader than those of the United States delegation — and because, on the other hand, possessing exquisite tact and a great desire to prevent the failure of a high purpose in an assembly of which he was the promoter, he went further in order to come to an agreement with the Latin American delegates than in all probability the United States delegation would have deemed themselves authorized to go.[26]

The invitation of Secretary Bayard with its statement of the topics provided by the law of May 24, 1888, was used as the program of the Conference. The actual accomplishment of the desiderata set forth in the program was not great. A customs union was not thought practicable, and the committee which considered it recommended in its stead separate reciprocity treaties. The proposal for the adoption of a common silver coin was reported adversely and was not accepted. The project of the completion of a railroad connecting North and South America was recommended. There were several agreements upon pro-

[25] Romero, "The Pan-American Conference," *North American Review*, CLI (September, 1890, and October, 1890).
[26] *North American Review*, CLI, 366.

jected treaties in regard to patents, trade marks, and copyrights. The chief attention of the Conference was devoted, however, to the evolution of some plan for international arbitration. There were various schemes suggested but no agreement was reached, so Mr. Blaine drafted an arbitration scheme in order to have some basis upon which the Conference might work.[27] His project was much modified before the final adoption on April 9, 1890. Arbitration was to be obligatory for all controversies except those which, in the opinion of one of the nations involved in the controversy, compromised her independence. In the recommendation as signed, the United States was given no more power and no more important a position than the least of the Latin American States. Mr. Blaine accepted all modifications of his scheme and expressed himself as ready to agree to any movement insuring peace.[28]

The Conference closed on April 19, 1890. The farewell address of Mr. Blaine contained a statement which is at the same time a justification of the Conference and an expectation which has been proved by time:

The extent and value of all that has been worthily achieved by your Conference can not be measured today. We stand too

[27] Romero states that this was the only time when Mr. Blaine seemed excited. In his effort to secure the acceptance of the arbitration scheme, he came down from the chair and supported the motion as a delegate.

[28] A brief summary of the work of the Conference may be found in the article of Wilgus, cited above, and in W. S. Robertson, *Hispanic American Relations with the United States*, 393-394. The reports of committees and discussions may be found in *International American Conference*, I and II.

near it. Time will define and heighten the estimate of your work; experience will confirm our present faith; final results will be your vindication and your triumph.[29]

The Conference over, its recommendations were taken back to the several states represented to be approved or rejected. The arbitration scheme which Mr. Blaine had so long and so ardently desired was not adopted. The only practical result of the Conference appeared to have been the establishment of an International Bureau of American Republics, which was destined to be a permanent and very valuable agent for the collection and dissemination of information. But, as Mr. Blaine said, the achievement of the Conference "cannot be measured today." [30]

[29] *International American Conference*, II, 1166-1167.

[30] Mr. Wilgus in the *Hispanic American Historical Review*, V, 700-701, gives two quotations, one from the *Nation*, April 24, 1890, and the other from the New York *Tribune*, April 20, 1890, between which, he says, the truth lies. The *Nation*: "The closing scene of the Pan-American Conference is said to have been extremely affecting, Mr. Blaine being almost moved to tears. . . . If the emotions of the conference were due to the small results achieved, they were fully justified." The *Tribune*: "The Congress has ended but the work of American unification has barely begun. The ground has been leveled, the way has been opened for securing united action on the part of the eighteen commonwealths, which will promote the enlightened self interest of each and the common welfare of all; and it now remains for the United States to take the initiative and to complete a great work of high civilization. By conciliatory diplomacy, by the opportune negotiations of treaties, by energetic and intelligent action and perseverance, and patience and tact, the State Department can accomplish great and memorable results for American civilization. In this work it must have the individual support of public opinion in America. From this day the Monroe Doctrine passes by processes of diplomatic

It is necessary, further, to examine the part played by Mr. Blaine himself, as expressive of the policy of the United States in the Conference and to show the course which he took in carrying out the recommendations of the Conference. Mr. Romero stated that most of the Latin American delegates had come to the Conference with the apprehension that the United States would attempt to gain political and commercial predominance over the other States of the continent. He stated further:

There is nothing that can be shown to prove that this was the purpose of the United States. Its delegates did not propose in the conference anything seemingly intended to accomplish such an end. Judging, therefore, by facts and results, these apprehensions were entirely ungrounded.[31]

Mr. Blaine did not at any time attempt to control the action of the Conference nor to force any decisions upon its delegates. Mr. Romero stated that not only did Blaine, apparently, not have a preconceived plan but he even refused to express an opinion on any subject or to give instructions to the United States delegates when they called upon him.[32] His entire aim seemed to be to allow full freedom for discussion and decision without any pressure or suggestions from the United States. He, undoubtedly, was fully aware that the surest way to prevent the success of the Conference

evolution into a stage of higher development. There is an American continental policy to be worked out and consummated."

[31] *North American Review*, CLI, 358.

[32] *Ibid.*, 410.

would be to permit the domination of the United States and he showed exceptional tact and restraint in his conduct of the sessions.[33]

It is an interesting commentary upon Mr. Blaine's attitude toward Hawaii that in March, 1890, Congress passed a resolution authorizing the President to extend that kingdom an invitation to the Conference.[34] The Conference adjourned before the Hawaiian acceptance was received. Mr. Blaine wrote:

This government regrets the circumstances no less, not only by reason of the peculiar importance of Hawaii as one of the geographical extremes of the American system, but also in view of those well known qualities which would have rendered your participation of signal value to the work of the Conference.[35]

The attention of the Conference had been to a great extent devoted to consideration of measures designed to foster and promote trade between the United States and Latin America. The work of the committee of the Conference in charge of commercial relations was influenced and hampered by the fact that during the months in which the Conference was in session, Congress was occupied with the McKinley tariff, the discussion of which was, naturally, followed most closely

[33] The years which had elapsed since 1881 had brought much disappointment and disillusion to Mr. Blaine. It is doubtful whether he could have conducted a conference in 1881 with so much disinterestedness and impartiality.

[34] The message of President Harrison in December had recommended the adoption of such a measure.

[35] Blaine to Carter, May 3, 1890. MS. Notes to the Hawaiian Legation, 1890.

by the delegates. Secretary Blaine was vitally interested in the McKinley Bill, for he felt that its proposals
to take the duties off sugar and coffee, to impose them
upon hides, and raise those on wool would prevent any
success in negotiating reciprocity agreements. The
United States would have nothing to offer to the Spanish American nations in return for commercial concessions. Before the close of the Conference he wrote a
letter to Representative McKinley stating:

It is a great mistake to take hides from the free list, where
they have been for so many years. It is a slap in the face to the
South Americans with whom we are trying to enlarge our trade.
It will benefit the farmer by adding five to eight percent to the
price of his children's shoes.

It will yield a profit to the butcher only, the last man who
needs it. The movement is injudicious from beginning to end
— in every form and phase.

Pray stop it before it sees the light. Such movements as this
for protection will protect the Republican party into a speedy
retirement.[36]

On June 4 he sent the report of the Conference recommending reciprocity treaties to the President with
a report in which he stated that Argentine was irritated
by the hides and wool regulations of the McKinley
tariff, and that there were other hindrances to trade
with South America. European trade there was increasing while ours was decreasing. The United States
would be the greatest gainer from any reciprocity
agreements which might be negotiated. He felt that

[36] Blaine to McKinley, April 10, 1890, Hamilton, *Blaine*, 677.

wool, hides, and sugar gave us a basis for successful bargaining with Latin America. He, therefore, recommended that the present tariff bill be amended to authorize the President to declare the ports of the United States free to all the products of any nation of the Western Hemisphere, whenever and as long as such nations admitted a certain list of our products free of duty and imposed no export duty upon their own products.[37]

President Harrison submitted the report and the letter of the Secretary of State to Congress on June 19 with a message in which, without actually doing so unprecedented a thing as to ask for the amendment Mr. Blaine desired, he called attention to the fact that the "real difficulty in the way of negotiating profitable reciprocity treaties is that we have given freely so much that would have had value in the mutual concessions which treaties imply." [38] This message, accompanied by Blaine's letter of June 4, opened a struggle in Congress, which was both interesting and unusual. Senator Hale introduced an amendment to the McKinley Bill embodying Mr. Blaine's proposal. The proposition received little favor in the Senate. Mr. Blaine was very active in his opposition to the placing of sugar on the free list with no *quid pro quo* from the nations thus favored, and he intervened directly in the attempt to

[37] Blaine's letter may be found in *Congressional Record*, 51 Cong., 1st Session, pp. 6256-6259. It was accompanied by various tables showing our trade with South and Central America.

[38] Richardson, *Messages and Papers*, IX, 74.

procure some measure of reciprocity. This public criticism of a measure before Congress by a Secretary of
State was most unprecedented and was looked upon
with great disapproval. Mr. Blaine was, of course,
aware that his step was most unusual, but he felt that
the situation demanded it. He conducted a campaign
of education by writing letters to members of Congress
and other influential citizens on the subject, which were
given to, and written to be given to, the press.[39] He
addressed public meetings and conferred with committees. In short, he was as active as though he were still
a member of the House of Representatives.[40]

The activities of the Secretary of State were unsuccessful in moving the Ways and Means Committee of
the House but had great effect upon the public, especially upon the mid-west farmers, and the members of
Congress heard from their constituencies in no unde-
cided manner. Such statements as: "There is not a section or a line in the entire bill that will open the market
for another bushel of wheat or another barrel of pork"
caught the ear or the eye of the Middle West and Congress was forced to pay attention.[41] The McKinley Bill
as finally passed on October 1 was a partial response
to all the agitation although it did not completely satisfy Mr. Blaine. It placed sugar and other tropical

[39] Edward Stanwood, *Tariff Controversies*, II, 279, quotes letters
to the Mayor of Augusta, Maine, and to Senator Frye of Maine.

[40] Stanwood, *James G. Blaine*, 327. He told a friend at this time
that he would give two years of his life to be back on the floor of the
Senate or House for this debate.

[41] Hamilton, *Blaine*, 684 ff.

products on the free list but authorized the President to impose duties on those products when, in his opinion, a nation exporting them did not extend similar favors to the United States or treated the products of the United States in a way which he might deem "reciprocally unequal or unreasonable." [42]

As soon as Mr. Blaine became sure that a reciprocity measure, however grudging and retaliatory in nature it might be, was certain, he called in Mr. John W. Foster and employed him to take charge of the reciprocity negotiations.[43] By the terms of the law these agreements were not of the nature of treaties and did not require the action of the Senate. They were to be negotiated by executive action and were to run for the life

[42] Stanwood, *Tariff Controversies*, II, 281. The general reciprocity provision of the McKinley Act reads: "That with a view to secure reciprocal trade with countries producing the following articles, and for this purpose, on and after the first day of January, 1892, whenever and so often as the President shall be satisfied that the government of any country producing and exporting sugars, molasses, coffee, tea and hides, raw and uncured, or any such articles, imposes duties or exactions upon the agricultural or other products of the United States, which in view of the free introduction of such sugar, molasses, coffee, tea and hides into the United States he may deem to be reciprocally unequal and unreasonable, he shall have the power and it shall be his duty to suspend, by proclamation to that effect, the provisions of this act relating to the free introduction of such sugar, molasses, coffee, tea and hides, the production of such country, for such time as he shall deem just, and in such case and during such suspension duties shall be levied, collected and paid upon sugar, molasses, coffee, tea and hides, the product of or exported from such designated country as follows, namely:" There follows a schedule of duties.

[43] The work of Mr. Foster in negotiating the reciprocity agreements is discussed in his *Memoirs*, II, 6-19.

of the tariff act or until the President should decide to alter them. The Secretary of State addressed a circular note to the diplomatic representatives in Washington of the countries which might be interested, calling their attention to the law and asking what changes their governments would make in their tariff regulations in order to secure the advantages offered in the McKinley Tariff.

Brazil was the first country to respond to the invitation to negotiate, and a schedule of American goods to be admitted free into Brazil was arranged and an agreement signed on February 5, 1891.[44] Other American States followed. Mr. Foster went to Cuba and to Spain and was successful in negotiating agreements securing reciprocal commercial advantages. There were negotiations with the British West Indies, carried through with the consent of Great Britain. Germany became interested because of her beet sugar industry and signed a reciprocity agreement. In all, the activities of Mr. Foster and of the Secretary of State netted some twenty reciprocal trade conventions. Venezuela, Colombia, and Haiti were the only Latin American States to decline any arrangement, and President Harrison issued the proclamation imposing the prescribed duties on their "sugar, molasses, coffee, tea and hides."[45]

This reciprocity movement, which had thus received

[44] "Correspondence with the Legation of Brazil at Washington," *U. S. Foreign Relations*, 1891, p. 43 ff.

[45] Foster, *Memoirs*, II, 16.

so promising a start, was destined to survive only until a Democratic Congress rescinded the McKinley Act. It had proved sufficiently valuable to the Spanish American States to cause them to protest, albeit unavailingly, when the agreements came to an end.[46] Mr. Blaine had labored long, had defied precedent, and had forced Congress to concede his point, only to have it proved again that the United States had, as yet, no conception of his vision of a hemisphere welded together by bonds of common interest and knit in a commercial union.

It is in this matter of the International American Conference and its resultant reciprocity movement that there may be discerned the full measure and character of Mr. Blaine's Spanish American policy. From the viewpoint of American imperialism he lived in a period of transition, belonging as much to the age of Manifest Destiny and to the period of Seward's schemes of expansion as he did to the new movement of economic penetration in which the European nations were involved. His eagerness to further the domination of the United States in the Western Hemisphere was tempered by a sincere desire for international peace. Arbitration of all disputes between American States was a vital point in his policy. The futility and waste of the constant wars and disorders in Spanish America were ever present in his mind. In his efforts to build up trade and intercourse between the United States and its neighbors, he was expressing the most farsighted and clear-visioned thinking of his party and his period. The

[46] *Ibid,,* 17.

steady advance of the United States in commerce and and in prestige was to be accompanied by peace, prosperity, and mutual good feeling throughout the hemisphere. He had a conception of a real Pan Americanism based upon friendship and mutual interests; a conception so often lost sight of in the years to come, that Pan Americanism has come to mean a different thing both to the United States and to Latin America than it did to Secretary Blaine in the days of the first International Conference.

CHAPTER VIII

HAWAII: A PART OF THE AMERICAN SYSTEM

THE extension of the Monroe Doctrine into an active American policy was one of the chief tenets of Secretary Blaine's policy. This new conception of a continental system and of an American foreign policy which should center itself upon the Western Hemisphere, promoting peace and increasing commerce, was extended by Blaine to include the Hawaiian Islands. European interest was to be curtailed and supplanted there as well as in Latin America.

Blaine's interest in Hawaii was of long standing. His biographer, Stanwood, states that from early manhood he favored the acquisition of the Islands.[1] Luther Severance, a predecesor of Blaine on the Kennebec Journal, had been appointed in 1850 by President Taylor first commissioner of the United States to the Sandwich Islands. In a speech in the House of Representatives on December 10, 1868, Blaine stated:

Whatever, therefore, may be before us in the untrodden and often beclouded path of the future — whether it be financial embarrassment, or domestic trouble of another and more serious type, or misunderstandings with foreign nations, or the exten-

[1] Stanwood, *Blaine*, 359.

sion of our flag and our sovereignty over insular or continental possessions, that fate or fortune may peacefully offer to our ambition — let us believe with all confidence that General Grant's administration will meet every exigency with the courage, the ability and the conscience which American nationality and Christian civilization demand.[2]

President Garfield, also, had very definite ideas in regard to the position which the United States should assume with reference to Hawaii. Writing to Hinsdale, whom he appointed minister to Hawaii, he said that the condition of the Hawaiian kingdom was such as to cause anxiety. It was feared that the King might plan either the sale of the Islands to some European power or some commercial treaty which would embarrass the United States. "We shall probably soon have more delicate or important diplomatic work in that direction than at any previous time in our history."[3] Garfield was, apparently, ready to sustain Blaine in this field as vigorously as in that of Latin American relations.

The relations between the United States and Hawaii had always been close. In 1819 a group of missionaries had gone there from Boston, and ever after the bond between the United States and Hawaii was strong. The descendants of these missionaries became leaders in Hawaii although they maintained constant contact with the home of their fathers. The growth of American whaling in the Pacific furnished another point of con-

[2] Stanwood, *op. cit.*, 101.
[3] Smith, *Garfield*, II, 1167.

tact, for the whalers spent part of every year in Hawaiian ports. From the earliest days the United States was interested in rumors that French or Russian or English influence might control the Islands and insisted upon the independence of Hawaii from such control. After the Mexican War, when the tide of settlement swept along the Pacific coast, the Government of the United States first entertained ideas of annexation.

Secretary Marcy, in 1834, authorized the American commissioner to make a treaty with Hawaii providing for the establishment of a protectorate under the United States flag. The Islanders wished, however, to be accorded statehood in the Union, so a treaty was negotiated to incorporate them as a state.[4] The death of the Hawaiian King and the succession of a monarch more under British influence put an end to the negotiation. It is doubtful whether the Senate would have ratified such a treaty had it been completed, but the desire of the Islanders is significant. The growth of the sugar industry, largely stimulated by American capital, together with the importance of the American market for sugar caused a movement for a reciprocity treaty with a desire expressed on both sides for the annexation of Hawaii to the United States. The reciprocity treaty was defeated in the United States Senate

[4] *U. S. Foreign Relations*, 1894, Appendix II, "Hawaii," pp. 127-129. This volume is entirely devoted to Hawaii and contains the entire correspondence from the beginning of diplomatic relations. Every document was printed except one dispatch from John S. Stevens, October 8, 1892. See Appendix I of this volume.

in 1870, and the subject of annexation was dropped although Seward expressed himself in favor of it.[5]

In 1874, the movement toward closer commercial relations between the United States and Hawaii began anew, and on January 30, 1875, a reciprocity treaty was signed in Washington and in June, 1876, went into effect. By its terms certain products of Hawaii, including unrefined sugar, were to be admitted free of duty into the United States, and certain American manufactured products were placed on the Hawaiian free list. Altogether, practically free trade was established between the two countries. The most significant part of the treaty was the agreement made by the King that he would not, so long as the treaty was in force,

lease or otherwise dispose of or create a lien upon any port, harbor, or other territory in his dominions, or grant any special privilege or rights of use therein to any Power, State or Government, nor make any treaty by which any other nation should obtain the same privileges, relative to the admission of articles free of duty, thereby secured to the United States.[6]

Protest was at once made by the British Government on the ground that the Hawaiian Government had, in making the treaty, violated the treaty with Great Britain of 1852, which was on "the most favored nation"

[5] Seward to McCook, September 12, 1867, *U. S. Foreign Relations,* 1894, Appendix II, p. 143. Also Edmund James Carpenter, *America in Hawaii: A History of the United States Influence in the Hawaiian Islands.*

[6] *U. S. Foreign Relations,* 1894, Appendix II, 164-167. Article IV quoted above is on page 166.

basis. The discussion over this point went on for several years, growing more and more acrimonious, until
it was feared that Great Britain might resort to force
in order to cause the Hawaiian Government to accord
equal privileges to British commerce.[7]

Secretary Blaine had been in office only a few weeks
when he received information that Great Britain was
causing difficulty in the relations of the United States
and the Hawaiian Islands. By the treaty of 1875, it
was a flagrant violation of that treaty for Hawaii to
extend its advantages to other nations because of "most
favored nation" clauses in other existing treaties. If
Hawaii were to accede to the demands of Great Britain,
the benefits which the United States derived from the
provisions giving her special favors in the Hawaiian
market would be worthless. In April, 1881, Blaine took
up the matter in a letter to James Russell Lowell, the
United States minister in London, closing with this
warning:

The position of the Hawaiian Islands in the vicinity of our
Pacific coast, and their intimate commercial and political relations with us, lead this government to watch with grave interest, and to regard unfavorably, any movement, negotiation, or
discussion aiming to transfer them in any eventuality whatever
to another power.[8]

About the same time Secretary Blaine received word
that King Kalakaua was setting forth on an extensive

[7] Carpenter, 50.

[8] Blaine to Lowell, Manuscript Instructions, Great Britain, April
23, 1881.

tour of Asia and Europe. A feeling that he might be tempted to alienate some portion of his kingdom in return for commercial or financial assistance caused Blaine to send out on April 22, a long circular letter to the American ministers in those countries which the King was to visit. He called attention to the fact that although the Treaty of 1875 forbade any such alienation of territory, the convention might be terminated upon twelve months notice after it had been in operation seven years. The position of the Hawaiian Islands in the vicinity of the Pacific coast and the political and commercial interest of the United States in them caused the United States to "watch with grave interest and to regard unfavorably" any negotiation calculated to transfer them in whole or in part to another power. He instructed each minister to watch the conduct of the King and if necessary to warn the Government to which he was accredited of the attitude which the United States would take.[9]

Apparently nothing occurred to make them feel that such action was necessary. A newspaper report of an intention on the part of the King to sell his kingdom led at once to a note from that royal personage to his representative in Washington, instructing him to state to Mr. Blaine that no such intention was entertained. Blaine replied that the President had placed no credence in such a report.[10] The episode was trivial, but it

[9] Blaine to White, Manuscript Instructions, Germany, April 22, 1881.

[10] Blaine to E. H. Allen, September 10, 1881, Manuscript Notes to the Hawaiian Legation.

serves to illustrate Blaine's watchfulness over the affairs of the island kingdom of the Pacific.

During the summer of 1881, Blaine received word from James M. Comly, American minister at Honolulu, of British claims to refunds on customs duties because of demands, based on "most favored nations" clauses in British-Hawaiian treaties, for the advantages of our reciprocity treaty. The British commisioner had apparently been exciting distrust of the United States and had assured Hawaiian authorities of British protection against the imperialism of the United States.[11] The British representative was also endeavoring to obtain from Hawaii a convention providing for the importation of coolie labor from British Asiatic possessions and giving an English resident control over all cases arising concerning such immigrants.[12]

On June 30, 1881, Blaine sent a long dispatch to Comly discussing the treaty question and urging him to avoid any difficulty with Hawaiian authorities but to impress upon the Hawaiian Government the fact that the United States relied upon it to carry out the treaty provisions in good faith. Comly was told that the United States wished the representations to be in the line of encouragement rather than "complaint of any anticipated derelictions." [13]

Again on November 19, Blaine returned to the attack with a forceful note. After a discussion of the pro-

[11] Comly to Blaine, June 6, 1881, *U. S. Foreign Relations*, 1881, 622.

[12] Manuscript Dispatches, Hawaii, Vol. 20, No. 178, July 4, 1881.

[13] Blaine, *Political Discussions, Legislative, Diplomatic and Popular*, 388-390.

posed coolie convention and the difficulties its completion would cause both Hawaii and the United States, Comly was instructed to ask for an interview with the Secretary for Foreign Affairs and to communicate to him the views of the United States. The Government of the United States had always respected Hawaiian independence and had always declined to assume a protectorate, but it desired to strengthen the Hawaiian Government and develop the commerce and enterprise of the islands.

This policy has been based upon our belief in the real and substantial independence of Hawaii. The government of the United States has always avowed and now repeats that, under no circumstances, will it permit the transfer of the territory or sovereignty of these islands to any of the European powers. . . . It is too obvious for argument that the possession of these islands by a great maritime power would not only be a dangerous diminution of the just and necessary influence of the United States in the waters of the Pacific, but in case of international difficulty it would be a positive threat to American interests too important to be lightly risked.[14]

A few days later Blaine sent a supplementary and explanatory dispatch to Comly in the course of which he extended his policy in regard to Hawaii still further. "The policy of this country with regard to the Pacific is the natural complement to its Atlantic policy." Hawaii was the key to the maritime dominion of the Pacific states, as Cuba was the key to the Gulf trade. Under

[14] Blaine to Comly, November 19, 1881, *U. S. Foreign Relations,* 1881, 633.

no circumstances could the United States permit any change in the territorial control of the Islands which would " cut them adrift from the American system." The desire of the United States was for a prosperous independence for Hawaii and for a closer union of all American States. But the United States

firmly believes that the position of the Hawaiian Islands as the key to the dominion of the American Pacific demands their neu- rality, to which end it will earnestly co-operate with the native government. If, through any cause, the maintenance of such a position of neutrality should be found by Hawaii to be imprac- ticable, this government would then unhesitatingly meet the altered situation by seeking an avowedly American solution for the grave issues presented.[15]

On the tenth of December, Blaine wrote to Lowell at London a summary of the efforts of foreign coun- tries to gain the same footing in Hawaii as the United States. He reiterated his position that Hawaii was a part of the American system of states, and that, al- though favorably inclined to native rule, "we could not regard the intrusion of any non-American interest in Hawaii as consistent with our relations thereto." [16]

There was no diplomatic controversy over Hawaii at this time and no open discussion of the situation, but these dispatches show very clearly Blaine's intention to include the Hawaiian Islands in the scope of the Mon- roe Doctrine as definitely as any of the States of the American continents. Here, as elsewhere, his policy

[15] Blaine to Comly, *U. S. Foreign Relations*, 1881, p. 635.
[16] Blaine to Lowell, December 10, 1881, *ibid.*, 569.

was simple, decisive, and inclined to be aggressive. Although he undoubtedly looked toward ultimate annexation of Hawaii, his attitude was most circumspect.[17] It was only European intervention that he deplored. He may, perhaps, have felt that peaceful penetration would eventually bring the desired result if the United States were free from competition in the Hawaiian field.[18]

[17] Stanwood, *Life of Blaine*, 359.

[18] This belief is clearly expressed in a confidential dispatch to Comly, December 1, 1881, *U. S. Foreign Relations*, 1894, Appendix II, 169-170. "A single glance at the census returns of Hawaii for half a generation past exhibits this alarming diminution of the indigenous element amounting to one and one-half per cent per annum of the population. Meanwhile the industrial and productive development of Hawaii is on the increase and the native classes, never sufficiently numerous to develop the full resources of the Islands, have been supplemented by an adventious labor element, from China mainly, until the rice and sugar fields are largely tilled by aliens. . . . I have shown in a previous instruction how entirely Hawaii is a part of the productive and commercial system of the American states. So far as the staple growths and imports of the Islands go, the Reciprocity Treaty makes them practically members of an American Zollverein in an outlying district of the state of California. So far as political structure and independence of action are concerned Hawaii is as remote from our control as China. This contradiction is only explicable by assuming, what is the fact, that, 30 years ago, having the choice between material annexation and commercial assimilation of the Islands, the United States chose the less responsible alternative. The soundness of the choice, however, evidently depends on the perpetuity of the rule of the native race as an independent government, and that imperilled, the whole framework of our relations to Hawaii is changed if not destroyed. . . . There is little doubt that were the Hawaiian Islands, by annexation or distinct protection, a part of the territory of the Union, their fertile resources for the growth of rice and sugar would not only be controlled by American capital, but

There is no reason to believe that when Blaine came into office again in 1889, his point of view as to the island kingdom had changed. Nothing had happened in the intervening years to cause any change of opinion. It is, however, very difficult to find any definite statement of that judgment or any clear thread showing the connection between Secretary Blaine and subsequent events in the Islands.[19] All conclusions as to his influence upon events are by inference only and cannot depend upon his official statements nor, so far as can be discovered, upon confidential or private ones.

In June of 1889 President Harrison appointed as United States minister to Hawaii, Mr. John L. Stevens of Augusta, Maine. Mr. Stevens was a man of some diplomatic training; he had been minister to Sweden and Norway and had acquitted himself with credit. He

so profitable a field of labor would attract intelligent workers thither from the United States. . . . A purely American form of colonization in such a case would meet all the phases of the problem."

The Monroe Doctrine appears to have received a new and economic interpretation in Blaine's dispatches in 1881. The states in the "American System" were to be reserved, if possible, for the commerce and economic penetration of the United States.

[19] It is a significant fact that there are no instructions from Blaine to Stevens in this period, of greater length or importance than the merest acknowledgment of the receipt of dispatches. Practically all of the material on Hawaii has been printed. *U. S. Foreign Relations,* 1894, Appendix II, contains a reprint of all documents printed before, and Gresham stated that he had withheld only one document. (See Appendix I of this volume.) The Archives of the State Department revealed no others. The one withheld was kept back because of personalities contained in it and not because of the importance of the subject matter. Mr. Stevens, unfortunately, left no memoirs nor private papers which are available.

had been an editor of the Kennebec *Journal*, a post which Blaine also had filled, and he had for many years been a friend of the new Secretary of State. It is quite obvious that Stevens was a Blaine appointee. He sailed for Hawaii in August. There is no record of any instructions from Mr. Blaine at the time of the appointment which would serve as a guide to the minister. Stevens probably visited Blaine prior to his departure, and it is safe also to conjecture that instructions were sent him in unofficial, informal correspondence of which the Department of State has no record.

When Mr. Stevens reached Hawaii in the fall of 1889, he found the political situation in the Islands far from stable. A constitution, promulgated by the King in 1887, had created a limited monarchy with a responsible ministry. This change had been brought about by the foreign element in the Islands, which was steadily increasing, and which represented the wealth and enterprise of the kingdom. This element was composed of the old "missionary people" (descendants of the early missionary settlers) together with the newer commercial and industrial "sugar" group. As the foreign element grew and became more influential, it was equally apparent that the natives, aristocracy as well as lower classes, were diminishing in numbers and in political power. This was one cause for unrest. The foreign element was, however, not entirely a unit. The greater part of it, undoubtedly, was of American nationality or extraetion and favored ultimate annexation of the Islands to the United States. There were other groups which were in opposition and, in general, they seem to have been led by the British commercial interests and to have favored the royal party as opposed to the constitutional or liberal and progressive faction of the Government.

The material for any number of disputes and revolutions was at hand. In August, 1889, George Merrill, Stevens' predecessor, reported that there had been an unsuccessful attempt at a revolution in the course of which he had had marines landed from an American man-of-war to safeguard American lives and property.[20] It seemed to Merrill and, later, to Stevens, wise to have an American warship constantly in Hawaiian waters.[21]

Stevens found another situation in Hawaii, which closely concerned the United States, and which became enmeshed in the web of politics and intrigues which constituted the "government." The reciprocity treaty of 1875 with the United States still had several years to run, but the sugar interests of Hawaii, alarmed at the prospect of a Republican tariff, wished to make their position secure by a new treaty which should definitely place sugar on the free list. Mr. Stevens, who was from the beginning distinctly in favor of closer relations with Hawaii, at once identified himself with this

[20] Stevens to Blaine, *U. S. Foreign Relations*, 1894, II, 280.

[21] Letters were exchanged in the fall of 1889 on this subject between the Departments of State and Navy. Both Admiral Kimberly and Stevens asked for naval support, especially for the period of the Hawaiian elections in February, 1890. In 1891 the petition was repeated.

group in business and political circles and urged the cause of the new treaty. He wrote that the British and French interests opposed the idea of a new American treaty and added:

I am much impressed by the strong American feeling pervading the best portion of the population and which is especially manifest among the men of business and property. There is no doubt that reciprocity is doing much to Americanize these islands and to bind them to the United States.[22]

In October, 1889, the Hawaiian cabinet published an "Explanation of the Government position in Regard to a new Treaty with the United States." This pamphlet stated that it was the desire of the Government to increase the commerce with the United States, and that the immediate cause of the movement for the treaty was the agitation in the United States to lower sugar duties and to pay bounties to producers of American sugar. The effect of such legislation would be to annul the advantages of the existing reciprocity treaty. A new treaty should contain, if possible, complete reciprocity and identical treatment in regard to bounties and privileges. The Hawaiian Government would like a further clause containing a positive guarantee by the United States of the independence and autonomy of Hawaii and was willing to concede in return American control of Hawaii's treaty-making power.[23] In other words, in the fall of 1889 the Hawaiian Government

[22] Stevens to Blaine, October 7, 1889, *U. S. Foreign Relations*, 1894, II, 292.

[23] *Ibid.*, 293-295.

was prepared to become a dependency or protectorate of the United States.

This treaty project was not carried out in the winter of 1889-90, and the McKinley Tariff, which was passed by the House of Representatives early in 1890, caused a violent reaction in Hawaii. Stevens wrote in May that placing sugar on the free list would destroy the sugar industry in Hawaii and injure the interests of many Americans. He felt that Hawaii needed a 50 per cent specific duty on raw sugar.[24] As a result, probably, of the tariff tendencies in the United States, the American group in the Hawaiian cabinet lost its influence over the King, and Stevens was greatly disturbed by the prominent part played by a certain Canadian, named Ashford, who held the office of attorney general. Ashford opposed the idea of a new treaty with the United States and favored an ocean cable and steamship connection with Vancouver, a project of the Canadian Pacific Railway Company, and a reciprocity treaty with Canada. It was thought that Ashford was in the pay of the Canadian Pacific, if not an agent of Sir John Macdonald.[25]

After the McKinley Tariff became a law, the Hawaiian Legislature passed resolutions stating that, since the Act diminished the value to Hawaii of the existing treaty of reciprocity, the Hawaiian Government should,

[24] Stevens to Blaine, May 20, 1890, *ibid.*, 319.
[25] Stevens to Blaine, May 28, 1890, *ibid.*, 321. This is of interest when viewed in the light of United States-Canadian relations as a whole in this period. See Chapters XIII and XIV.

while guarding most zealously the freedom, autonomy and independent sovereignty of the King of Hawaii, enter into negotiations with the U. S. Government for a treaty looking to the
extension of the principle of reciprocity between the two countries to other articles which may be the product or manufacture
of the two countries with a view to the continuance and increase
of the mutual benefits which have hitherto accrued to both
countries under the existing reciprocity treaty.[26]

The position of Hawaii, thus disregarded in the Mc-
Kinley Tariff Act, was not entirely forgotten. The
protests of Mr. Stevens and the resolutions of the Hawaiian Legislature received the attention of the Department of State, and the message of President Harrison in December, 1890, recommended that Congress
repair the wrong done Hawaii by the Tariff Act, which
"might otherwise seem to be a breach of faith on the
part of this Government." [27] On February 10, 1891,
Secretary Blaine wrote to the Hawaiian minister, Mr.
Carter, that it was the expectation of the Committee on
Foreign Relations to secure the passage of a bill reliev-
ing Hawaii from the effect of the McKinley Tariff
Act.[28]

King Kalakaua, always vacillating between the liberal or American group and the reactionary faction,
was about to take advantage of the temporary unpopularity of the former element to rescind the constitution.
He was prevented, possibly by the representations of

[26] *U. S. Foreign Relations*, 1894, II, 339.

[27] Richardson, *Messages and Papers*, IX, 110.

[28] Blaine to Carter, February 10, 1891, Manuscript Notes to Hawaiian Ministers, Archives of State Department.

Mr. Stevens and the British minister, from taking this step and early in 1891 sailed to the United States with the intention of aiding in the negotiation of a new treaty.[29]

His death in San Francisco shortly after he reached the United States altered the situation. His successor was his sister, Queen Liliuokalani, who was from the first anti-American and reactionary. The political situation in Hawaii was, from that time, very unstable and unsatisfactory. The Queen and the Court party were in the minority but were able to obstruct all legislation and were ready to use any means, even unconstitutional ones, to gain their ends. They opposed the negotiation of a new treaty with the United States and were, undoubtedly, back of the movement for a new constitution which, if successful, would have made possible a return to the old autocratic government.

The damage wrought the sugar industry by the McKinley Tariff, and the reactionary attitude of the Queen, which threatened to prevent any remedy, and which, indeed, threatened the constitution itself and the control it had given to the commercial interests, were the causes for the growth of annexationist sentiment in Hawaii from the fall of 1890 on, to the time of the revolution in 1893. From the point of view of the sugar planters and the commercial interests, the situation was intolerable. Revolution and annexation seemed to them the only remedy.

[29] *U. S. Foreign Relations*, 1894, II, 339. Stevens and the English minister apparently agreed on all except economic issues.

Stevens early identified himself with this annexation-ist, anti-royal faction and from September, 1891, to his recall wrote often and at length in favor of annexation. There is no document in the correspondence which shows either the approval or disapproval of Mr. Stevens' opinions or activities. In all this period there was no note or instruction sent Stevens from the Department of State other than the merest formal acknowledgment of reports and dispatches from Hawaii. The silence was undoubtedly that of perfect consent and approval, for the Secretary of State had long been on record as favoring ultimate annexation. What Stevens' original instructions had been can only be inferred by his conduct in office, but it is obvious that Blaine gave him no advice and no orders now that circumstances had changed and events were moving rapidly toward revolution. It seems safe, therefore, to infer that Mr. Stevens was neither exceeding his instructions nor incurring official disapproval. The statements made in his dispatches, therefore, may be considered to be representative of the policy of the Department of State as expressed by Blaine in a letter to President Harrison, "I think there are only three places that are of value enough to be taken, that are not continental. One is Hawaii, the others are Cuba and Porto Rico. Cuba and Porto Rico are not imminent and will not be for a generation. Hawaii may come up for decision at any unexpected hour and I hope we shall be prepared to decide it in the affirmative." [30]

[30] Letter to Harrison of August 10, 1891, quoted in Hamilton, *Blaine*, 692.

In spite of the anti-American attitude of the Queen and the Court, there was still a great deal of demand for a new treaty with the United States, and the campaign through the winter of 1891-1892, culminating in the legislative elections in February, was fought on that issue. Stevens was, of course, heartily in favor of it and wrote long dispatches on the subject, arguing that reciprocity must be more complete, that there must be more diversified agriculture in Hawaii, that the Islands were of commanding importance in the Pacific, and that the United States must retain control of Hawaii. He felt that the Islands were of vast importance to the United States and must remain under the

increased fostering care of the United States or fall under foreign control. A niggardly, hesitating and drifting policy towards them would be as unwise as unstatesmanlike. There is certainly no possible objection to negotiating and carrying into effect a full free trade treaty with them, for the aggregate of their products would be relatively so small compared with the vast productive resources and requirements of the United States as to make little perceptible difference in American markets and prices.

Believing that the views I have herein expressed are in accord with much in the past course of the American Government and in harmony with the opinions of the President and of the Secretary of State, I submit them for what they are worth. As an American citizen, loving my country and caring for its welfare and its future greatness, I can say no less. As an official representative of the Government of the United States in these special circumstances I can properly say no more.[31]

[31] Stevens to Blaine, September 5, 1891, *U. S. Foreign Relations, 1894*, Appendix II, 350-352.

The Hawaiian elections in February, 1892, resulted in no appreciable improvement of the political situation. The new cabinet was weak and divided into factions. Ashford, the Canadian member, was avowedly opposed to a new treaty. A new party appeared in the legislature, composed of so-called "Liberals," who were opposed to the treaty and later favored a new constitution. They were dominated by the Queen's favorites at Court and were, Stevens said, "irresponsible white voters, half castes and a large majority of the native Hawaiians." [32]

Stevens wrote after the election, that the annexation sentiment was increasing, and that he saw no prospect of improvement in the feverish political situation until the Islands became either a part of the American Union or a possession of Great Britain. He felt that annexation to the United States was the policy which should be adopted for the good of all concerned, and that, in the meantime, a war ship should be constantly at Honolulu. [33] A month later he wrote asking for definite instructions in case of revolution. Should the United States officials aid a deposed government, or should they only protect American property and citizens? What should be done about the disposal of American forces? [34]

These were significant questions in the light of subsequent events. It is equally significant that Blaine made no answer but left the decision to Stevens. In

[32] Stevens to Blaine, February 8, 1892, *ibid.*, 181.

[33] Stevens to Blaine, February 8, 1892, *ibid.*, 181.

[34] Stevens to Blaine, March 8, 1892, *ibid.*, 182.

April Stevens wrote that the more radical opponents of the Queen were strong enough to capture the government buildings, but that the more responsible citizens favored only pacific measures and looked toward the approaching meeting of the newly elected Legislature for some amelioration of conditions. He believed that if the conservative wing of the annexationists could have definite encouragement from the United States, they could "carry all before them." [35] This plea, also, was met by discreet silence on the part of the Secretary of State. Mr. Stevens' activities were not, on the other hand, in any way curtailed.

The new Legislature had been quietly elected and was believed to have a safe majority of the wealthy, pro-American element, many of them of American blood.[36] When it met, the old, weak cabinet, dominated by a Tahitan favorite of the Queen, was voted out. The new cabinet chosen by the Queen was not accepted by the Legislature and a deadlock at once followed. For two months the legislative majority struggled for the principle of a responsible ministry. In this struggle the American and German elements in the capital supported the Legislature, and the British sided with the Queen.[37] The anti-American group favored a coup d' état and a new constitution restoring an absolute monarchy.[38] There was the usual unsavory tangle of diverse economic interests: English sugar

[35] Stevens to Blaine, April 2, 1892, *ibid.*, 356.
[36] Stevens to Blaine, May 21, 1892, *ibid.*, 357-359.
[37] Stevens to Blaine, September 14, 1892, *ibid.*, 183.
[38] Stevens to Blaine, October 31, 1892, *ibid.*, 186.

houses versus American, the adherents of the Canadian Pacific Railroad's policy of a cable and a steamship line versus its opponents, and the advocates of a new English loan to the royalists versus those who wished dependence upon the United States. On November 8 Stevens reported the end of the deadlock and the triumph of the Legislature.[39] The new cabinet was composed of wealthy, responsible men, three of them of American blood, one of English, and only one of mixed parentage. It was the triumph of the American interests. Stevens was jubilant and stated: "I am happy to say that my official and personal relations with this ministry are likely to be most friendly and cordial." [40]

This triumph of the Legislature did not produce calm, for the defeated royal party went on with its intrigues, and the chasm between the Legislature and the Executive, between the adherents of the constitution and those of the autocratic Queen was wider, if possible, than before. Revolution from one side or the other was expected by all parties. Stevens spent much time and energy in urging the annexation policy upon the Secretary of State, now Mr. John W. Foster. He stated that the United States must at once decide between the annexation of Hawaii and a protectorate over the Islands in which there should be a customs union and an absolute cession of Pearl Harbor. He,

[39] Stevens to Foster, November 8, 1892, *ibid.*, 376. Blaine retired in June, but the news apparently did not reach Stevens until November. There was no change in instructions, and Foster evidently gave him the same free hand and silent approval accorded by Blaine.

[40] *Ibid.*

personally, favored the former plan for "the golden hour is at hand." [41] He sent long reports on the financial, agricultural, social, and political conditions of the Islands, made use of the usual bogey-man of English acquisition, and in general did all he could to call forth some action from the Department of State. Foster, however, followed Blaine's policy of silence. He neither reproved nor applauded Stevens' enthusiasm and awaited the turn of events. President Harrison's message to Congress of December 6 admitted that "our relations with Hawaii have been such as to attract an increased interest, and must continue to do so." He felt that cable connections were necessary and admired the development of Pearl Harbor. He said further:

Many evidences of the friendliness of the Hawaiian Government have been given in the past and it is gratifying to believe that the advantage and necessity of a continuance of our close relations is appreciated. [42]

In the meantime Hawaii was quiet in the lull before the storm. The long awaited and expected revolution occurred in January, 1893. An attempt on the part of the Queen to grant a new constitution but essentially restoring an absolute monarchy was countered by a revolution to destroy the monarchy and establish a republic. Stevens was, most opportunely, absent from Honolulu during the ten days preceding the revolution and could thus disclaim all responsibility for its inception. Most opportunely also for the revolutionists, he

41 Stevens to Foster, November 20, 1892, *ibid.*, 383.
42 Richardson, IX, 316.

returned in time to summon American marines from the warship in the harbor to defend American "lives and property" and incidentally to place these seamen so that they gave ample protection to the forces of the revolution. Stevens was the first representative of a foreign power to recognize the provisional government. A commission was at once dispatched to the United States to negotiate a treaty of annexation, and the work of Stevens was over.[43] On February 1, he wrote to Foster, "The Hawaiian pear is now fully ripe and this is the golden hour for the United States to pluck it." [44]

The annexation treaty was negotiated with great speed and was sent to Congress on February 15, just one month after the revolution, with a message which reads exactly like Stevens' dispatches of the year previous.[45] The monarchy was called "effete" and the Queen's government "weak and inadequate." "Only two courses are now open — one the establishment of a protectorate by the United States, and the other annexation full and complete." The President advised prompt action upon the treaty.

The letter which Secretary Foster sent to the President with the treaty and accompanying documents merits a little examination because of the light it casts upon the policy of the administration. Some of the statements quoted may seem, in view of Mr. Stevens' dispatches, to need some qualification:

[43] Stevens to Foster, January 18, 1893, *U. S. Foreign Relations*, 1894, Appendix II, 386.

[44] *Ibid.*, 294.

[45] Richardson, IX, 348.

The change of government in the Hawaiian Islands thus chronicled, was entirely unexpected so far as this government was concerned.

At no time had Mr. Stevens been instructed as to his course in the event of a revolutionary uprising.

The landing of the marines was at the request of citizens and in accordance with the practice of protecting lives and property.

The marines, when landed, took no part whatever toward influencing the course of events. Their presence was wholly precautionary, and only such disposition was made of them as was calculated to subserve the particular end in view. . . . They remained isolated and inconspicuous until after the success of the Provisional Government.

There is not the slightest indication that at any time prior to the formal recognition in full accord with the long-established rule and invariable precedents of this Government did the United States Minister take any part in promoting the change, either by intimidating the Queen or by giving assurance of support to the organizers of the Provisional Government.[46]

It is undoubtedly true that Stevens had had no instructions as to what to do in case of revolution, but it is hardly accurate to state that the revolution was unexpected, or his attitude toward it unforeseen. In the same way, the landing of the marines was in accordance with custom, but the disposition made of them was such as to aid the revolutionists rather than to protect American property. They were, it is true, quiet, but their presence caused the collapse of the Queen's forces.[47]

[46] U. S. Foreign Relations, 1894, Appendix II, 199.
[47] See Blount's Report, ibid.

The recognition of the *de facto* government was in accordance with the practice of the United States, but it is apparent that Stevens did not hesitate long in deciding that it was really *de facto*.

The treaty was not ratified in the last days of the Harrison administration and was withdrawn from the Senate by President Cleveland. The problem of Hawaii during the Cleveland term does not fall within the scope of this study, however much it merits attention. Hawaii remained a republic but did not become a territory of the United States until 1898.

In the treatment of this episode, the assumption has been that Stevens represented the policy of Secretary Blaine. The two men had long been friends and neighbors in Augusta. To say that a man was an active Republican from Maine was to say that he was a Blaine adherent through and through. Stevens was a Blaine appointee. Both men were on record as favoring ultimate annexation. Stevens went to Hawaii without any official instructions, at least, without any instructions which appear in the files of the Department; and he received no such instructions during his stay in the Islands. If there were any communications from Secretary Blaine, or, after June, 1892, from Mr. Foster, they were of a confidential nature, and no copies were kept in the files. It seems safe to state, therefore, that Stevens was probably correct when he said he felt sure that he represented the opinions of the President and of the Secretary of State. The inference seems to be that the administration was playing an opportunist part. As annexation sentiment grew in the Islands, it was to be neither openly encouraged nor discouraged, and when "the pear was ripe" the United States, if it did not pluck it, would at least allow it to fall into its eagerly awaiting hands. Secretary Blaine retired in June, 1892, and cannot, of course, be considered in any way responsible for whatever means Mr. Stevens may have taken in the winter of 1892-1893 to make the revolution possible and successful, and it is only fair to state that the most minute search of Mr. Blount, Cleveland's investigator, did not show that Stevens had any nefarious dealings with the revolutionary leaders. They were his friends and he approved their conduct. Perhaps his own statement that "I am doing my utmost to blend reticence and prudence with firmness and vigor and as far as possible shall protect American influence and interests here," [48] adequately expressed his attitude.

[48] Stevens to Foster, October 8, 1892, confidential, Manuscript Dispatches, Hawaii, No. 70, Vol. 25. This is the only Stevens dispatch unpublished. See Appendix I for complete dispatch.

CHAPTER IX

THE SAMOAN CONFERENCE, 1889

ALTHOUGH Mr. Blaine extended the Monroe
Doctrine to the Hawaiian Islands and considered
their acquisition both desirable and inevitable, there is
no evidence that he was similarly interested in any other
group of Pacific islands. The conference which met in
Berlin in the spring of 1889 gave to him his only contact with the long standing and complicated controversy
over the Samoan Islands and at the same time furnished
the only diplomatic incident in German-American relations during the periods when he was Secretary of
State. The commercial development of Samoa began
about 1857 when the house of Godeffroy and Sons of
Hamburg established its headquarters at Apia for trade
in the products of the Pacific. The interest of Germany
in the Islands dates from this event and is throughout
the whole period identified with the commercial interests of the German firm. The diplomatic history of the
Islands, which began with 1872 and ended with their
annexation by Germany and the United States in 1899,
may be divided into three periods: first, that of formulation of treaties with the United States, Germany, and
Great Britain, 1872-1879; second, the period of disturbance ending in the Samoan Conference in 1889;

and, third, the ten years in which an unsuccessful attempt was made to carry out the provisions of the treaty which ended that Conference. The closing months of the second period fall in the time when Blaine was again in charge of the Department of State.[1]

The diplomatic interest of the United States in the Samoan Islands dates from the unofficial visit of Commander Meade, of the U.S.S. "Narragansett," in 1872, who made an agreement with the native chiefs for exclusive right to a naval station in Pago Pago Harbor. The next year Colonel Steinberger was sent out by Secretary Fish on a special mission of investigation.

---

[1] For the development of the Samoan controversy prior to 1889, the account follows that of Miss Jeannette Keim in *Forty Years of German-American Political Relations*, Ch. V, "Samoa: The United States and Germany in the Pacific," and the summary given in Moore's *Digest of International Law*, Vol. I. Robert Louis Stevenson, *Footnote to History: Eight Years of Trouble in Samoa*, is valuable for the years just prior to the Berlin Conference. The printed source material for the controversy is found in the following list of United States Documents:

House Executive Document No. 161, 44 Congress, 1st Session;
Senate Executive Document No. 2, 46 Congress, 1st Session;
House Executive Document No. 238, 50 Congress, 1st Session;
Senate Executive Document No. 102, 50 Congress, 2nd Session;
Senate Executive Document No. 31, 50 Congress, 2nd Session;
House Executive Document No. 119, 50 Congress, 2nd Session;
Senate Executive Document No. 68, 50 Congress, 2nd Session;
Senate Miscellaneous Document No. 81, 51 Congress, 1st Session;
Foreign Relations for the period, especially 1889.

There are German *White Books* and British *Blue Books* for the controversy and some of the correspondence to 1886 is reprinted in *Staatsarchiv*, XLIV. *Die grosse Politik der europäischen Kabinette* contains a few incidental references, and *Archives diplomatiques* publishes only the protocols of the Conference of 1887.

He found the native government weak, apparently in fear of the increasing German dominance, and forwarded for the Samoans an appeal for annexation to the United States. Steinberger recommended annexation but the anti-imperialistic feeling and policy of the United States in that period was an obstacle. In 1877 one of the Samoan chiefs, La Mamea, visited the United States and offered a protectorate over the Islands. This was refused but a commercial treaty was concluded and Pago Pago Harbor was ceded to the United States.

This Treaty of 1878 is of great importance in the events of the later period, for it contained an article stating:

If, unhappily, any differences should have arisen or shall hereafter arise, between the Samoan government and any other government in amity with the United States, the government of the latter will employ its good offices for the purpose of adjusting those differences upon a satisfactory and solid basis.[2]

Just what the Samoans thought was meant by this article is difficult to discover. "Good offices" apparently came much nearer protection in their minds than any one in the United States meant or understood by the term. The article was, probably, only a friendly gesture in return for a treaty in which the advantages lay entirely on one side.

Germany and Great Britain each secured by treaty the following year a harbor and similar commercial

[2] Article V, Treaty of 1878.

privileges. These treaties compromised native autonomy, in that laws which concerned nationals of the two
countries were to be approved by the home government
of those nationals. Neither treaty contained a "good
offices" clause. Shortly after this a general convention
was drawn up, which practically neutralized and turned
over to the consuls of Great Britain and Germany the
government of Apia, the center of foreign commercial
interests. The United States was asked to adhere to
this convention and assisted in the municipal government, and, although the Senate never approved the
convention, American consuls in practice took part in
the administration.[3]

The Samoans resented foreign interference and exploitation and disliked having their conduct and mode
of life regulated. There followed a period of confusion and controversy in which civil war between native
chieftains was entangled with interference on the part
of the German consul and the representative of German commercial houses. The English and American
consuls were not exactly disinterested spectators, and
the situation was complicated by the quarrels and intrigues of the various factions among the foreign population.

The crisis occurred in 1884 when Dr. Stuebel, the
German consul, forced upon the joint kings, Malietoa
and Tamesese, an agreement which placed, for all prac-

[3] Each nation had, therefore, acknowledged Samoan independence.
Yet Great Britain and Germany had compromised it. It was further
limited by the convention establishing the Municipality of Apia.

tical purposes, the government of the islands in German control. The British and American representatives at once protested, while Malietoa refused to carry out the agreement and appealed to Great Britain for annexation and protection. This action sealed his fate. Germany from that time on supported the co-king, Tamesese. In 1885 the German flag was raised in the Islands, but the act was disavowed by Bismarck, who protested his adherence to the idea of the equality of the three foreign powers. Malietoa appealed to the consul of the United States, who raised the American flag, only to haul it down again when his act was disavowed by Secretary Bayard. It was apparent that some measures must be taken to reach an agreement as to policy.

Early in 1886 Secretary Bayard suggested that Germany and Great Britain authorize their respective ministers at Washington to confer with him and that, as a preliminary step, the three nations each send a commissioner to Samoa to investigate actual conditions there. The invitation was accepted, and the commissioners were duly dispatched. It is interesting to note that all three commissioners reported against a tripartite control. The German commissioner felt that Germany's predominating commercial interests entitled her to sole control, while the American felt that, for that very reason, the control should not be German but American, since the slighter interests of the United States made impartial administration more possible.

In the meantime Great Britain and Germany had

come to agreement on the various colonial questions that had been troubling their diplomatic relations. It needed only the warning from Germany that continued opposition in such relatively remote and unimportant regions as Samoa and West Africa would deprive England of German support in Egypt and the Near East, to cause England to agree to support Germany in the coming conference.[4]

The Washington Conference met in June, 1887, foredoomed to failure. Secretary Bayard submitted a plan on the basis of Samoan independence and autonomy, providing for a tripartite supervision, which he hoped would be temporary. Germany's plan dismissed the idea of native autonomy as impossible and tripartite control as impracticable and suggested a mandatory government depending, in theory, upon the three Governments but, in fact, upon Germany alone, for the "Advisor to the King" was to be nominated by the power having a preponderating influence. Great Britain agreed with Germany.

When no agreement seemed possible, the Conference

[4] *Die grosse Politik der europäischen Kabinette, 1871-1884,* IV, 143, No. 790. Count Herbert von Bismarck to Count von Hatzfeld, March 19, 1886. A long letter warning England against opposition in colonial affairs ends thus:

"Fortdauernde Friktionen auf kolonialen Gebieten können schliesslich zu einer politischen Gegnerschaft überhaupt führen und England würde seine Rechnung schwerlich dabei finden, wenn es in Ägypten und im Orient bezahlen müsste, was seine Beamten in Sansibar und Apia verschuldet haben."

See also Zimmermann, *Geschichte der deutschen Kolonialpolitik,* 288 ff.

was adjourned, and two years of great confusion and tension ensued. Germany declared war upon Malietoa "personally," finally deporting him, and made Tamesese sole king. The Samoans rebelled and, under the leadership of Mataafa, made war upon Tamesese, who was completely under the control of an efficient German prime minister.

Robert Louis Stevenson calls the period from December of 1888 to March of 1889 the "Furor Consularis," and the circumstances fitted the name. The German consul, Knappe, undoubtedly wished the annexation of Samoa, but he was not supported by Bismarck.[5] The American consul quarreled violently with Knappe, and the British consul was not popular in either camp.[6] British, German, and American war vessels were sent to the harbor at Apia, and the slightest indiscretion on the part of naval officers might well have precipitated a conflict.

[5] Pendleton to Bayard, February 1, 1889. Confidential correspondence printed for the use of the American Commission to Berlin included in a manuscript volume of dispatches from the United States Commission. Pendleton reported that Bismarck remarked that the German consul at Apia appeared to have quite lost his head and that the Imperial Government had no desire to transcend the Samoan treaties.

[6] Carl Schurz to Bayard, January 30, 1889. Quoted in Carl Schurz, *Writings*, V, 1-6. Schurz reported to Bayard an interview with Count Arco-Vally, the German minister, in which Count Arco had insisted upon the friendship of Germany for the United States. He called the hostility a newspaper and consular conflict and deprecated the fact that the American consuls had been inferior to the English and German in all mental equipment and social standing. Both Schurz and, later, Bayard admitted the truth of this statement.

In January, 1889, President Cleveland sent the whole correspondence on Samoa to Congress with a message declaring that Germany was aiming at a predominance in Samoa which would destroy the independence of the Islands and the equality of position of the foreign powers. Much feeling was aroused, and Congress appropriated money for the protection of the interests of the United States. Secretary Bayard protested against the German policy through the United States minister at Berlin. Prince Bismarck had not the slightest intention of going to war over Samoa, and his replies were most pacific and conciliating.[7] He proposed to Lord Salisbury that the British Government unite with Germany in inviting the United States to a conference at Berlin in "resumption of the consultation which took place between the representatives of Germany, England, and the United States in 1887, at Washington." He stated that Germany did not intend to put in question the independence of the island group nor the equal rights of the powers. Bayard accepted

[7] Pendleton to Bayard, February 9, 1889. Correspondence printed for use of American Commission. "He (Bismarck) remarked that untrue statements and intemperate comments by the press, telegraphed from America and elsewhere, which were in marked contrast with considerate official utterances, had created in the minds of many the impression — a most erroneous one — that grave difficulties existed between the German and American Governments. There existed, he said, nothing to cloud the traditional pleasant, amicable relations between the two governments and peoples and nothing thus affecting them could or should arise." Bismarck was willing that the foregoing remarks should go to the Secretary of State but asked that they be not published.

the invitation but asked that there be a suspension of hostilities in Samoa and a truce on the basis of the *status quo*. The Cleveland administration came to an end, and the appointment of the American Commission at the Berlin Conference was left to the incoming administration.

On the 16th of March, before news of the approaching settlement reached far-off Samoa, a hurricane swept down upon the crowded harbor of Apia. One ship only, out of the thirteen war vessels of the three nations sheltered there, escaped at least partial destruction. All thought of combat was over.[8] The disaster cleared the air, and the possibility of any indiscretion in the Islands which might imperil the coming conference no longer needed to be feared by the diplomats.

On March 18 President Harrison appointed as commissioners to the Conference, John A. Kasson, a former minister to Germany; William Walter Phelps, the newly appointed minister to Germany; and George H.

[8] This disaster gave Stevenson material for one of his most dramatic chapters in *Footnote to History*, Ch. X. This closes with the statement, which has some inaccuracies:

"Then, in what seemed the very article of war, and within the duration of a single day, the sword-arm of each of the two angry powers was broken; their formidable ships reduced to junk; their disciplined hundreds to a horde of castaways, fed with difficulty, and the fear of whose misconduct marred the sleep of their commanders. Both paused aghast; both had time to recognize that not the whole Samoan archipelago was worth the loss in men and costly ships already suffered. The so-called hurricane of March 16th made thus a marking epoch in world-history; directly, and at once, it brought about the congress and the treaty of Berlin; indirectly, and by a process still continuing, it founded the modern navy of the States."

Bates, who had been sent to Samoa as investigator by Bayard in 1886.[9] The German commissioners were Count Herbert Bismarck, Baron von Holstein, and Dr. Krauel, and the British were Sir Edward Malet, Mr. Charles Stewart Scott, and Mr. Joseph Crowe.

In the interval before the meeting of the Conference, it was obvious that Prince Bismarck was preparing the German public for a change of policy in regard to Samoa. Mr. Pendleton reported that, although there was a jingoistic tone in some circles, the German press as a whole expressed satisfaction with the idea of a conference.[10] At a parliamentary dinner Bismarck spoke of Samoan affairs and remarked emphatically that the idea should be "utterly excluded" that on account of this "little matter" the friendly relations with the United

[9] Bates's appointment was natural under the circumstances but caused considerable difficulty. His report in 1887, just published, had been unfavorable to Germany and, furthermore, in the April and May numbers of the *Century Magazine* there appeared from his pen articles on the Samoan question in which he publicly assailed Germany on the ground of bad faith, deception, and insulting conduct. Bates had been appointed before the articles appeared but was not withdrawn when the articles caused criticism. When the Commission reached Berlin, Count Herbert Bismarck at first refused to meet Mr. Bates but an interview was at last arranged by Kasson in which Bates humbly stated that he had tried to stop the publication of his articles after he had been appointed but could not do so and that the recent appearance of the German *White Books* might have altered his opinions. Count Herbert, thereupon, spoke coldly to him, and the Conference was permitted to proceed. See Manuscript Dispatches, Germany, Vol. 48, letter from Pendleton to Blaine, April 13, 1889, and Manuscript Dispatches, Samoa, April 29, 1889.

[10] Pendleton to Blaine, February 25, 1889. Manuscript Dispatches, Germany, Vol. 48.

States could be disturbed.[11] The German newspapers frankly predicted a retreat from the previous extreme position in regard to Samoa.[12] In the German *White Book*, which appeared in March, 1889, Bismarck disavowed the conduct of Dr. Knappe, the German consul general at Samoa, and asserted that his entire conduct of affairs in working for annexation and in proclaiming martial law was without authorization. The London *Times* for March 23, commented:

> Such is the way in which Prince Bismarck disavows his agents and rehabilitates himself in the confidence of the United States previous to the Samoan Conference which will set everything right again.[13]

[11] Pendleton to Blaine, March 4, 1889, *ibid.*

[12] Quotation from the Berlin *Freisinnige Zeitung*, February 26, 1889, *ibid.*

[13] Quotations from the London *Times*, March 23, 1889, contained in a volume of manuscript correspondence in the Archives of the State Department, entitled "The Samoan Conference," which contains the confidential dispatches from and to the American Commission, the correspondence printed for the use of the commissioners, and numerous newspaper clippings, reports, etc. The *Times* article gives the following quotations from Bismarck's preface to the *White Book*:

"This (Dr. Knappe's) repeated statement that he had been commissioned or empowered by the Imperial Government to declare war, or even martial law, was arbitrary or due to an error difficult to explain. . . . It seems to me that his touchiness in the matter of the respect he claimed, together with the letter of Capt. Brandeis of December 13 last, and the presence at Apia of three German ships of war deprived Herr Knappe of that *sangfroid* which alone could enable him to retain a clear view of the situation and its possible consequences. In his correspondence, too, with his colleagues, he seems to have written in a brusque and excited tone, which sometimes even took the form of threats against the other consuls. You are aware

Stevenson paid Bismarck a tribute, which the careful historian may wish to modify, when he wrote:

The example thus offered by Germany is rare in history; in the career of Prince Bismarck, so far as I am instructed, it should stand unique. On a review of these two years of blundering, bullying, and failure in a little isle of the Pacific, he seems magnanimously to have owned his policy was in the wrong. He left Fangalii unexpiated; suffered that house of cards, the Tamasese government, to fall by its own frailty, and without remark or lamentation, left the Samoan question openly and fairly to the conference. . . .

To the more cynical, Bismarck's conduct may be explained by interest and expediency, but the effect was the same — Germany retreated.[14]

that the demands put forward by Consul Knappe when negotiating with Mataafa that Germany should take over the administration of the islands, including their representation abroad, were unwarrantable, and that he was telegraphed to from here to withdraw them at once. The further statements in his report that all the Samoans would prefer to see the islands annexed by Germany, but that nevertheless there was little hope that the rebels would give way are partly contradictory and partly lack practical import, as without the assent of England and America the political status of Samoa cannot be aimed at.

"It is incomprehensible to me how Herr Knappe should again recur to this idea of annexation, seeing that from his experience in the Foreign Office as well as his instructions, and our recent correspondence with him he must have known that all thought of annexing Samoa are in direct contradiction to the policy pursued by me in accordance with the ideas of the Emperor."

[14] *Footnote to History*, 268.

Bismarck telegraphed to Count Arco-Vally, German minister in Washington: "Ich persönlich wäre dafür, dass wir uns wenn irgend möglich auf anständige Weise gänzlich aus Samoa herausziehen, denn dieses wird niemals einen wirklich greifbaren Wert für uns darstellen,

The instructions given by Secretary Blaine to the American commissioners are dated April 11, 1889. They are comprehensive and extremely conservative in tone. There is no trace of aggressive policy and no apparent desire to commit the United States to closer relations to Samoa.[15] The commissioners were instructed to study the correspondence and the protocols of the 1887 Conference.[16] Mr. Blaine stated that the United States desired a speedy and amicable solution of all the questions involved and

that, while it will steadily maintain its full equality of right and consideration in any disposition of those questions, it is as much influenced by an anxious desire to secure to the people of Samoa the conditions of a healthy, prosperous, and civilized life, as it is bound by its duty to protect the rights and interests of its own citizens wherever their spirit of lawful enterprise may carry them.

He hoped and believed that no one of the three powers

sondern höchstens dazu dienen, unser Verhältnis zu Amerika, vielleicht später auch einmal zu Australien, und dadurch zu England zu gefährden." Hermann, Freiherr von Eckardstein, *Lebenserinnerungen und politische Denkwürdigkeiten.*

[15] In the interview already referred to between Carl Schurz and Count Arco-Vally, the German minister had observed that some persons feared lest Mr. Blaine might be in favor of annexing the Samoan Islands to the United States or, at least, of establishing an American protectorate. Schurz thought that there was no basis for such an idea and was reassured by Bayard, who wrote on March 9 that he had just seen Blaine for the first time in seven years and thought him much enfeebled and much less likely to pursue an aggressive policy than in 1881. Carl Schurz, *Writings*, V, 19.

[16] Instructions in full, *U. S. Foreign Relations*, 1889, 195-204, and in a resumé, 349-353.

wished to encroach upon Samoan independence and he wished it clearly understood that the Berlin Conference was merely a continuation of the Washington Conference, for the United States would not admit that events since 1887 had changed the basis for consideration. In other words, the Conference of 1887 was initiated for the purpose of establishing peace and a stable native government on the basis of local autonomy and the equality of the treaty powers, and the Conference of 1889 must be conducted on the same basis.

The subjects upon which the commissioners were given instructions fell under five heads. They were to ask for a restoration of the *status quo* of 1887 in order to restore the equality of the treaty powers. They were to attempt to obtain a stable government with native autonomy and, if intervention should appear to be necessary, it was to be avowedly temporary in character and preparatory to complete autonomy. They were to secure a settlement of the land question on a basis of equity and the saving of a reasonable amount of land to the natives. There should be prohibition or regulation of the importation and sale of firearms and intoxicating liquors. The commissioners were to use their own judgment in renewing the municipal government of Apia.

By a comparison of these instructions with the policy of Secretary Bayard, as outlined in the Conference of 1887, it may be seen clearly that Blaine was far from taking an advanced or aggressive position. The Bayard scheme had contemplated the preservation of the native government with the addition to the king and vice-king, of an executive council of three secretaries, who with the king and vice-king would form the executive council. These secretaries were to be nominated, one each, by the three treaty powers and appointed by the king. They were to be foreigners but were to retain their extra-territorial powers. Mr. Blaine was avowedly afraid of any such plan. He far preferred an absolute autonomy, for, as he said:

This scheme itself goes beyond the principle upon which the President desires to see our relations with the Samoan government based, and is not in harmony with the established policy of this government. For, if it is not a joint protectorate, to which there are such grave and obvious objections, it is hardly less than that, and does not in any event promise efficient action.[17]

Secretary Blaine feared that the tripartite scheme would merely transfer to the executive council the disputes which had produced the "Furor Consularis," and yet, since many able men who had studied the question advocated a tripartite control, Blaine did not, in his instructions to the commissioners, rule it out of discussion, but contented himself with insisting that such control must be temporary and based upon the equality of the powers. He wished no permanent break to occur in the American tradition. Extending and revivifying the Monroe Doctrine for the American system of states, he was quite willing to keep up the converse of the Doctrine — abstinence from contact with European affairs. The Monroe Doctrine might be extended to

[17] *U. S. Foreign Relations*, 1889, 201.

include Hawaii but not necessarily the Samoan Islands, and "entangling alliances" were to be avoided if possible. It remains to be seen in how far the American Commission carried out the Secretary's wishes.

The Conference met on April 29 and the "General Act" was signed on June 14.[18] There were in all some nine sessions. Mr. Kasson stopped in London for a few days on his way to Berlin and had what was, apparently, a very pleasant interview with Lord Salisbury in which the latter did not commit himself to any definite plan or policy. Kasson expressed the hope that the English members of the Conference might be able to exercise a little more latitude in discussing the pending questions than they had at the Washington Conference. Upon obtaining, in answer to this indirect attempt to discover whether England was still bound to support Germany, no response save a laugh and the remark that Lord Sackville certainly was not famous for talking, Kasson grew more bold and remarked that the English-speaking race seemed better adapted to promote civilization and peace than was Germany, and that it might be natural for England and the United States to agree on the Samoan question. Salisbury replied that England had too little interest in Samoa to

[18] The General Act and the protocols may be found in *U. S. Foreign Relations*, 1889, 353 ff., and in *Sen. Exec. Doc.* No. 81, 51 Cong., 1st Session (No. 2698). The correspondence from and to the commissioners of the United States was not published and was of a confidential nature. It forms a volume in the Archives of the State Department entitled "The Samoan Conference" and will be referred to, hereafter, under that name.

take an active part in the Islands and that the German interest was far greater. He acknowledged that he had no faith in the success of the tripartite scheme and had been responsible for Lord Sackville's support of Germany in 1887. Kasson obtained from him, however, two avowals which gave him considerable satisfaction. In view of the opposition of the United States, the proposition to which Germany and Great Britain had adhered in 1887 would have to be abandoned, i. e., the plan for a foreign control of the Islands exercised by the power having the greatest interest involved. Salisbury thought also that Prince Bismarck was tired of the whole question. He refused to express any opinion as to a substitute for the two plans offered for consideration at the Washington Conference.[19]

Mr. Kasson proceeded to Berlin where he met the British ambassador, Sir Edward Malet, whose views on the Samoan question are of considerable interest in that they represent the solution of 1899 rather than the work accomplished by the Conference of Berlin.[20] Had the British ideas been put into effect, the ten years of uneasiness under tripartite control might have been avoided. But the United States was not, in 1889, ready for such a solution. Kasson learned that Lord Salisbury was considering whether it might not be possible to divide the islands so that each Government could take sole foreign jurisdiction of one of them. This notion was quite in keeping with the various steps in

[19] Kasson to Blaine, London, April 24, 1889, "Samoan Conference."
[20] Kasson to Blaine, Berlin, April 27, 1889, *ibid.*

the partition of Africa, which had been occupying the attention of the Foreign Office for some time. Sir Edward Malet offered, as his personal opinion, the proposition that the three powers divide their national influence so as to be, by common consent, dominant in different regions; the Americans, for example, in the Sandwich Islands, the English in the Tonga Islands, and the Germans in Samoa.

This diplomatic give and take with no regard for the wishes and independence of the native government did not fit in with the instructions of the American Commission, which were emphatically in favor of the preservation of that autonomy. Kasson replied that any such idea was beyond his instructions. Malet suggested, also, that it was worth considering "for example, if the Island of Tutuila, where our interests lay especially in the bay of Pago Pago, was separately managed by us in connection with local chiefs, everything there would move harmoniously. So with the Germans at Upsolu." Kasson replied that under the treaty with Samoa, the United States was bound in honor to use her good offices for the benefit of the natives in Samoa, and he feared trouble if any of them were turned over to the Germans, against whom there was so much animosity among the Islanders. Sir Edward, thereupon, expressed the polite hope that England might aid in reconciling the views of Germany and the United States and the opinion that both schemes advanced at the Washington Conference would have to be abandoned.

It is quite apparent that had the United States been

ready to give up the idea of native autonomy and the integrity of the native kingdom, the British representatives would have proposed a partition scheme of some sort, which would have anticipated the settlement of 1899 and might have settled other colonial questions which were irritating British-German relations. Such a proposal would undoubtedly have been agreeable to the German representatives. It may be considered, therefore, that it was this American refusal to give up the idea of native autonomy and to assume the burden of empire which caused the Conference to act along lines which both Lord Salisbury and Prince Bismarck disapproved, and to arrive at a solution for whose success they entertained grave doubts.

On April 28, the last day before the opening of the Conference, Kasson had a visit from Count Herbert Bismarck, in which the latter proposed the abandonment of the German mandatory scheme and the appointment of three officers to act conjointly in the region in possession of the foreigners. The natives were to be allowed to rule themselves, and Malietoa would be freed by Germany.[21] The predicted retreat of Germany had taken place. Malietoa, so long a captive, was to return and some form of a tripartite control was to be formulated. Prince Bismarck preferred always to enter a conference on the basis of preliminary agreements

[21] Kasson to Blaine, April 28, 1889, Telegram, "Samoan Conference." From the time of the opening of the Conference most of the correspondence was telegraphic. Secretary Blaine followed the work of the Conference closely and sent frequent additional instructions.

between the powers involved, so that the work of the conference might proceed smoothly and no disagreement appear in the published protocols.

Secretary Blaine responded to the report of Count Bismarck's proposition by a telegram instructing Kasson to insist upon some form of direction in the establishment of the native government, in order that one of the powers might never again be able to make war on Samoa without the consent of the other two.[22] Blaine tried also to secure recognition of the exclusive rights of the United States to Pago Pago, as granted by the Treaty of 1872.[23] Kasson answered that he could not well raise the question because of the English and German harbor concessions which would be raised,[24] and Blaine withdrew his insistence.[25] Blaine telegraphed also that the commissioners insist upon a clause prohibiting the importation of intoxicating liquors.[26]

Meantime the work of the Conference went on. It was easily agreed that there must be some sort of judge or tribunal to decide upon the customary contested elections of the native kings and to deal with the disputes over land titles and other disputes involving foreigners.[27] It was a delicate question to decide just who, among the native claimants, should be recognized as king. Malietoa had long been in exile under German

[22] Blaine to Kasson, May 3, 1889, *ibid.*
[23] Blaine to Kasson, May 4, 1889, *ibid.*
[24] Kasson to Blaine, May 5, 1889, *ibid.*
[25] Blaine to Kasson, May 6, 1889, *ibid.*
[26] Blaine to Kasson, May 5, 1889, *ibid.*
[27] Kasson to Blaine, May 4, 1889, *ibid.*

control. Tamasese had been vice-king and had been recognized by Germany as king but was *persona non grata* to the other powers and to the larger proportion of the natives. Mataafa, the leader of the majority of the Islanders, was able and patriotic but unacceptable to Germany because of the firing upon the German sailors in December, 1888. Germany would not object to any candidate except Mataafa. Germany wished, also, to obtain a punitive indemnity for the German sailors killed in the ill-fated expedition of December 17-18.[28] Blaine replied that he was quite willing to exclude both Mataafa and Tamasese because of the civil war, and that he preferred to exclude Malietoa also because he was weak and had long been under German influence. He refused the idea of an indemnity for Germany because he did not wish Samoa under financial obligation to Germany, and, also, because he did not wish the Islands to be reduced to absolute penury.[29]

For all the seeming accord, things were not going well at Berlin. Mr. Kasson had managed to keep all the correspondence in his own hands and had carried on long and confidential conversations with Count Herbert and the German delegation. He had been minister to Germany and had a large Berlin acquaintance and he, apparently, felt himself the chief of the American Commission. Their commissions, however, were of equal merit, and the instructions had been sent them

[28] Kasson to Blaine, May 9, 1889, "Samoan Conference."
[29] Blaine to Kasson, May 11, 1889, *ibid.*

in common. The Department of State had in no way distinguished among them, and Kasson's two colleagues resented their exclusion and protested to Blaine.[30] Kasson was, furthermore, so closely in touch with the German view that he was in danger of making concessions which seemed unimportant to him, but which his colleagues disapproved, and which the Secretary of State, himself, had, in some cases, forbidden. Kasson felt that Germany was making very real concessions in surrendering Malietoa, and that her prestige might be maintained by restoring him to the throne and granting the German demand for an indemnity.[31] Kasson proposed in the Conference, against the wish of the American Commission and perhaps at German instigation, the withdrawal and disarmament of Mataafa's forces. Phelps and Bates both preferred that any such disarmament should await the results of the Conference, the former going so far as to state that Tamasese had no substantial native support and that "Mataafa represents the sacrifice, nationality, and heart of Samoa." [32]

To desert Mataafa entirely seemed too great a concession to German prestige. The English were anxious to effect a compromise by a restoration of the *status quo* of 1887, which had been the tenor of Blaine's original instructions. That would mean that Malietoa would become king once more, and that Tamasese and Mataafa would be excluded without any necessity for an

[30] Bates to Blaine, May 11, 1889, *ibid.*
[31] Kasson to Blaine, May 12 and 13, *ibid.*
[32] Phelps to Blaine, May 12, *ibid.*

election, which might, in the unsettled condition of things, be dangerous.[33]

On May 14 Blaine sent a series of telegrams to the commissioners individually and collectively in which he expressed his surprise and regret that any differences had arisen. He urged upon them perfect frankness and cooperation and gave assurance that they were all of equal power. All dispatches were to be seen by each representative, and joint action was to be the rule. Blaine had already expressed his willingness to see Malietoa resume the kingship and his refusal to consent to an indemnity for Germany. He now agreed with Phelps that all questions of the disbandment of Mataafa's forces should await the adjournment of the Congress.[34]

Mr. Kasson was indignant at the accusations of usurpation of authority and offered to withdraw from the Conference "to escape tricephalous jealousies." [35] He did not, however, carry out this intention but appears to have taken a less prominent part in the negotiations thereafter. The path of the American Commission was by no means smooth, for Mr. Bates became as outspokenly anti-German as Kasson had been pro-German and would agree to no concessions desired by the Imperial representatives. He wrote long dispatches to Blaine stating his opinions and urging the danger of losing everything by too much compromise and concili-

---

[33] Phelps to Blaine, May 13, "Samoan Conference."

[34] Blaine to Phelps, May 14, *ibid.*

[35] Kasson to Blaine, May 13, 1889, *ibid.*

ation. He disapproved Kasson's scheme for a powerful judge to decide upon elections, land disputes, and cases involving foreigners. He held that the exclusion of Mataafa from the kingship was fatal to the avowed basis of the negotiations — Samoan independence. An indemnity for Germany was unjust. Samoa, rather, should demand the indemnity. He felt that the United States had ample basis for bargaining in claims for the acknowledgment of the wrongful deportation of Malietoa, the unjustifiable war on the natives, and the interference with Americans, and he could neither be content nor be quiet.[36]

Mr. Phelps appears to have maintained a sane, middle-of-the-road course. He had resented and joined with Bates in protesting against Kasson's exclusion of them in the early days of the Conference, but when that difficulty was settled, he worked steadily for a sensible compromise of the disputed minor issues. It must be kept clear, moreover, that after Bismarck's preliminary concessions only American stiff-necked refusal to be generous in arranging details could have blocked the work of the Conference. Germany was conceding much, but she did wish consideration for her views on the system to be established for the government of Samoa.

[36] Bates to Blaine, May 15, *ibid.* Mr. Bates's articles in the *Century* had closed with remarks about war being preferable to dishonor "which in a nation should crimson the cheek of every citizen as readily as the blow of a gauntlet did that of a knight of old." His fire-eating propensities seem not to have been entirely curbed during the Conference.

Mr. Blaine seems to have leaned at times toward the extreme views of Bates, but in general he agreed with Phelps in a willingness to make minor concessions. In a telegram of May 16, he supported Bates and instructed the Commission that no king was to be forced upon the Islanders, who should decide for themselves in a free election. He felt it unwise to have but one judge and recommended that all power which it was necessary to delegate to foreigners be shared equally by the three powers.[37] Two days later Mr. Phelps wrote Blaine that Germany would recognize Malietoa but never would accept Mataafa, and that the only alternative was an election of a third person. Samoa possessed no such candidate, and the future would be perilously unsettled.[38] Even Bates finally agreed that the insistence upon Mataafa would mean the break up of the Conference and that the United States, unless willing to go to war to support Samoa, had better accept Malietoa.[39] On May 19 Blaine cabled that the President consented to the restoration of Malietoa and the *status quo* of 1887 provided that the three powers be equally represented in the executive government and that an impartial judge be assured.[40] He recommended

[37] Blaine to the Commission, May 16, *ibid.*

[38] Phelps to Blaine, May 18, *ibid.*

[39] Bates to Blaine, May 18, *ibid.*

[40] Blaine to the Commission, May 19, *ibid.* There was discussion as to which Government should nominate the judge and the Conference finally agreed that he should be nominated by the Lord Chief Justice of England. Blaine agreed (May 20) to this plan but said he preferred a neutral judge.

that the powers pay the salaries of the foreign officials.

On May 27, the agreement reached by the Conference was completed and sent to Washington for approval. It provided that Samoa should be neutral territory and that no power should have separate control.
Samoa was to have an independent government, Malietoa would be restored, but his successor would be
chosen by free election. There was to be a supreme
court under the jurisdiction of a single judge called the
Chief Justice, nominated by the Lord Chief Justice of
England, who should have jurisdiction over everything
arising under the General Act. There was to be a commission to settle land disputes, made up of representatives of each of the three powers, and it was to complete its work within two years. The municipal council
of Apia was renewed and was to be elected by the residents of Apia. The importation and sale of firearms
and intoxicating liquors were to be carefully regulated.[41]

The confidential reports which the three commissioners sent to Blaine were as diverse as their opinions had
been throughout the Conference. Kasson felt that
Great Britain had been fair throughout, had acquiesced
when Germany and the United States agreed, and had
worked for adjustment elsewhere. He felt that the
Commission had fulfilled its instructions in the restoration of the *status quo* and in the government given Samoa and wished to ". . . renew the expression of
my conviction that Germany has been honest in her
desire for an honorable and durable settlement of the

[41] See *U. S. Foreign Relations*, 1889, for the text of the General Act.

Samoan question. The conduct of Count Bismarck in the Conference has been both honorable and conciliatory and leaves us no occasion for complaint." [42]

Mr. Bates considered that the treaty did not fulfil the instructions which Blaine had given the American commissioners. He felt that the Commission had been confronted throughout by the united opposition of England and Germany and that the General Act might be deprived of any success by that opposition. There had been, in his opinion, a "complete subordination of American to European influence," and he gave some half dozen reasons for that belief.[43]

Mr. Phelps sent a brief dispatch, written after a perusal of Bates's dispatch, in which he stated that he thought that all of Bates's points were badly taken except the one that the plan laid too great a burden of expense upon Samoa in providing that the Samoan Government pay all the foreign officials.[44] Phelps felt, however, that it could not be helped since Great Britain flatly refused to pay the salaries, being "painfully sensitive at asking their parliaments for one extra dollar." [45] Mr. Phelps felt that the General Act provided the best possible solution and came very close to the letter of the Secretary's instructions. He was satisfied with the

[42] Kasson to Blaine, June 5, 1889, "Samoan Conference."

[43] Bates to Blaine, June 6, *ibid.*

[44] This point seems well taken. Stevenson in the *Footnote to History*, 305-306, stated that the monthly salaries of the foreign officials amounted to $1155 while the King received $95, less than the private secretary of the Chief Justice.

[45] Phelps to Blaine, June 7, "Samoan Conference."

attitude of the powers and considered the compromises and concessions of no great moment. Mr. Sewall, a former consul in Samoa, had gone to Berlin as an aide to the Commission and he, too, sent a report modeled after the lines of Mr. Bates's but rather more condemnatory of the entire proceedings.[46]

Assailed by these reports, two in condemnation and two in approval of the work of the Congress, Mr. Blaine set to work to formulate his own opinion. On June 8, he cabled his criticisms to the Commission.[47] The restoration of Malietoa and the withdrawal of the German demand for an indemnity were satisfactory, but the President wished a declaration that no reprisals against the Mataafa forces would ever be undertaken, and that the supreme court should not take cognizance of any offense committed before its organization. The President was surprised at the extent of powers given to the Chief Justice. Such powers were too great, and inconsistent with his judicial character. He was a court of last appeal as a land judge and also had power to decide on the elections and the executive action of the King. Such power made him a political autocrat. If he was to be appointed by the Chief Justice of England, the instructions given the American Commission had been disregarded, for their cardinal point had been the equality of the treaty powers. The President did not approve either the extent of the powers nor the method of appointment of the Chief Justice of

[46] Sewall to Blaine, June 6, *ibid.*
[47] *Ibid.*

Samoa. He would prefer the nearest approach to the conditions where the three consuls would be the inter-mediaries between the treaty powers and the native government.

Mr. Blaine had ignored all the jealousies and suspicions of Mr. Sewall and Mr. Bates and had based his criticism on what seemed to him the vital defects of the scheme and the places where the original instructions of the American delegates had not been carried into effect. The criticism that the General Act was self-contradictory since it expressly guaranteed local autonomy and then took it away by entrusting all the essential powers of government to the Chief Justice was made repeatedly after 1889 and was undoubtedly one of the reasons for its failure. The dislike which Mr. Blaine felt for the plan to have this powerful judge nominated by Great Britain may have been due to a suspicious attitude toward the British Government which seems to have been natural to him, but there can be no denying the fact that it did destroy the equality of the three powers and, coupled with the clause providing that the Chief Justice could be dismissed by any two of the powers, made for European control in Samoa. It is equally true, on the other hand, that Secretary Blaine had given his consent to the separate articles of the General Act as they had been agreed upon, and his criticisms of such a fundamental part of the scheme as the powers of the Chief Justice came rather late in the proceedings. It may have been that the conflicting reports of the inharmonious and disagreeing American Commission confused the issue.

The Commission replied to the Secretary's criticism in a cable on June 9, one clause of which brought an answer which has since become famous:

The President does not know the irritability of those who believe they have yielded already in all essentials to claims of the United States; nor the danger of asking now too many changes. On that account we want him to try to give further weight to those points upon which three such different minds as ours have agreed. First: demands for many radical changes in detail could easily induce Germany and England to withdraw, if not from the conference, at least from their assent to important points already yielded. Second: the government by three consuls has been tried and found unsatisfactory. Third: no other scheme seemed a better substitute than an impartial representative of civilization, equally responsible to the three powers, such as could be found in an English judge properly selected. The nationality of the judge and his method of selection was an exclusively American suggestion and against the English proposition.[48]

The clauses in the cablegram just quoted which aroused Mr. Blaine's ire were those referring to the "irritability" of the German and English delegates and the nationality of the judge. A reply was immediately sent to the Commission, which was in the nature of a sharp reproof. The "irritability" had, apparently, been transferred, by suggestion, to the Secretary of State!

In what essentials the United States gains under the project

[48] Crosby (Secretary of the Commission) to Blaine, June 9, *ibid.*

I am unable to determine. This government will never consent to absolutely rob Samoa of all autonomy and to install an English judge as the ruler of the islands. The modifications in detail which the United States demand will be sent to you at once. If you will read my no. 18 you will learn that the President would much have preferred a judge selected from a neutral nation to one from England.[49] I now learn for the first time that the English proposition originated with you. Had the commission informed us of successive steps in the conference modifications could have been suggested during deliberations. Irritability on the part of your English and German associates is not a determining factor with the government of the United States.

The last sentence of this cablegram must have been the source for all the rumors and reports based upon the reference in Miss Hamilton's life of Blaine that at the Samoan Conference, Secretary Blaine defied Prince Bismarck, out-bluffed him, and won a great diplomatic victory.[50] In reality, the cablegram came at the close

[49] See note 40.

[50] Hamilton, *Blaine*, 659. "The negotiations were delicate, the situation was not without peril. Once the committee cabled to the Secretary the conviction that they must compromise; that Bismarck was angry, and that without yielding somewhat they feared everything would be lost. Mr. Blaine cabled in response that 'The extent of the chancellor's irritability is not the measure of American rights.' He could be irritable himself on occasion and he knew for how little it counted. The negotiations were brought to a happy conclusion. In constant close communication and entire sympathy with the Secretary, the commissioners by their skill and patriotism secured the treaty of Berlin." The atmosphere of happy accord given by the last clauses of this quotation must have caused the Americans who had composed the Commission to smile!

of the negotiations, was a reproof to the American plenipotentiaries, and probably never came to the knowledge of Prince Bismarck, whose attitude throughout had been one of indifference to details and of conciliation, so long as German prestige did not receive damage. Nor can it be said that Mr. Blaine's bombast produced any great result other than to relieve his feelings to such an extent that he was willing to accept the General Act with but one alteration.

Mr. Kasson replied to the criticism by again tendering his resignation. "I take full share and more of responsibility for the clauses objected to and should be relieved at once of further duty." [51] Mr. Phelps wrote explaining that the clause providing for an English judge had been suggested because it seemed that only an Anglo-Saxon could be trusted with judicial power over half-civilized nations.[52] Mr. Blaine sent a long list of minor changes in detail for the consideration of the Conference, closing his dispatch with the pithy remark that the "President will not be hurried into any agreement he does not understand, nor will he assent to any provisions he does not approve." [53] On the next day Mr. Blaine cabled that he did not recall his consent to an English judge but did insist that his powers be judicial only, and on the day following (June 12) he suggested that if the judge was to have political powers he should be nominated by the King of Sweden and Nor-

[51] Kasson to Blaine, June 10, "Samoan Conference."
[52] Phelps to Blaine, June 10, *ibid.*
[53] Blaine to the Commission, June 10, *ibid.*

way.[54] This suggestion seems to have caused some relief to the commissioners, and Phelps cabled suggesting that if the powers should yield on an English judge, the United States might give up all the minor objections made by Blaine and thus avoid delay.[55] Blaine, therefore, authorized them to sign "if the judge is appointed by a neutral and has no retroactive jurisdiction." [56]

The Conference met for its eighth session, the first since May 29, as soon as Mr. Blaine's cable of authorization arrived and at once proceeded to complete the agreement. Count Bismarck and Sir Edward Malet reported that their Governments had accepted the provisions of the treaty, and that they were ready to sign. Mr. Kasson said that the American plenipotentiaries were authorized to sign with only two modifications. The first was that the judge should have no retroactive jurisdiction, and it was at once agreed to. The other proposed the substitution of a nomination of the Chief Justice from a neutral nation by the King of Sweden and Norway for the nomination by the Lord Chief Justice of England. Count Bismarck at once agreed, subject to the approval of his Government, and it was moved that the Conference adjourn pending the receipt of instructions from the three Governments.[57] It is ob-

[54] Blaine to the Commission, June 11 and 12, "Samoan Conference."

[55] Phelps to Blaine, June 12, *ibid.*

[56] Blaine to the Commission, June 13, *ibid.*

[57] Protocol for the Eighth Session, *Sen. Mis. Doc.* No. 81, 51 Cong., 1st Session, 69-71.

vious that the alteration to satisfy Mr. Blaine had been agreed upon by the three commissions prior to the session of the Conference.

The proposition as to the nomination of the judge was cabled to Secretary Blaine, who, at first, tried to provide that the king select a Swede as judge. Upon being informed that the clause was the best that could be obtained,[58] he at once cabled "No objection. Concede the point." [59] There was now no further obstacle and the Conference at once met to affix the formal signatures to the General Act, and the Samoan Congress was over.

In transmitting the protocols and the Act to the Senate, President Harrison said he was pleased to find in it "an honorable, just, and equal settlement" and Secretary Blaine hoped "that this act may be conducive to the good government of Samoa under native autonomy and to the lasting settlement of the vexed questions which have agitated the three powers in their complex relations to these islands." [60] It was, however, ultimately unsatisfactory and partly for the reasons Blaine had feared: the local autonomy was but a name and the real governmental power was in foreign hands, the government was too great a financial burden upon the Islanders, and it met with no satisfaction nor approval.

The United States soon regretted the participation to which it was pledged. Mr. Blaine had disapproved

[58] Commission to Blaine, June 14, 1889, "Samoan Conference."
[59] Blaine to the Commission, June 14, *ibid.*
[60] *Sen. Mis. Doc.* No. 81, 51 Cong., 1st Session.

Bayard's plan of 1887 but had in the end accepted under protest one much like it. The United States was bound, contrary to its traditional policy, to a partnership, almost an alliance, with European nations. When the Cleveland administration came in, there was an effort on the part of the President and his Secretary of State, Walter Q. Gresham, to rid the United States of this obligation, even though it went no further than Cleveland himself was willing to go during his first administration. Congress was invited to consider the taking of steps looking to the withdrawal of the United States from the bonds of the treaty.[61] A readjustment in Samoa did not seem expedient, however, until 1899, when, after the Spanish war had pledged us to imperialism and Great Britain was involved in the South African war, the Islands were annexed, Tutuila to the United States and the rest of the Islands to Germany.

From the point of view of American foreign policy the General Act of the Berlin Conference represents merely a temporary deviation and not a permanent emergence from the tradition of isolation from world politics. Secretary Blaine pursued no aggressive or far-reaching policy and was not enthusiastic over the results of the Conference, which, it is clear, imposed much more of an obligation upon the United States than his original instructions warranted. To the end of the Conference he worked to obtain a larger measure of auton-

[61] See Cleveland's Annual Message, December 3, 1894, and December 5, 1895, Richardson, IX, 531 and 635. Also *U. S. Foreign Relations*, 1894, 511.

omy for the natives and a more temporary foreign influence in the Islands. There is not the slightest evidence that he had any desire to extend American influence in Samoa. The problem there was, in his mind, essentially different from that in Hawaii.[62]

[62] The subject of the Berlin Conference has been treated at a much greater length than its importance merits for the reason that there has been heretofore, so far as could be discovered, no use made of the confidential manuscript dispatches from the Conference. The printed material gave only the invitation to the Conference, the instructions to the Commission, the formal protocols, and the General Act. The quarrels of the plenipotentiaries and their discordant views, the trials and tribulations of the Secretary of State, and the compromising spirit of the foreign powers make an interesting chapter in American diplomacy.

CHAPTER X

INTEREST IN THE FAR EAST

SECRETARY Blaine was genuinely interested in Hawaii and had been brought by force of circumstances into direct contact with the Samoan controversy, but his interest did not extend to the Far East. He came into office in 1881 with a well-formulated opinion on the subject of the exclusion of the Chinese from the United States, but upon all other matters relating to the Far East, he appears to have had little knowledge and less interest. Chinese immigration was a domestic question and one of considerable political as well as economic importance. Mr. Blaine had made speeches upon the subject in the House of Representatives and had written Garfield in regard to the matter before the beginning of the new administration.[1] The Treaty of 1880 with China, which permitted the suspension of the immigration of Chinese laborers, and which afforded protection for other classes of Chinese in the United States and for such laborers as were already resident, was not ratified until after Garfield's inauguration. The first Exclusion Act, carrying out the permission implied in the treaty, was passed in 1882 and was for a ten-year period. Both political parties were in favor of exclusion and each was, at times, inclined to

[1] See above, p. 18.

use the passage of more stringent legislation as a bid for votes during the months preceding a presidential election. No president cared to be on record as failing to approve such legislation, regardless of the critical situation in which diplomatic negotiations might happen to be.

Although the Act of 1882 would not expire for some four years, the public in 1888 was clamoring for more absolute exclusion of Chinese labor. Many measures were introduced in Congress, some complying with, and more that contravened, the Treaty of 1880. Secretary Bayard endeavored to obtain from China a treaty which would permit the legislation demanded, by an agreement forbidding all immigration. The treaty as negotiated in Washington was ratified by the Senate but not by the Chinese Government. This lack of ratification irritated Congress, which had begun legislation to carry it into effect, and just before the presidential election, the Scott Bill was passed by an overwhelming majority of both parties. President Cleveland signed it on October 1, and it at once went into effect.[2]

The Scott Act did not limit the period for which the Chinese laborers were to be kept from the shores of the United States and prohibited the return of all who had gone to China for a visit, whether or not they had obtained certificates of readmission. Even those Chinese entitled to return to the United States who were al-

[2] *U. S. Foreign Relations*, 1888 and 1889. For a good secondary account of the whole Chinese immigration question from the diplomatic viewpoint see Tyler Dennett, *Americans in Eastern Asia*, Ch. 28.

ready at sea were to be turned back when they reached this country. This act was most extraordinary and in complete contravention of the treaty, which guaranteed to the Chinese already resident in this country their right to "go and come of their own free will and accord" and to receive all the "rights, privileges, and immunities and exemptions which are accorded to the citizens and subjects of the most favored nation." The Chinese minister, Chang Yen Hoon, at once, and very naturally, protested against the Act on the ground that it violated both the spirit and letter of the treaty.[3] Chang stated that he had understood in the treaty negotiations of the preceding year that Cleveland would veto any bill which contravened the terms of the Treaty of 1880. Bayard, in reply, denied that any such pledge had been made but admitted that he, himself, had never approved of the bill, but that Congress had desired it and was quite independent of the Executive.[4]

With the change of administration the correspondence lapsed. Mr. Blaine's personal views on the subject were well known. His party had been pledged to exclusion and there seemed no remedy obtainable. Throughout the whole Harrison administration there was practically no intercourse between the Chinese legation and the State Department. The communications of the Chinese minister went unanswered and his protests received no attention. Mr. Dennett says:

[3] Chang Yen Hoon to Bayard, January 26, 1889, *U. S. Foreign Relations*, 1889, 121 ff.

[4] Bayard to Chang Yen Hoon, February 2, 1889, *ibid.*, 122.

The American Government was in a position, notwithstanding its legality as sustained by the Supreme Court, utterly indefensible from the viewpoint of diplomacy. . . . It is becoming for Americans in criticizing the actions of other governments in Asia to be humble if not charitable.[5]

The Chinese minister received some encouragement from the fact that the Supreme Court, in the spring of 1889, declared that although constitutional the Scott Act was in contravention of the Treaty of 1880. He addressed on July 8 a long and very able note to Mr. Blaine, summarizing the situation thus far and asking a remedy. He stated:

In my country we have acted upon the conviction that where two nations deliberately and solemnly entered upon treaty stipulations, they thereby formed a sacred compact from which they could not honorably be discharged except through friendly negotiations and a new agreement. I was, therefore, not prepared to learn . . . that there was a way recognized in the law and practice of this country whereby your government could release itself from treaty obligations without consultation with, or the consent of, the other party to what we had been accustomed to regard as a sacred instrument.[6]

On July 15, Mr. Wharton answered this note with the brief statement that it would receive "careful and prompt attention."

The action of the Department of State in carrying out Mr. Wharton's promise can be judged from the

[5] Dennett, *Americans in Eastern Asia*, 548.
[6] Chang Yen Hoon to Blaine, July 8, 1889, *U. S. Foreign Relations, 1889*, 132-139.

fact that when a new Chinese minister arrived during the next year, one of his first communications was a note very like that of July 8, 1889, written on March 26, 1890.[7] On October 1, Tsui wrote again:

It has filled me with wonder that neither an acknowledgment of its receipt nor a reply thereto, has up to this been received. Knowing how carefully and courteously you observe all the requirements of diplomatic intercourse, I have not attributed this neglect to any personal choice on your part. I have persuaded myself that your silence has been enforced by some controlling reasons of state which have, in your opinion, made it prudent that you should still defer for a time the answer which my government has for many months been very anxious to receive.[8]

This appeal produced an answer, of a sort, after the long and complete silence. Mr. Blaine wrote that the questions involved were the subject of careful consideration, and that at an early date he hoped to convey to Tsui the views of the President.[9] Upon the opening of Congress, Tsui wrote asking that that body be urged to take action to assure the Chinese Government that the United States would maintain its treaty obligations in full force. He mentioned the fact that he had not received the promised reply to the previous communications in regard to the violation of treaty rights.[10] Mr. Denby, United States minister to China, was asked by

[7] Tsui Kwo Yin to Blaine, *U. S. Foreign Relations*, 1890, 211.
[8] *Ibid.*, 228.
[9] Blaine to Tsui, October 6, 1890, *ibid.*, 229.
[10] Tsui to Blaine, December 4, 1890, *ibid.*, 229.

the Chinese Government to inquire as to response to the Chinese notes. He, too, returned evasive replies.[11]

Throughout the whole of 1891 there appears to have been no correspondence upon the matter between the Chinese legation and the Department of State.[12] It was the season of one of the periodic outbreaks against foreigners in China, and the authorities of both countries were engaged in discussion of riots, difficulties of missionaries and merchants, and indemnities.

The original Exclusion Act of 1882, amended in 1884, did not expire until 1894 but the approach of another presidential election caused Congress to pass further restrictive measures. The enactment of the Geary Act of May 5, 1892, put into operation the most stringent regulations affecting the Chinese which had, up to that time, been devised. Parts of the law, such as the condemnation to hard labor without a trial by jury, of Chinese violating the certification clauses of the law, were later declared unconstitutional, and the entire law was in violation of the Treaty of 1880, which was still in effect.[13] After the passage of the bill and before President Harrison signed it, Tsui made one last protest and appeal in behalf of the treaty. He wrote Blaine:

[11] *Sen. Exec. Doc.* No. 54, 52 Cong., 2nd Session.

[12] There is none printed in *U. S. Foreign Relations*, 1891, nor in *Sen. Exec. Doc.* No. 54, 52 Cong., 2nd Session, which contains most of the correspondence. No additional correspondence was found in the Archives of the Department of State.

[13] For an analysis of the legislation of this period see Moore, *Digest*, IV, 190 ff.

Your own silence on the subject must be understood to be recognition that what we have charged is true. In fact, your own Supreme Court has admitted that. Now, the Congress, in this bill which has just been voted, has a provision that this bad law [the Scott Act] shall be kept in force.[14]

The signature of the President was affixed, however, upon the same day upon which Tsui made his appeal and Mr. Blaine resigned without having replied to the series of communications from the Chinese minister which began with the note to Bayard on February 26, 1889.

In November, 1892, Mr. Tsui wrote to Foster, giving another summary of the one-sided correspondence. He once more asked action on the part of the coming Congress on the objectionable clauses in the exclusion legislation. On December 10 Mr. Wharton, again Acting Secretary, replied in a note which for the first time in the course of the correspondence gave the view of the Executive on the existing legislation. The Chinese notes were now answered but only by the suggestion that the laws of the United States be given sanction by a new convention in conformity with them.[15] In March, 1894, such an immigration treaty was signed.

The action of the Government of the United States in the decade preceding 1894 was incontestably wrong and in violation of its pledged word to China. The fact that the mass of public opinion of both parties favored

[14] Tsui to Blaine, May 5, 1892, *U. S. Foreign Relations*, 1892, 149.
[15] Wharton to Tsui, December 10, 1892, *Sen. Exec. Doc.* No. 54, 52 Cong., 2nd Session, 41-43.

the action of Congress does not alter the fact that the acts of Congress violated the Treaty of 1880 with China. Nor does the fact that the Executive, under the circumstances, could not alter the conduct of the legislative branch of the government, excuse the Secretary of State for his studied avoidance of the issue and the discourtesy of the long disregard of the communications of the Chinese legation. There is every indication that Mr. Blaine agreed in principle with the action of Congress and that this approval, coupled with his conviction that the treaty had been violated, prevented his making any response to the Chinese protests.[16]

Mr. Blaine had been interested in this question of Chinese exclusion primarily from its domestic side and had, apparently, little or no interest in any other question involving the Far East. The trade of the United States with China and the Orient was not at that time considerable. Mr. Blaine was engrossed with his policy in regard to Latin America and saw no occasion to change the policy of his predecessors in regard to Europe or Asia. He was, however, to take action in regard to an oriental region, hitherto little known to the citizens of the western world, which has been con-

[16] The Chinese Government showed its resentment for the exclusion acts by a refusal to receive Harrison's appointee, Mr. Henry Blair, as minister from the United States. See Harrison's Message, December 9, 1891, Richardson, IX, 186. This refusal left the legation in charge of Cleveland's appointee, Mr. Charles Denby, who had the unusual experience of being retained in office through all of Harrison's administration. Cleveland reappointed him in 1893, and he continued in Peking until 1898.

sidered one of the most important steps ever taken by the United States in Far Eastern affairs. It must be admitted, however, that negotiations with Korea which Blaine in 1881 authorized Commodore Shufeldt to make were undertaken at the desire of Shufeldt himself, who had become interested in the Orient, and not because the Secretary of State had any particular concern in the matter. If a treaty opening Korea to intercourse with the western world could be brought about easily and without expense or unpleasant results to the United States, well and good. Any credit therefrom would redound to the glory and prestige of the United States and to the credit of the Department of State. Otherwise there was no value in the negotiation.

In 1876 Japan had succeeded in forcing, without bloodshed, a treaty of amity and commerce upon Korea, the "hermit kingdom," whose only relations with the outside world had, theretofore, been with China. The treaty provided for the opening of several ports, provided for the reciprocal reception of diplomatic representatives, granted Japan extra-territoriality in criminal cases and was, in general, similar to those imposed upon China and Japan by foreign powers. Its most important clause was one acknowledging the integrity and independence of the Korean kingdom, thus disavowing the vague but traditional Chinese suzerainty over Korea.[17] This was an entering wedge for Japan, which already had fairly definite ideas as to her future expansion and penetration of Asiatic territory.

[17] Tyler Dennett, *Americans in Eastern Asia*, 446-447.

Russia, moving eastward and southward from Siberia, had also come in contact with and had designs upon the little kingdom whose greatest desire it had been to remain undisturbed.

The United States, as well as other nations, had an interest in the fate of Korea. William H. Seward had, as a part of his farflung, imperialistic policy, initiated a movement to open Korea.[18] Its failure did not prevent further efforts in succeeding administrations, which were in turn to fail. After the Japanese-Korean Treaty in 1876, Japan wished to obtain an acknowledgment of the position of leadership in Asiatic affairs which she felt she had reached and intimated that all nations wishing to deal with Korea should negotiate through Japanese channels.

The Navy Department of the United States was interested in the fate of seamen shipwrecked on the coast of Asia, and in 1878 Secretary Thompson dispatched Commodore Shufeldt to visit Korea and endeavor to open negotiations with the Government.[19] Evarts had little apparent interest in the project but gave it his approval so far, at least, as measures to protect shipwrecked mariners were concerned. The attempt made by Shufeldt to get in touch with Korea

[18] *Ibid.*, 450. Mr. Dennett states that, "The movement to open Korea . . . was by far the most important political action undertaken by the United States in Asia until the occupation of the Philippines in 1898. To disturb Korea in any way was to disturb the equilibrium of the Far East."

[19] Dennett states (p. 456) that the United States Government was apparently unaware of taking any important step.

through Japanese assistance soon revealed the fact that Japan was not at all ready to see Korea opened to the trade of other nations. The effort of Shufeldt to penetrate Korea through the Japanese consul at Fusan failed, and Shufeldt went back to Nagasaki to await an answer to a letter sent through the Japanese Government at Tokio. Korea responded to this rather insincere effort on the part of Japan by an unqualified refusal to receive negotiations. Russia, Great Britain, France, and Italy, all made unsuccessful attempts in the same period (1876-1880).[20] Korea was still the "hermit kingdom" so far as western nations were concerned.

In the meantime the presence and mission of Shufeldt became known to the astute Viceroy, Li Hung Chang, at Tientsin. He saw at once the significance of the Japanese schemes and fearing, also, the Russian interest in Korea, he determined to further the desires of the Government of the United States. A Korea open to world trade was far less a menace to China than a Korea controlled by Japan or swallowed up by Russia. The United States was on record as desiring the maintenance of the integrity of the government and territory of the Far Eastern nations and had a more disinterested view toward them than any other nation. If Korea must be disturbed, Li Hung Chang felt that it would be better to have the *status quo* altered by the United States than by any other agency. China was, he knew, in no position for a war with either Russia or Japan. If diplomacy could check the ambitions of either power,

[20] J. W. Foster, *American Diplomacy in the Orient*, 320 ff.

he would make use of any scheme that seemed expedient.

Li Hung Chang, therefore, sent for Shufeldt, offered to assist him in opening negotiations with Korea, and complimented him by offering him a position in the Chinese navy. Commodore Shufeldt, satisfied that the way was then open for the accomplishment of the mission, returned to the United States to report and to receive further instructions. Mr. Blaine, upon becoming Secretary of State, took a more enthusiastic attitude toward the project than had his predecessor, and in March, 1881, Shufeldt was detached from sea duty and sent back to China with orders from both the State and Navy Departments.[21]

The instructions given Shufeldt by Blaine ordered him to report to Mr. Angell, the United States minister to China. On his way to Pekin he was to stop at Tientsin from which place he was to report any information he might obtain as to the readiness of the Korean Government to open negotiations for a treaty of amity and commerce.[22] Later instructions to Shufeldt show that Blaine desired a commercial treaty similar to those with China and Japan. It must contain a "most favored nation" clause, provisions for extraterritorial jurisdiction of United States consuls and for a diplo-

[21] For the narrative to this point the account in Dennett, Ch. 24, has been followed. The correspondence for 1881-1882 in the Archives of the State Department has been consulted for the Shufeldt negotiations themselves. Instructions, China, Vol. 3; Dispatches, Vols. 57-59.

[22] Blaine to Shufeldt, May 9, 1881, Manuscript Instructions, China, Vol. 3.

matic representative at the capital. The fact that Blaine did not believe that the United States had any direct interests in Korea is shown by this statement:

> While no political or commercial interest makes such a treaty urgent, it is desirable that ports of a country so near to Japan and China should be opened to our trade and to the convenience of such vessels of our navy as may be in those waters and it is hoped that the advantage resulting from the growing and friendly relations between those great Empires and the United States will have attracted the attention and awakened the interest of the Corean government.[23]

The opening of Korea had long been Commodore Shufeldt's great ambition. The United States would gain a certain prestige if Korea's first treaty with the western powers should be with it. Blaine could see no disadvantages in authorizing Shufeldt to proceed, provided every precaution was taken to avoid a repulse. If he so desired, Shufeldt was also given permission to accept a position in the Chinese navy.

The Commodore reached China in June, 1881, but did not find it as simple to negotiate his treaty as he had expected. Li Hung Chang was no longer as apprehensive of a war with Russia as he had been a year earlier.[24] The representatives of the European powers in China placed every difficulty in Shufeldt's path, and his position in Tientsin became so embarrassing that he was almost ready to drop the whole project.

[23] Blaine to Shufeldt, November 14, 1881. Manuscript Instructions, China, Vol. 3.

[24] Angell to Blaine, July 16, 1881. Manuscript Dispatches, China, Vol. 57.

In December, 1881, however, the Viceroy assured Shufeldt that Korea was ready to negotiate. He insisted that a treaty should recognize China's sovereignty over Korea. Mr. Holcombe, who was in charge of the legation at Peking, wrote that the position of Korea was really entirely independent, and that Li Hung Chang was anxious to have Korea acknowledge a dependency upon China. He was also, Mr. Holcombe believed, moved by a fear lest Russia seize Korea. He felt that the only value of the treaty to the United States would be in prestige, and for that reason, that we should be the first nation to obtain a treaty, if we made one at all.[25] A few days later Holcombe wrote that Li Hung Chang was determined to control the negotiations for the treaty, and that he was anxious to counteract Japanese influence in Korea.[26]

Secretary Blaine retired from office December 16, 1881, and the treaty which was at length negotiated in the spring of 1882 was under the direction, nominally at least, of his successor, Mr. Frelinghuysen. As a matter of fact, Commodore Shufeldt's requests for instructions from Mr. Frelinghuysen on the question of acknowledging Chinese sovereignty over Korea remained unanswered and the Commodore, rather than lose his coveted treaty, made what bargain he could and signed the treaty (May 22, 1882). The compromise with Li Hung Chang provided that Shufeldt

[25] Holcombe to Blaine, December 19, 1881, Manuscript Dispatches, China, Vol. 58.

[26] Holcombe to Blaine, December 29, 1881, *ibid.*

should write a letter to Li, officially stating that the assistance of China had been asked in making the treaty "because Korea was a dependency of China." He would also send to the President a letter from the King of Korea, stating that the treaty had the consent of China.[27]

The treaty thus signed opened Korea to western trade and intercourse. It became the model for other treaties which Korea made with European powers. The supplementary letters which Li had demanded were unpublished and worthless, and no clause acknowledging the supremacy of China appeared in any of the treaties.[28] Shufeldt accomplished his mission and fulfilled his ambition. The treaty, as signed, in practically every detail corresponded with Blaine's instructions, but the Commodore returned a disillusioned man. He wrote:

I have little faith in the friendship of China for any nation and believe that friendship to be measured by the pressure brought to bear upon it, and I desire to repeat my conviction, that if a treaty is made with Corea, it will be owing to circumstances surrounding that country which are as threatening to China as to Corea itself and not from any particular friendship for the United States.[29]

The treaty, although actually negotiated after Frelinghuysen took over the office of Secretary of State,

[27] Dennett, 460.

[28] Dennett, 461. Mr. Dennett states that the Treaty of 1882 was Li Hung Chang's greatest mistake and marks a step in the dismemberment of the Chinese Empire.

[29] Shufeldt to Frelinghuysen, April 10, 1882, Manuscript Dispatches, China, Vol. 59.

was in accordance with the Blaine instructions and any credit for it, if credit is due, belongs to Blaine and to Shufeldt, whose project it virtually was. There is no evidence that Blaine looked upon it as anything more than an occasion to assert the prominent position of the United States in world affairs. The importance of Korea in Far Eastern politics in its relation to China and Japan seems not to have been considered by him.

CHAPTER XI

MINOR QUESTIONS ARISING FROM THE IMMIGRATION PROBLEM

IN the years when Mr. Blaine was Secretary of State, the United States came into contact with European nations in a very slight degree. The questions at issue were not of great importance and in general were of two classes. They arose either out of some phase of the immigration problem or from some commercial difficulty. One of the minor, but important and often irksome and difficult, duties of the Department of State has been the protection of the interests and persons of those naturalized citizens of the United States who have returned to the lands of their birth for visits of varying duration. European nations did not, until recent years, admit the possibility of expatriation[1] and held such visitors as liable for military service and other obligations to the state. Naturalized Americans have ever been inclined to claim abroad the rights they held in the United States, and the Department of State has sometimes insisted upon demanding for citizens of the United States rights in a foreign country not granted there to natives of like race or color. At times citizens

[1] The treaties recognizing this right began with that with England in 1870.

of the United States both native and naturalized have called loudly for protection when their acts abroad have been contrary to the laws of the country which they were visiting but not to the laws of the United States. The problem of when such citizens were entitled to protection and how far the United States Government should go in aiding them has always been one difficult of solution.[2]

Two episodes of such character came up for Blaine's attention during the years when he was Secretary of State. In dealing with one of them he attempted to develop a new and positive policy; in the other he took the lines laid down by earlier and later secretaries. Neither question was settled by him nor for some time thereafter. The first of these problems was that of the status in Russia of Russian Jews who had become American citizens and then returned to Russia for business or pleasure and who asked for protection from the laws enacted against Jews. This request was on the basis of the treaty between Russia and the United States which granted to the citizens of each, reciprocal privileges of travel and temporary residence. This problem was of some interest during both of the periods when Blaine was Secretary of State. The second had to do with cases, arising under the coercion laws of Great Britain, of Irish Americans who violated, or were alleged to have violated, these laws while sojourning in Ireland or in England.

Mr. John W. Foster was appointed minister to

[2] Charles G. Fenwick, *International Law*, 156 ff.

Russia in 1880 [3] and upon his arrival at his post found a dispatch from Secretary Evarts instructing him to approach the Russian Government on the question of the Jews, only when the laws of Russia injuriously affected American citizens, but that at such times he was to take action consistent with the theory of religious freedom held by the United States. Mr. Foster soon had two cases to deal with, that of Henry Pinkos and that of Wilczynski. Both were Jews and naturalized citizens of the United States and both were engaged in trade in St. Petersburg. Under peculiarly difficult circumstances both were forced to give up their business and leave the city and the country, the only reason given by the Russian Government being that they were Jews. Both appealed to the American legation and the two cases formed the basis of communications between Foster and the Russian Foreign Office. The United States based its action on its duty to protect its citizens wherever they might be and also upon the clause in the treaty with Russia which gave Americans the right to reside in all parts of Russia. M. de Giers, the minister of foreign affairs, held that American Jews were subject to the same regulations and laws as Russian Jews, and that the Jews were a very troublesome group in Russia, which it was necessary to treat with especial

[3] J. W. Foster, *Diplomatic Memoirs*, 163. "One of my predecessors at the Russian Court, who called on me in New York before sailing, told me that I would have very little to do at the Legation; that I might have to go to the Foreign Office about once a month to get a poor American Jew out of trouble but that I would find very little else of an official character to occupy my time."

rigor. The Russian Government, therefore, could not abrogate the proscriptive laws. Russia, however, recognized that American Jews were generally of the better class and appreciated the position of the United States Government in the matter. The Russian Government agreed, therefore, to accord Jews who were American citizens all the privileges given other foreigners, provided the legation would apply in each case for such privileges, certifying the citizenship of each applicant.[4] Mr. Foster stated in his *Memoirs* that he had not found the American Jews treated any more harshly than those of other nationality, and that after his remonstrances in the two cases of Pinkos and Wilczynski, he had no further complaints because of any action of like character on the part of the Russian Government.[5]

Mr. Blaine came into office during this negotiation, which was to last through the summer of 1881, and wrote asking for copies of all Russian laws dealing with the Jews and for all the facts in regard to the difficulties experienced by foreign Jews in Russia. His desire was for some sort of joint representation by foreign nations in St. Petersburg or, at the least, for joint action on the part of Great Britain' and the United States. Foster was instructed to discover whether such

[4] Foster to Evarts, December 30, 1880, *U. S. Foreign Relations, 1881*, 996. This is a long dispatch and a complete survey of the situation. In his *Diplomatic Memoirs*, Vol. I, Mr. Foster gives a good summary.

[5] Foster, *Diplomatic Memoirs*, I, 166. Foster to Blaine, August 29, 1881, Manuscript Dispatches, Russia, 1881.

action would be acceptable or not. Mr. Blaine's ideas in regard to it may be best examined in his own words:

One other point may not improperly be adverted to, Sir Charles Dilke seems to deem it an essential consideration in these matters, "whether any protest is likely to be of use." If the like view animates the several governments whose citizens or subjects may be aggrieved in Russia, it is quite certain no good will come from the unsupported action of any of them in the premises and a policy of discreet inaction on the part of all of them would seem the most natural outcome of the matter, and the one which the Russian government would be most interested in bringing about. Some sort of concurrence of views on the subject would appear to be desirable, and I have, therefore, to request you in conversation with your colleagues and especially with the British Ambassador, to impress them, discreetly but unequivocally with the earnest purpose of this government to endeavor to bring about such an equalization of the status of foreigners in Russia, irrespective of faith, as will comport with the enlightened spirit of the age.[6]

On July 29, Mr. Blaine wrote a very long and very able note to Mr. Foster, giving a history of the whole question of the treatment of Jews in Russia and the position taken by the United States in regard to its citizens who were affected by the Russian laws. He stated that the United States did not differentiate between native-born and naturalized citizens, nor citizens of different creeds. They all had equal rights under the laws and treaties of the United States and were entitled to equal protection abroad. The Treaty of

[6] Blaine to Foster, June 22, 1881, Manuscript Instructions, Russia, 1881, XVI.

1830 with Russia had given reciprocal privileges to the citizens of the two countries, and for many years there was no complaint as to its interpretation on either side. He hoped that there would be a mutually agreeable conclusion to the difficulty arising out of the treatment of the Jews, and that if the treaty stipulations were not sufficient in the eyes of Russia to determine the questions of nationality and tolerance or to secure for Americans in Russia the rights accorded to Russian citizens in the United States, there might be an additional agreement on these points:

You can further advise him (De Giers) that we can make no new treaty with Russia nor accept any construction of our existing treaty which shall discriminate against any class of American citizens on account of their religious faith.[7]

All of Mr. Blaine's efforts were fruitless, for on August 29, Foster reported that De Giers held that the treaty did not exempt Jews who were citizens of the United States from having the laws of Russia in regard to Jews applied to them. This view was more in accord with international law than that taken by Blaine, for it is customary for one nation to demand for its citizens located in another country only those privileges accorded by that country to its own citizens of the same class, race, or religion.[8] De Giers, however, reaffirmed his willingness to grant exemption to such American

[7] Blaine to Foster, July 29, 1881, Manuscript Instructions, Russia, 1881, XVI. The note is given in extract in *U. S. Foreign Relations, 1881.*

[8] Fenwick, *International Law,* 157. Hyde, *International Law,* I, 266-267.

citizens as the minister might make application for.[9] Russia would grant as a favor in particular cases that which we demanded as a right.

The move toward joint action in an attempt to further the cause of religious toleration in Russia met with no success. Mr. Foster reported that the British ambassador said that he did not think that he could co-operate with the United States minister in representations to Russia respecting the condition of Jews who were Russian subjects.[10] Blaine believed that the Russian Government contemplated even more restrictive measures in regard to Jews and determined to forestall it if possible. The British ambassador to Russia proving cold to his project, he wrote to Lowell at London, November 22, instructing him to "bring the subject before the formal consideration of the British government in a firm belief that community of interests will lead to common action." He felt that it would be a terrible thing to behold a return of the Ghetto of the Middle Ages and hoped to initiate a movement which might also include other powers and which would influence Russia to ameliorate the condition of the Jews.[11] Nothing came of this movement and Mr. Blaine went out of office without in any way ameliorating the anti-Jewish legislation in Russia, although he had obtained

[9] Foster to Blaine, August 29, 1881, Manuscript Dispatches, Russia, 1881.

[10] Foster to Blaine, November 13, 1881, Manuscript Dispatches, Russia, 1881.

[11] Blaine to Lowell, November 22, 1881, Manuscript Instructions, Great Britain, 1881, XXVI.

a sort of gentlemen's agreement whereby the Jews who were naturalized American citizens were to be relieved from the burden of the Russian laws against their race.

Between the winter of 1881 and Mr. Blaine's return to office, there was some recurrence of difficulty and some slight interest expressed by Congress in the status of the American citizens who met with difficulties in Russia on account of their race and religious beliefs.[12] By 1890, however, the chief interest of the United States was in the evident effect that the oppression of the Jews in Russia had upon the general problem of immigration, which was beginning to interest the Government and citizens of the United States. There were not, in this later period, pressing cases of injuries done to American citizens in Russia, but the steadily increasing influx of Russian Jews to this country presented a fresh aspect of the whole situation. In August, 1890, Congress asked President Harrison for information regarding the enforcement of the edicts against the Jews in Russia. The correspondence was accompanied by a report from Mr. Blaine,[13] which stated that although he knew of no new edicts, the immigration of the Russian Jews presented a great problem.

In February, 1891, Charles Emory Smith, United States minister to Russia, reported a long conversation with M. de Giers on the subject of the treatment of the Jews, which had been initiated by De Giers, who as-

[12] *House Exec. Doc.* No. 192, 47 Cong., 1st Session. *House Mis. Doc.* No. 55, 49 Cong., 2nd Session.

[13] *House Exec. Doc.* No. 470, 51 Cong., 1st Session.

sured him that no new or harsh legislation was contemplated by the Russian Government. De Giers admitted that the Jews had a very real grievance but
maintained that the question was a manysided one and
very difficult to solve. Mr. Smith stated that we regarded the question as a purely Russian domestic problem except where American citizens were concerned,
but that the United States would, of course, be very
happy to see an amelioration of the condition of the
Jews.[14]

There did occur in 1891, in spite of De Giers' assurances, a more stringent enforcement of many of the
anti-Semitic laws and many Jews emigrated.[15] The situation was complicated by a famine of great severity
due to crop failures in Russia, and the number of emi-
grants steadily increased.[16] In December of 1891 President Harrison made the situation the occasion of an
extended reference in his annual message to Congress:

This government has found occasion to express, in a friendly
spirit, but with much earnestness, to the Government of the
Czar its serious concern because of the harsh measures now
being enforced against the Hebrews in Russia. By the revival
of anti-Semitic laws, long in abeyance, great numbers of those
unfortunate people have been constrained to leave the Empire
by reason of the impossibility of finding subsistence within the
pale to which it is sought to confine them. The immigration of

[14] Smith to Blaine, February 10, 1891, *U. S. Foreign Relations*, 1891,
734.
[15] Smith to Blaine, October 20, 1891, *ibid.*, 744.
[16] Mr. Blaine estimated that about 1889 the number had been
200,000 yearly.

these people to the United States . . . is largely increasing, and is likely to assume proportions which may make it difficult to find homes and employment for them here and to seriously affect the labor market . . . the sudden transfer of such a multitude . . . is neither good for them nor for us.[17]

True as these observations were and real as was the interest of the United States in the question, it cannot be said that the Harrison administration advanced its solution in any respect.

Naturalized citizens of the United States were causing difficulties for the United States in one other region in 1881. Ireland was in the midst of one of its periods of great agitation over the execution of the land laws. Many Irishmen were arrested and imprisoned for long periods of time under the Coercion Act of 1881. In 1881 several Irishmen who had resided for some time in the United States and who claimed United States citizenship were arrested in Ireland or in England for the violation of British laws. The question presented to the minister of the United States and the Department of State was a delicate one. In the first place it must be ascertained whether, in each case, the person appealing to the United States for protection was a citizen of the United States or not.[18] If his citizenship should be definitely proved, then it must be discovered by examination of the facts in the case whether he had violated any of the British laws. In the third place, if

[17] Richardson, *Messages and Papers*, IX, 188.

[18] Great Britain had, since 1870, admitted the right of British citizens to expatriate themselves.

the violation should be proved, it must be decided whether there were to be questions raised as to the legality of applying the Coercion Act in its entirety to American citizens.

The minister of the United States, Mr. Lowell, soon came to the conclusion that the Irishmen claiming United States citizenship were not always citizens, and that, even if they were, they were usually as guilty of violation of the laws as were other Irishmen who were British citizens. Lord Granville quite naturally refused to admit that citizens of the United States were entitled to any different treatment from that meted out to citizens of Great Britain who were arrested for violation of the same laws.[19]

The case of Michael P. Boynton is one of the famous ones of that period and illustrates very well the difficulties involved. Boynton was arrested early in March as being "reasonably suspected of inciting some of the Irish to murder and commit acts of violence." He at once claimed protection of the United States on the ground that he was an American citizen and that the warrant for his arrest had contained no charge.[20] He was at once asked to give evidence that he was an American citizen. It was known that he had resided in the United States, and that he had received a passport from Secretary Seward in 1866, which had long since expired. Boynton claimed citizenship on two grounds: first, that his father had taken him to the United States as a child and had become naturalized, thus conferring

[19] Lowell to Blaine, June 4, 1881, *U. S. Foreign Relations*, 1881, 533.
[20] According to the new Act of 1881 — the so-called Coercion Act.

citizenship on his minor children; second, Boynton himself had served in the United States Navy during the Civil War and had thus confirmed and made unquestionable his citizenship. The proof for both of these statements was difficult to obtain, and pending such proof Lowell felt he could make no inquiries into the arrest.[21]

The case caused much excitement among the Irish in the United States, and the Senate asked for the facts and the correspondence. Blaine wrote to Lowell that he had reported to the President upon that occasion that the evidence presented by Boynton was not such as to prove his claim to citizenship under the laws of the United States. Mr. Blaine went on to state quite clearly his point of view in regard to such cases in general, admitting, however, that he had not as yet seen a copy of the "Coercion Act" of 1881. The retroactive nature of the act was a factor that was difficult for the United States to accept, as were the warrants without definite charge and the possibility of long imprisonments without trial or the production of proof.

That the fact of American citizenship could, of itself, operate to exempt anyone from the penalties of a law which he had violated, is, of course, an untenable proposition. Conversely, however, the proposition that a retroactive law, suspending at will the simplest operations of justice, could be applied without question to an American citizen, is one to which this government would not give its anticipatory assent.

Had Boynton's citizenship been proved, since his of-

[21] Lowell refused to accept the passport of 1866 as evidence of the citizenship of Boynton and was upheld by Blaine.

fense had been committed subsequently to the passage of the act, all that could have been done for him would have been a request for a speedy trial and the production of proof of his guilt. Lowell was given this hypothetical case for use in any contingency which might arise in the future.[22]

The case of Joseph B. Walsh, who was arrested in March, 1881, presented a further opportunity for the expression of Blaine's position, for the status of Walsh as a citizen of the United States was unquestionable. In writing Lowell in regard to Walsh, the Secretary of State reasserted the absence of any disposition to interfere with the administration of local or general laws in Great Britain but protested against the summary proceedings used in the cases arising out of the Coercion Act.

If American citizens while within British jurisdiction offend against British laws, this government will not seek to shield them from the legal consequences of their acts, but it must insist upon the application to their cases of those common principles of criminal jurisprudence which in the United States secure to every man who offends against its laws, whether he be an American citizen or a foreign subject, those incidents to a criminal prosecution which afford the best safeguard to personal liberty and the strongest protection against oppression under the forms of law, which might otherwise be practiced through excessive zeal.

Blaine held that the right of an accused to know the specific crime with which he was charged and to a

[22] Blaine to Lowell, May 26, 1881, *U. S. Foreign Relations*, 1881, 530.

speedy trial by an impartial court and jury was incontestable. Lowell was instructed to investigate and

make such temperate but earnest representations as in your judgment will conduce to his speedy trial, or in case there is no specific charge against him, his prompt release from imprisonment.[23]

Lowell made the representations requested but received a flat refusal from Lord Granville to give him any information other than that contained in the warrant itself or to treat American citizens arrested under the act in any way differently from British citizens. Lowell stated, accurately enough, that this was a position which might be justified by precedents in our own diplomatic history.[24] There the matter rested through the period of Blaine's term of office. Frelinghuysen continued the protests with much the same effect. As the Irish situation became less tense and as the American protests rolled up, the British authorities became reluctant to arrest naturalized citizens of the United States, provided such citizenship were known.[25]

Secretary Blaine and Mr. Lowell were the objects of much criticism on the part of the Irish in the United States and their sympathizers for failure to take more energetic action, but that they did all that was proper under the circumstances is shown by a statement of Lowell's to the effect that:

[23] Blaine to Lowell, June 2, 1881, *U. S. Foreign Relations*, 1881, 532.
[24] Lowell to Blaine, July 15, 1881, *ibid.*, 541.
[25] Lowell to Frelinghuysen, March 14, 1882, *U. S. Foreign Relations*, 1882, 206.

Naturalized Irishmen seem entirely to misconceive the process through which they have passed in assuming American citizenship, looking upon themselves as Irishmen who have acquired a right to American protection rather than as Americans who have renounced a claim to Irish nationality.[26]

In the case of the Italians who were killed by a mob in New Orleans in 1891, Mr. Blaine faced another and quite different angle of the immigration problem. The incident is of very little importance in a study of his foreign policy but throws some light upon his views in regard to the duties and problems of his office. The situation in its simplest terms was this. New Orleans had a large and rapidly growing Italian colony, composed partly of substantial and worthy citizens and partly of the riff-raff of Italian, especially Neapolitan and Sicilian, desperadoes. The Italian consul, Corte, estimated that there were probably one hundred or more Italians in New Orleans who were convicts escaped from Italian prisons or men wanted for diverse crimes by the Italian police. There was, undoubtedly, a gang or band of Italians in New Orleans which was a branch of, or similar to, the Mafia or Cormorra or Black Hand societies of southern Italy. This band had terrorized parts of New Orleans, and in October, 1890, the chief of police, D. C. Hennessy, was murdered, presumably by some members of the organization, just as he was about to produce evidence tending to break it up.

New Orleans was notoriously ill-governed, and its

[26] *Loc. cit.*

mayor seems to have been peculiarly inefficient and unwise. He made diverse threats against the entire Italian
colony and caused a number of promiscuous arrests
upon very little evidence. The trial of those accused
of complicity in the murder of the chief of police was
more or less of a farce, for it became evident that several of the jurors had been bribed or coerced to bring
in a verdict of acquittal regardless of the evidence. The
citizens of New Orleans organized a sort of "vigilance
committee," known as the Committee of Fifty, which
was pledged to investigate and bring the guilty to justice. Mass meetings were held and much popular feeling was stirred up. The Italian colony was greatly
perturbed and the consul notified Baron Fava, the
Italian minister, who appealed to Blaine to see that all
Italians involved were protected and that those accused
should have a fair trial.[27] Mr. Blaine responded by
telegraphing Governor Nicholls of Louisiana and was
assured that no violence need be apprehended.

After the trial popular feeling in New Orleans ran
high. The mayor made no effort, apparently, to stem
the tide. Meetings were held and a mob was allowed
to gather undisturbed by the police. The governor
refused to call in the troops without the request of the
mayor, and the sheriff refused the entreaty of the governor of the parish prison in which the Italians were
confined, for additional guards to protect the prison-

[27] "Correspondence in Relation to the Killing of Prisoners in New
Orleans, March 14, 1891," *U. S. Foreign Relations*, 1891, 658. This
document contains practically all of the correspondence in any way
connected with this incident up to April, 1892.

ers.[28] The mob broke into the prison and eleven persons of Italian origin were lynched. Five of them had not been tried, three had been acquitted, and three were being held for re-trial. It was unknown how many of them had been naturalized and were citizens of the United States, but there was little doubt that several were still Italian subjects. They were all suspected of having been members of the secret society held to be responsible for the death of Mr. Hennessy, and all had more or less unsavory reputations.

The Italian Government at once sprang to the defense of its citizens in the United States. Baron Fava protested against the lack of protection given the Italians by the municipal authorities in New Orleans and demanded that the guilty be speedily brought to justice.[29] The Secretary of State telegraphed to Governor Nicholls:

Our treaty with that friendly government . . . guarantees to the Italian subjects domiciled in the United States "the most constant protection and security for their persons and property," making them amenable, on the same basis as our own citizens, to the laws of the United States and of the several states in their due and orderly administration. . . . The Government of the United States must give to the subjects of friendly powers that security which it demands for our own citizens when temporarily under a foreign jurisdiction.[30]

Mr. Blaine hoped that all offenders might be brought

[28] Consul Corte to Fava, March 15, 1891, *U. S. For. Rel.,* 1891, 669.
[29] Fava to Blaine, March 15, 1891, *ibid.,* 666.
[30] Blaine to Nicholls, March 15, 1891, *ibid.*

to justice at once, and that the Italians might be protected from further violence.

The governor in reply stated that everything was
quiet again, and that the mob violence had been directed
against the particular individuals, and that the race or
nationality of the victims was not a factor in the case.
It was fairly clear from the first that it would be difficult to get any prosecution of the leaders of the mob by
the authorities of the City of New Orleans or the State
of Louisiana.

The Italian Government became more and more insistent in its cablegrams. The prime minister, Marquis
Rudini, was peremptory in his demand that the guilty
be brought to justice and insistent that Baron Fava
demand an indemnity, which "we trust will be granted
directly. A simple declaration, though cordial and
friendly, is not sufficient; we want positive facts." [31]
By March 25, Italian public opinion had become "justly
impatient," and Rudini threatened the recall of his
minister if immediate measures were not taken.

Mr. Blaine, thus daily assailed by the Italian Government, endeavored to find out how many of the murdered Italians had been subjects of the Italian king, and
what measures were being taken by Louisiana. Owing
to the dual nature of the government of the United
States, there was little else that the federal Executive
could do. He wired the United States minister at Rome
to explain carefully to Marquis Rudini the character of
the government of the United States and the necessity

[31] Rudini to Fava, March 19, 1891, *ibid.*, 671.

for a thorough investigation of the facts before any decision should be reached.[32]

On March 31 Baron Fava left Washington in accordance with the orders of his Government, leaving the legation in charge of a chargé d'affaires. His last note to Secretary Blaine stated that the reparation demanded by the Italian Government consisted of:

(1) The official assurance by the Federal Government that the guilty parties be brought to trial.

(2) The recognition, in principle, that an indemnity is due to the relatives of the victims.[33]

Mr. Blaine's answer to these demands was characteristic. He stated that the Government of the United States was quite unable to give the assurances which Rudini demanded. The State of Louisiana was in charge of bringing the offenders to trial, and the Federal Government could not act until it was clear that justice was not being done. "Even if the National Government had the entire jurisdiction over the alleged murderers, it could not give assurance to any foreign power that they should be punished." He recognized the principle of indemnity in case it should be proved that they had been wronged by a violation of their treaty rights, and he again promised a thorough investigation. The note ended with the curt statement:

I have also informed him that in a matter of such gravity the Government of the United States would not permit itself to be unduly hurried; nor will it make answer to any demand until

[32] Blaine to Porter, March 29, 1891, *U. S. For. Rel.,* 1891, 675.
[33] Fava to Blaine, March 31, 1891, *ibid.,* 676.

every fact essential to a correct judgment shall have been fully investigated through legal authority. The impatience of the aggrieved may be natural but its indulgence does not always secure the most substantial justice.[34]

The Government of the United States was faced once more with one of those unpleasant situations where the very nature of the federal system blocked the way of the National Executive in a matter of treaty obligations.[35] The United States was bound to make secure the lives and property of the Italians resident within its limits, but the trial of offenders against that security must be carried on by the State of Louisiana. Mr. Blaine had been rather abrupt in his statement of the position in which he found himself, but he had some cause for irritation in the impatience and arbitrary demands of the Italian Government, which was, apparently, as much affected by the political situation in Italy as it was by the wrongs of its subjects in the United States.[36]

On April 14, Mr. Blaine wrote a long note to Marquis Imperiali, giving the history of the treatment of

[34] Blaine to Marquis Imperiali, April 1, 1891, *ibid.*, 676-677.

[35] See the articles by Godkin in the *Nation* for 1891, LII, 232, 294, 296, 337. Godkin was no admirer of Blaine's but he felt that Blaine had done all he could in this case.

[36] Porter to Blaine, April 1, 1891, *U. S. Foreign Relations*, 1891, 678. "Parliament is to reassemble on the 14th instant, and I discovered, as I thought, that the fear of not being able to satisfy it that proper vigor has been exercised by the ministry occasioned profound anxiety and was tempting to a course more extreme than would otherwise, perhaps, be adopted. Being a coalition ministry, it dreads the risk of attempting to withstand an adverse popular feeling, however temporary."

similar cases by the Government of the United States since the days of Daniel Webster. He stated that the United States was pledged to grant to foreigners within its limits only the protection accorded its own citizens, that "foreign residents are not made a favored class." He felt that there was no claim of indemnity unless it should appear that the public authorities had connived at the mob action or were guilty of gross negligence. If that sort of situation should be proved, and if Louisiana failed to take steps to punish those guilty, then the President would feel that a case had been established that should be submitted to Congress for action upon the question of an indemnity.[37] And so the matter stood throughout the rest of 1891.

The message of President Harrison on December 9, 1891, reopened the incident with a frank expression of regret for the "most deplorable and discreditable incident." He stated that the temporary absence of the Italian minister had retarded the correspondence, but that a friendly conclusion was not to be doubted.

In the reopened negotiation, the Italian Government insisted upon a recognition of the principle that an indemnity was due, before Baron Fava should return to the United States. The amount of the indemnity was of minor importance. Mr. Whitehouse, the American chargé in Rome, answered that he felt that the President's message of the preceeding December had given the required admission of the principle.[38] Congress

[37] Blaine to Imperiali, April 14, 1891, *U. S. For. Rel.,* 1891, 683-685.
[38] Whitehouse to Blaine, March 14, 1892, Manuscript Dispatches,

took the step indicated by the President and appropriated 125,000 francs to be given the Italian Government for distribution among the families of the victims. On April 12, Mr. Blaine communicated this action to Marquis Imperiali with the hope that friendly relations would be resumed, and upon the same day the Marquis declared the resumption of diplomatic intercourse.

The incident closed with this inevitable result that the United States Government endeavored to assuage by a money payment the injury done to its treaty obligations by the government of one of the states of the federal union. Whether by any more conciliatory conduct Mr. Blaine could have changed the result is a difficult question to answer. Italy's impatience and peremptory demands for categorical statements seemed impossible to meet, and it may have been that neither Government was averse to permitting the investigation to take its course while the suspension of diplomatic relations made interference difficult. Public opinion in Italy was appeased, and the United States grew used to the idea of an indemnity in the months that intervened. There can be little doubt that the conduct of this diplomatic episode influenced Mr. Blaine in his treatment of the similar case in regard to the murder of the sailors of the U.S.S. "Baltimore," which occurred in Chile later in the same year.[39] His patience in that incident was more exemplary and was thought by many to be carried to an unusual extreme.

Italy, Vol. 25, and Marquis Imperiali to Blaine, March 27, 1892, Manuscript Notes from the Italian Embassy, Vol. 13.

[39] See above, Chapter VI.

CHAPTER XII

THE CONTROVERSY IN REGARD TO AMERICAN PORK

A QUESTION of some importance to American commerce arose in 1881 and, strangely enough, continued through the intervening period, to be settled by Blaine in 1891. The entry of American pork into the markets of Europe, a question economic in the main, consumed an amount of attention from the diplomatic representatives of the United States out of all proportion to its importance. The Archives of the State Department for the period from 1880 to 1892 are full of dispatches and notes of instruction on the subject. The question became entangled with various political questions both at home and abroad and was the ever-present or perennially re-appearing *bête noir* of many a diplomat in the service of the United States.

In its simplest terms the issue was this. American pork, especially such pork products as ham, bacon, and lard, was found or, at least, reported to be dangerous to health on account of the presence of organisms producing trichinosis. The habit of certain Europeans of eating such pork products uncooked was a contributing factor in making some pork unsafe for human consumption, for proper cooking would have rendered harmless any such parasites if they had been present. It is probably safe to say that there was some cause for the accusations against American pork but probably little more than against the pork of other nations. The United States happened to be the greatest exporter of pork — that was all. In several of the European countries[1] the question of the protection of home industries played its part, for the exclusion of American pork undoubtedly stimulated the raising of native pork. There was an increasingly insistent demand that the United States institute some scientific and adequate system of inspection of meats designed for export, and the question was destined to trouble the State Department, as well as all those engaged in the pork business, until such a system was adopted in 1891.

It so happened that Mr. Blaine became Secretary of State just as the question came into the limelight in the winter of 1880-1881. The English consul in Philadelphia, Crump, sent the British Foreign Office, on December 21, 1880, a long report on the subject of American pork and pork products, stating that there had been a great mortality in the pork-raising parts of the United States from hog cholera, some 600,000 hogs having died in Illinois alone in the past year. He apparently confused cholera with trichinosis, for he stated that there was a danger to human life from eating the pork products exported from the United States, due to the presence of that parasite. Without verifying the

[1] France in the latter part of the period and Germany about the same time, 1889-1892.

report or making further investigation, the British Government published the Crump report in a *Blue Book* appearing in February. The London *Times* called attention to it and warned the public of the situation. At once a panic struck the European and British public and, incidentally, the pork market in the United States. On February 18, the French Chamber passed a decree prohibiting the importation of American pork pending an investigation by a parliamentary committee. A few days later Austria followed suit and it looked as though the panic would spread to other European countries and to England. The American exporters and packers at once called upon the State Department for aid in refuting the charges and allaying the fears abroad. American pork became a question of diplomatic importance and representations.[2]

The State Department rallied to the aid of the imperilled industry, and Evarts at once[3] sent out a telegram to all legations categorically denying the statistics given in the Crump report. When Blaine came into office he appointed a commission of members of the State Department to investigate and to report upon the whole question. He also began at once a correspondence with Sir Edward Thornton, the British minister to the United States, the purpose of which was to secure assistance in denying the statements of the Crump report. Mr. Blaine maintained that Crump

[2] *U. S. Foreign Relations*, 1881, gives the story of the episode. (*See* France, England, Belgium, Austria, Switzerland, and Spain.) Two or three notes from Blaine summarize the origins of the question.

[3] March 7.

had been misled by speculators who had hoped to force down the price of hogs on the livestock market, that the figures as to hog mortality had been grossly exaggerated, and, furthermore, that Crump had confused trichinosis with hog cholera. Trichinosis was a disease from which American hogs were almost completely free, while hog cholera was of no danger to human life.[4] The only satisfaction obtained from Thornton was the statement that Crump's figures seemed somewhat exaggerated, but that there was, apparently, basis for the report as a whole. Blaine was forced to make what use he could of such assistance.

Appeal to the British Government through Mr. Lowell was also of doubtful assistance. Lowell reported that, although Great Britain had no intention of prohibiting American pork and apprehended no danger from it, Lord Granville was disposed to believe the Crump report well-grounded. Lowell expressed a hope that Congress would take some action in regard to the inspection of pork products and stated his conviction that that would end all difficulties.[5]

There appears to have been no issue raised in Germany in 1881. Germany was also exporting pork and German pork was under suspicion for the same reason. In Belgium the public was excited, chiefly because of the French action, but the Government, upon investiga-

[4] Blaine to Thornton, March 9, 1881, *U. S. Foreign Relations*, 1881. See also Blaine to Lowell, March 17, *ibid.*, 515, and Blaine to Noyes, March 15, *ibid.*, 403.

[5] Lowell to Blaine, April 9, and April 13, 1881, *U. S. Foreign Relations*, 1881, 525.

tion, decided to do nothing more drastic than to issue a bulletin recommending the thorough cooking of all pork and pork products.[6] In Switzerland the same measures were taken.[7] In Spain the situation was slightly different. In February, 1880, both American and German pork had been prohibited. In July of that year the law had been modified, providing for the admission of pork from both nations after a microscopic inspection. This inspection was to be paid for by a tariff levied on the importation of the pork products. This law was in force in Spain in 1881 and was not altered during that year.[8] Austria prohibited American pork early in March, but the action was felt to be political in nature because of the fact that Austria exported pork and imported practically none. France was one of her best markets, and the prohibition was a pious second to that of France. Blaine urged the repeal of the Austrian law largely for the effect upon France.[9] These efforts proved unsuccessful.

It was in France that the chief difficulty was met in 1881. The law of February 18 prohibited the introduction of American pork into French ports and cut off one of the largest customers for the American products. Mr. Blaine instructed Noyes, the minister to France, to deny all rumors, to explain the errors in the Crump report, and to do all in his power to cause a repeal of

[6] Putnam to Blaine, April 30, 1881, *U. S. For. Rel.*, 1881, 67.

[7] Fish to Blaine, July 15, 1881, *ibid.*, 1163.

[8] Fairchild to Blaine, July 16, 1881, *ibid.*, 105.

[9] Blaine to Phelps, June 9, 1881, *U. S. Foreign Relations*, 1881, 55. Phelps to Blaine, July 2, 1881, *ibid.*

the law.[10] Early in June the report of the State Department investigation, which completely exonerated
the products accused of harboring the dread parasites,
was printed and sent to all representatives in Europe.
The report to Noyes was accompanied by a long note
explaining that the "Government of the United States
will yield to none in its earnest desire to accomplish all
which legislation or executive action can do to protect
the public health." Had the results been adverse, Blaine
went on, the United States would have been frank to
admit it and would have taken restrictive measures.
As the matter stood, Noyes was to do all that he could
to get a repeal of the law, for the action of France had
a bad effect upon other countries.[11]

In the summer of 1881 Levi P. Morton became
United States minister to France and he, too, labored
with the French Government for the repeal of the prohibitory decree. The ministry discussed establishing
laboratories at the ports of entry, where microscopic
examinations of imported pork products could be carried on, but dropped the idea as too difficult, slow, and
burdensome. In November, Morton had an interview
with Gambetta in which he urged the abrogation of the
decree. Gambetta replied that although he, personally,
did not share the public apprehension, he found it necessary to find some reason for the repeal which would
satisfy all prejudice. He asked if the United States
would not inaugurate a system of inspection of meats

[10] Blaine to Noyes, March 15, 1881, *ibid.*, 403.
[11] Blaine to Noyes, July 8, 1881, *ibid.*, 411-412.

designed for export. Such a measure, he felt, would cause the immediate repeal of the French law.[12] Mr. Blaine was extremely anxious to have some hopeful statement for the opening of Congress and did not feel it expedient to recommend restrictive legislation, but he was forced to retire from office without receiving any pledge from France.[13]

The question is a common one so far as diplomatic history is concerned, and Mr. Blaine had no marked success in handling it in 1881. He did not, in all probability, deviate from the path which Mr. Evarts or any other Secretary of State would have taken. His notes on the subject were able, facile, and plausible. He did not altogether succeed in convincing the reader that there was no fire at all as a cause for so much smoke, but there seems no reason to believe that his statements were not sincere. They show once again, moreover, that he was always ready and willing to do all in his power to encourage and aid American commerce in any of its channels.

In the interim between Mr. Blaine's terms of office the question of American pork became of increasing importance. In 1883 Germany also prohibited its importation on the ground that its consumption was dangerous to health. The Imperial Government passed

[12] Morton to Blaine, October 6, October 13, November 23, December 4, 1881, *U. S. Foreign Relations,* 1881, 430 ff.

[13] He wrote on November 25, a long and very able note to M. Outrey, the French minister, summarizing the entire question, giving the results of the investigations, and explaining the futility of the idea of microscopic investigation.

laws in the same period restricting the importation of American cattle by the introduction of very stringent quarantine measures. The European market for American meat products was very nearly cut off by these obstacles to importation in Austria, Italy, France, Germany, Spain, and Denmark. When Mr. Blaine again became Secretary of State in 1889, he returned to the fray with considerable zest. The packing interests and boards of trade throughout the Middle West were continually presenting petitions and protests to spur the Department of State to action.

Secretary Blaine wrote to Mr. Reid, minister to France, on June 11, 1889, that the Department regretted the lack of success in the attempt to get the succeeding French cabinets to repeal the prohibitory legislation. He felt it was an unnecessary and unjust discrimination against the United States. There had never been an authentic case of disease from eating American pork products. He regretted that the injury to farmers and packers of the United States should weaken the cordial relations of the two countries, and instructed Reid to bring the matter to the consideration of the French Government, cautioning him, however,

against proffering suggestions of retaliation on our part. Acts founded upon resentment work grievous injury to international relations; and while the interests affected in this country are doubtless exerting a potent influence among the representatives of the people, it may not be expedient to openly advert to the probability of Congressional action.[14]

[14] Blaine to Reid, June 11, 1889, *U. S. Foreign Relations*, 1889, 163.

Mr. Reid reported in the fall of 1889 that the prohibition was no longer based upon sanitary grounds but had become a part of the French protectionist program and that, although the cabinet was willing to repeal the decree, the Chamber contained a strong opposition.[15]

The matter rested without any accomplishment in the effort to remove European restrictions during the rest of 1889 and throughout 1890. In August of 1890 came the expected Congressional action, which, fortunately, took the form of an inspection of pork products designed for exportation rather than of retaliation against discriminations, and in March, 1891, came two supplementary acts to perfect the legislation and make it answer the European demands. Mr. Blaine at once renewed the correspondence in an effort to remove the restrictions. He now had something to offer in return for European action, and results were quickly attained.

On September 3, 1891, word was received of an Imperial German ordinance raising the prohibition on American pork products provided they had been examined in accordance with the American laws and had the prescribed certificates.[16] Five days later came the repeal of the restrictive legislation in Denmark.[17] In October the Italian restrictions were removed.[18] Early in December Austria and Hungary followed, and Mr. Grant sent Blaine congratulations on the splendid

[15] Reid to Blaine, October 19, 1889, *U. S. Foreign Relations*, 1889, 166.

[16] *U. S. Foreign Relations*, 1891, 528.

[17] C. E. Carr to Blaine, September 8, 1891, *ibid.*, 487.

[18] Whitehouse to Blaine, October 21, 1891, *ibid.*, 727.

Christmas gift to the American farmers.[19] At the same time the question received consideration in France. The French cabinet had long been willing to give up the prohibitory measure, which had been promulgated as a temporary one, but had so often been rebuffed by the protectionist Chamber of Deputies that the Government now persuaded the Chamber first to lay a duty on the importation of pork in order to bind that body to the policy of permitting the importation of that commodity. This being done, the cabinet issued decrees withdrawing the prohibition and providing for the admission of the American products subject to American and French inspection.[20]

It was a great satisfaction to Mr. Blaine to be able to announce to Congress the successful outcome of a controversy which had begun when he had been Secretary of State ten years before.[21] It cannot be said, however, that he contributed any more to that success than would any other Secretary of State nor that he followed a policy different from that which any one else would have pursued. It was the action of the Department of Agriculture in formulating, and of Congress in passing, the legislation which had so long been needed, which eventually caused the European nations to consider that all just cause for discrimination had disappeared.

[19] Grant to Blaine, December 5, 1891, *ibid.*, 31.

[20] Reid to Blaine, December 11, 1891, *ibid.*, 162.

[21] Harrison's Message to Congress, December 9, 1891, Richardson, IX, 181.

CHAPTER XIII

THE FUR SEAL CONTROVERSY

IT seems quite demonstrable that Blaine's real interest lay in the Western Hemisphere, and that the affairs of Europe and the East concerned him only where they directly affected the citizens of the United States. The fact that the foreign affairs of Canada were conducted by Great Britain threw one of the most important diplomatic controversies of the Blaine period into the field of Anglo-American relations. The controversy over the question of the killing of fur seals began when Canadian vessels entered the Bering Sea in 1886 [1] and was not completely settled until a joint treaty was negotiated by the United States, Japan, Russia, and Great Britain in 1911. The part of this controversy

---

[1] There was some dispute as to the date when Canadian sealers first entered the Bering Sea. Secretary Bayard stated it was in 1886. The Canadian Minister of Marine said Canadians had "long possessed the right of sealing." *Fur Seal Arbitration*, V, 283. This volume of the publication entitled *Fur Seal Arbitration* contains the documents submitted with the British case. They include Canadian as well as English documents and materials from the Colonial as well as the Foreign Office. It may be here noted that the *Canadian Sessional Papers* for the period contain only one paper on the controversy — and that a brief summary of the period 1886-1892. See *Canadian Sessional Papers*, 1892, Vol. 25, No. 11, 79-88, for the report of the Minister of Marine and Fisheries.

falling in the period of Harrison's administration was probably the most important and certainly the most interesting of any of its phases. The weak points of the Secretary of State are nowhere more clearly to be seen than in the Bering Sea dispatches, and yet nowhere else did he make more brilliant use of his abilities in defense of a weak case. It may, however, be said with equal truth that in these negotiations he appeared more bombastic than in any other controversy.

The question of who had the right to hunt seals in Bering Sea rose to diplomatic importance in 1886 when three Canadian vessels were seized by a United States revenue cutter some sixty miles off the Pribilof Islands, but its roots went back nearly one hundred years to the 1799 charter of the Russian American Company and Alexander I's ukase of 1821 prohibiting foreign vessels from approaching within one hundred Italian miles of the coasts under Russian sovereignty. This assertion of a *mare clausum* was protested both by the United States and Great Britain, and in 1824 and 1825 Russia retracted her claim to interfere with navigation or fishing in any part of the Pacific.[2]

In 1867 Russia ceded Alaska to the United States with all the rights and obligations given that region by all earlier treaties. This cession, "Seward's Folly," was

[2] The documents for the controversy from 1799-1899 may be found in *Sen. Exec. Doc.* No. 106, 50 Cong., 2nd Session. There is an excellent summary of the question in John Bassett Moore, *History and Digest of International Arbitration*, I, 755 ff. John B. Henderson, *American Diplomatic Questions*, has a good, unannotated, popular account of the controversy to 1900.

known to have but one industry of profit, the fur trade, and in 1870, the sole right to take fur seals, males less than seven years old, was conferred by a twenty-year lease upon the Alaska Fur Company, which assumed the responsibility for the care of the natives of the Pribilof Islands. A limit on killing was necessary for the protection of the fur seals, and regulation of the industry was demanded by the life habits of these peculiar animals.

The control of the fur seal industry being placed in the Treasury Department by the laws of 1868-1870, successive heads of that department from time to time had to provide details of administration. In 1872 Secretary Boutwell refused to send revenue cutters to prevent sealing by Australians in the passes between the Aleutian Islands, because he thought "the United States would not have the jurisdiction or power to drive off parties going up there for that purpose, unless they made such attempts within a marine league of the shore." [3] But in 1881, in answer to a question as to the meaning in the act of 1870 of the words "waters thereof" and "waters adjacent thereto," Acting Secretary of the Treasury French quoted the words of the treaty defining the boundary of 1867 [4] and added that all the

[3] Boutwell does not explicitly refer to Bering Sea, and in 1888 stated that he had referred only to the waters of the Pacific south of the Aleutian Islands.

[4] The western limit of the purchase was a water line beginning in Bering Straits and proceeding north and south as follows — due north from the intersection point of 170° east longitude and 65° 30' north latitude. In its southward course the line begins at the same point in the Straits and runs southwest so as to include in the territory ceded

waters within that line were the waters of Alaska Territory.[5] In March, 1886, when there were rumors that expeditions were fitting out to take fur seals in the Bering Sea, Secretary of the Treasury Manning directed customs agents on the Pacific coast to give publicity to the French letter, and a revenue cutter was sent to prevent illegal sealing. This marked a new phase in the affair, for the "Corwin" seized three Canadian vessels outside the three-mile limit and took them to Sitka for adjudication. The British Government immediately protested and the diplomatic controversy began.

Bayard, then Secretary of State, had to admit his lack of information concerning the action of the Treasury Department but after due consideration ordered the release of the vessels and the discontinuance of all pending proceedings. In April, 1887, when Sir Lionel Sackville-West, the British minister, asked assurances against seizures in the future, Bayard replied that the matter was under consideration.[6] There were several more seizures in the summer of 1887, and in October Judge Dawson of Alaska condemned the vessels taken and advanced the *mare clausum* theory, based on Russian claims of the early nineteenth century.[7]

the whole of the Aleutian Islands. Moore, *International Arbitrations*, I, 763.

[5] French to Ancona, March 12, 1881, *ibid.*, 769. It would be interesting to know whether Mr. French consulted Secretary of State Blaine in formulating this letter.

[6] West to Bayard, April 4, 1887, *Sen. Exec. Doc.* No. 106, 50 Cong., 2nd Session.

[7] Moore, *International Arbitrations*, I, 777 ff. John W. Foster states

In an identic note addressed to various European powers on August 19, 1887, Bayard, neither rejecting nor endorsing the measures taken by the Treasury and the Judiciary, asked for cooperation to protect the fur seals and the sealing industry in the Bering Sea. Russia and Japan responded at once, for they were anxious to aid their own fur industries. Great Britain acquiesced in principle and asked for a sketch of adequate regulations. In response Bayard, on February 7, 1888, proposed the establishment of a closed season from April 15 to November 1 for the region north of 30° north latitude. There seemed every probability of success in the negotiations, which were then carried on in London between Salisbury, the minister of foreign affairs, Phelps, the American minister, and M. de Stael, the Russian ambassador. Russia was eager for such an arrangement, and Salisbury assented to it in principle.[8]

The negotiations were blocked in May, however, for the British Government had referred the question of a closed season to the Canadian Government, which sent an adverse report.[9] This action on the part of Canada may have been due to the fact that the United States Senate was known to be opposed to the treaty, signed

in his *Diplomatic Memoirs*, II, 26, that the sending of the revenue cutter in 1886 was the work of the Alaska Commercial Company and that the Treasury Department knew little of it; also that the decision of the Alaska judge was made from a brief prepared by the lessees' agent in Washington and that the Attorney-General, upon learning of it, ordered the dismissal of the cases.

[8] *Sen. Exec. Doc.* No. 106, 50 Cong., 2nd Session, 84 ff.

[9] Colonial Office to the Foreign Office, April 25, 1888, *Fur Seal Arbitration*, V, 220.

on February 15, adjusting the dispute over the Northeast Fisheries.[10] Canadian leaders were also, doubtless, playing for the support of the Tory majority in British Columbia. On September 12, 1888, Phelps wrote to Bayard:

It is very apparent to me that the British Government will not execute the desired convention without the concurrence of Canada, and it is equally apparent that the concurrence of Canada to any such arrangement is not to be reasonably expected.[11]

Salisbury's initial willingness to accede to the wishes of the United States was due in part to a desire to restore amicable relations and in part to the fact that the British fur importers and manufacturers were advocating the protection of the seal fisheries.[12] His refusal to be a party to an agreement in opposition to the wishes of Canada was perfectly natural in view of a fixed policy to consider the wishes of the Dominion paramount in foreign questions which related principally to Canada.[13]

In the meantime Bayard had in the spring of 1888 promised that there should be no further seizures while negotiations were in progress. When the failure of the negotiations became apparent in the fall, Phelps wrote to Bayard:

[10] Moore, *International Arbitrations*, I, 784.

[11] *U. S. Foreign Relations*, 1891, 530.

[12] Foreign Office to the Colonial Office, September 3, 1888, *Fur Seal Arbitration*, V, 245.

[13] John George Bourinot, "Canada and the United States," *Papers of the American Historical Association*, Vol. V.

Under the circumstances, the Government of the United States must, in my opinion, either submit to having these valuable fisheries destroyed or must take measures to prevent their destruction by capturing the vessels employed in it. Between these two alternatives it does not appear to me there should be any hesitation.

He went on to argue that such a course would be in the nature of retaliation for the interference of Canada in the past two years with the Northeast Fisheries and ended his letter with the recommendation,

that the vessels that have been already seized while engaged in this business be firmly held, and that measures be taken to capture and hold every one hereafter found concerned in it. If further legislation is necessary it can doubtless be readily obtained.[14]

With this drastic proposal ended the diplomatic negotiations of 1888, which five months earlier had had such hope of success.

Before the end of the Cleveland administration one rather momentous step was taken by Congress in an attempt to clarify and define the issue by providing the "additional legislation" mentioned by Phelps. On February 25, 1889, a bill was introduced into the Senate to provide for the better protection of the fur seal and salmon fisheries of Alaska. The bill as passed by the Senate related only to the salmon fisheries but the House Committee on Merchant Marine and Fisheries added an amendment by which it was proposed that

[14] Phelps to Bayard, September 12, 1888, *U. S. Foreign Relations,* 1891, 530.

section 1956 of the Revised Statutes of the United States, which prohibited the killing of fur-bearing animals "within the limits of Alaska territory, or the waters thereof," should be interpreted as applying to all the waters of Bering Sea included in the treaty line of 1867. The amended bill went back to the Senate and was referred to the Committee on Foreign Relations because of its evident animus against other countries and its apparent assertion of the theory that Bering Sea was a *mare clausum*. The bill, as finally passed on March 2, declared the "waters thereof" "to include and apply to all the dominion of the United States in the waters of the Behring Sea," and it was made the duty of the President to issue each year a proclamation,

warning all persons against entering said waters for the purpose of violating the provisions of said section and he shall also cause one or more vessels of the United States to diligently cruise said waters and arrest all persons, and seize all vessels found to be, or to have been, engaged in any violation of the laws of the United States therein.[15]

Although this amendment to the laws of the United States dealing with the fur seal fisheries did not, in the end, declare that Bering Sea was included in the jurisdiction of the United States, it did, by its indefinite reference to the "dominion of the United States in the waters of Behring Sea" and its explicit warning to sealing vessels, put the legislative department on record as supporting the Treasury Department and the federal

[15] Moore, *International Arbitrations*, I, 765-767; *Revised Statutes*, Sec. 1956.

court in Alaska.[16] The fact that Cleveland signed the bill on March 2 gave evidence that the administration was ready to do the same and to follow the advice of Mr. Phelps given after the failure of the diplomatic negotiations. This bill, hurried through with so little consideration in the last week of the session, is reputed to have been due in large part to the efforts of Mr. Blaine, who had been appointed Secretary of State for the incoming administration.[17] At any rate, President Harrison issued the proclamation as prescribed by the bill in the early days of his administration, and it was duly reported to the British Foreign Office as the forerunner of difficulties for the next fishing season.[18]

During the spring of 1889 there was an attempt on the part of Russia to make common cause with the United States in behalf of their similar interests in the Bering Sea. Baron Struve, the Russian minister, was in Europe, and M. Rosen (later Baron Rosen), left in charge of the legation, was instructed to see if something could not be done in cooperation with the United

[16] The question came to the Supreme Court in the case of *In re Cooper* and was denied consideration because of the "well settled principle that an application to a court to review the action of the political department of the government, upon a question pending between it and a foreign power, and to determine whether the government was right or wrong, made while diplomatic negotiations were still going on, should be denied." 143 *United States Reports*, 472.

[17] Carl Russell Fish, *American Diplomacy*, 378. The Alaska Fur Company had a very strong lobby in Washington and several members of Congress were interested in the industry, notably Senator Elkins. See Gresham, *Life of Walter Q. Gresham*, II, 718 and 720.

[18] Edwards to Salisbury, Washington, March 23, 1889, *Fur Seal Arbitration*, V, 260.

States to put a stop to the depredations on the seal herds. The difficulty in the way of such action was the fact that those depredations occurred outside the three-mile limit. Baron Rosen, writing much later, said:

This difficulty could obviously be overcome only by securing the acquiescence of the principal maritime powers in a proposal, to be put forward by Russia and the United States, to undertake jointly the policing of the Behring Sea for the exclusive purpose of preventing the illegal killing of fur seals on the high seas. In obedience to the instructions received, I devised a plan of an agreement with the government of the United States to cover such a proposal and duly submitted it to the Ministry of Foreign Affairs. This plan having been approved, I was instructed to begin at once negotiations on the subject with the Department of State. Mr. Blaine likewise approved the plan when submitted to him, and we had very soon completed the drafting of the text of the proposed agreement.[19]

This proposed Russian-American agreement is of great importance in the light of subsequent events, for it shows the simple and direct method by which Mr. Blaine would have preferred to treat the question; and it foreshadows the argument used later when, after the failure of this negotiation, he was compelled to take up the question anew with Great Britain. So far as can be discovered, the negotiations between Baron Rosen and Mr. Blaine were never made public, and the papers setting forth the results of those negotiations have never before been published.[20] The convention which

[19] Baron Rosen, *Forty Years of Diplomacy*, I, 78 ff. This negotiation is mentioned also in Foster, *Diplomatic Memoirs*, II, 25.

[20] The papers relating to the negotiation and five drafts of the

was approved by the negotiators was in the form of a notice to other powers: whereas Russia and the United States were the sole owners of the only important breeding places of the fur seal, and whereas seal life was in danger of extinction unless open-sea killing were prohibited and the preservation of the seals considered an "absolute duty" imposed upon the two powers, they, therefore, had determined

with careful avoidance of all interference with the legitimate trade and commerce of other Maritime Powers, to exercise their indisputable right to preserve and protect this valuable seal industry.

To this end the two Governments were to issue regulations as to the number of seal skins to be taken from the islands. There was to be a closed season and no killing during migrations. Such killing was "absolutely forbidden and [would] be prevented by the two Powers with the use of force, if necessary." The convention ended with an expression of the belief that the other maritime powers would respect the measure.[21]

Of even greater interest than the draft of the proposed treaty are the memoranda which Baron Rosen

proposed convention between Russia and the United States may be found in the Manuscript Notes from the Russian Embassy, XIII, in the Archives of the State Department. The papers appear to be the result of a series of interviews between Rosen and Blaine and comprise five drafts for a treaty and two memoranda marked "Baron Rosen's papers." The subject matter has seemed of sufficient importance to justify the publication of the first and last drafts and of Baron Rosen's memoranda in an appendix to this volume, p. 373 ff.

[21] See Appendix II for final draft of the treaty.

left with the Department of State during the negotiation. In them he elaborated his ideas on the position of the two powers in undertaking the project of policing the seal industry. He emphasized the exceptional and unique nature of the pretensions they were making and admitted that the project was in opposition to the generally recognized principles of international law in regard to the high seas. He apparently wished to include a clause inviting the cooperation and accession of all maritime nations. He frankly stated the theory that the United States and Russia had property rights in the seal fisheries, and that they had a right to take measures necessary to protect their property. He felt that the proposed convention would put the question on its merits and would allay apprehension in regard to any vague claims of general maritime jurisdiction over the Bering Sea, "which claims would be sure to be strenuously resisted." He felt that the proclamation of the convention would be sure to have one of two results:

It would probably either lead to acquiescence in the course adopted by the two governments, or it would hasten the conclusion of the international agreement proposed by the United States in 1887, either of which results would be highly desirable, as it would put an end to the present state of uncertainty and would in the future preclude the possibility of complaints and claims with their attendant embarrassment and irritation.[22]

The final draft of the proposed convention had to be referred to Russia for approval before being signed, and Rosen and Blaine awaited a cabled reply. No re-

[22] See Appendix II.

ply came, and after two weeks the matter was dropped and Blaine went to Bar Harbor for the summer, to be joined later by a much crest-fallen Rosen, who could not imagine why a plan, begun under instructions and in draft approved by his Government, should have been pigeon-holed without a word. Years later he was informed that his report had been sent by De Giers to the various other members of the ministry, all of whom approved except the Minister of Marine, who feared that such a proposal might lead to complications with maritime powers whom Russia, in a naval way, could not face. De Giers, who had had difficulties with England in the Near East and in Central Asia, was much impressed and promptly dropped the plan, regardless of the discourtesy toward the United States.[23]

It is apparent from the evidence in this negotiation with Russia that the Secretary of State and Baron Rosen had gone into much detail in the discussion of their scheme, and that all the various implications of the question had been considered. Mr. Blaine had some definite idea before the controversy with Great Britain opened as to the argument which might be used by both sides. It cannot be said that he was ignorant of the international law involved nor that he failed to appreciate the difficulties which he must encounter in presenting the American case. Whether or not he made the

[23] Baron Rosen was extremely grateful to Mr. Blaine for the delicacy and tact with which he met the situation and for the friendliness and courtesy which refused to take offense at the apparent affront. Baron Rosen, *Forty Years of Diplomacy*, I, 80.

best of his weak position, and whether or not he played his part well can be determined only upon examination of the negotiations of the next two years.

On August 24 Mr. Blaine was notified by Edwardes, the British chargé, that rumors had reached London that the United States revenue cruisers had stopped, searched, and seized British vessels in Bering Sea outside the three-mile limit. He inquired whether the United States was in possession of the same information and asked that instructions be sent to the officers of such cruisers to prevent a recurrence of the seizures. He said that Bayard had assured the Foreign Office that there would be no further seizures pending the discussion of the question and ended by stating that Sir Julian Pauncefote, the newly appointed British minister, when he reached Washington would be ready to discuss the whole question, and that any settlement could only be hindered by such interference with British vessels.[24]

Blaine replied at once that so far he had no definite report, but that the rumors were probably correct. The Government of the United States earnestly desired the adjustment of the difficulties and would be prepared for the discussion when Sir Julian Pauncefote arrived.[25]

Edwardes wrote again in September asking for assurance that orders had been sent to Alaska to prevent any recurrence of seizures, saying that the recent re-

[24] Edwardes to Blaine, August 24, 1889, *U. S. Foreign Relations, 1890*, 358.

[25] Blaine to Edwardes, August 24, 1889, *ibid.*, 359.

ports "are causing much excitement both in England and in Canada." [26] Blaine answered that a categorical response would have been impracticable,

unjust to this government and misleading to the Government of Her Majesty. It was, therefore, the judgment of the President that the whole subject could more wisely be remanded to the formal discussion so near at hand which Her Majesty's Government has proposed.[27]

In October, after the facts of the seizure of the "Black Diamond" and the "Triumph" had been received, Salisbury sent his formal protest,[28] and the ground was prepared for the renewal of negotiations, to take place this time in Washington.

Meantime Canada was not being forgotten. Sir Charles Tupper, as high commissioner, was watching over Canadian interests in London and the Colonial Office kept in constant touch with the Canadian Government and at the same time with the Foreign Office. Sir John Macdonald, the Canadian premier, requested Sir Charles to urge upon Lord Salisbury the use of all diplomatic means to persuade the United States to abandon pretensions to control beyond the usual three miles.[29] The Canadian Minister of Marine and Fish-

[26] *U. S. For. Rel.,* 1890, 360, Edwardes to Blaine, September 12, 1889.

[27] Blaine to Edwardes, September 14, 1889, *ibid.,* 360-361.

[28] Salisbury to Edwardes, October 2, 1889, *U. S. Foreign Relations,* 1890, 362. There was some difference from the procedure of 1886-1887 in that the vessels seized were not taken to courts, condemned, and sold but were merely deprived of skins, ammunitions, etc., and ordered from Bering Sea.

[29] *The Life and Letters of the Right Honorable Sir Charles Tupper,*

eries, a son of Sir Charles Tupper, sent a long report on the question with particular attention to the fate of the vessels seized in 1886 and 1887, which had not yet been released. He recommended that the cases of these vessels be carried through to the Supreme Court of the United States by government subsidy, in order to have that body decide as to the legality of the seizures.

Sir Julian Pauncefote arrived in Washington late in October, 1889, and on November 1 reported a long conversation with Blaine in which the latter had refused to claim the Bering Sea as *mare clausum* but had maintained that the United States had a right to protect the fur seals. In regard to the project of negotiation, Blaine stated that since Great Britain had closed those of the preceding year, he felt that the proposal to renew them should come from her. He insisted that they be resumed in Washington and expressed a willingness that Russia should be included. Pauncefote, on his part, stated that he would have to have assistance from Canadian experts and brought up the subject of compensation for vessels seized in the past.[30]

In accordance with the procedure becoming customary in British diplomacy, the proposal to renew negotiations was referred to Canada, to be met by the arrogant response that it was held by the Canadian Govern-

II, 134. Macdonald's letter shows much animosity for Blaine and the feeling that Blaine would be opposed to all Canadian interests.

[30] Pauncefote to Salisbury, November 1, 1889, *Fur Seal Arbitration,* V, 386.

ment that no real danger of the extermination of the
seal fishery in Bering Sea existed, and that if the United
States was not of that opinion she should make the
proposals she considered necessary. If, however, the
renewal of negotiations was desired by Great Britain,
Canada would agree to it on four conditions:

(1) The United States must abandon all claims to
regard Bering Sea as *mare clausum* and revise any
legislation she might have passed which made any such
claims.

(2) There should be a direct representation of
Canada on the British Commission.

(3) Any conclusions resulting from the negotiations
would require the approval of Canada.

(4) Great Britain and the United States without
Russia should conduct negotiations for compensation to
British subjects for seizures.[31]

Pauncefote at once objected to these Canadian restrictions, for Blaine had flatly refused to have a Canadian commissioner or to negotiate, if all conclusions
must be subject to the approval of Canada.[32] Since the
United States had not officially made any claim to *mare
clausum*, that condition in the Canadian note was unnecessary. So far as the claims were concerned, the

[31] Salisbury to Pauncefote, December 7, 1889, *Fur Seal Arbit.*, V., 400.

[32] Blaine's persistent dislike and distrust for Canada appears in all
the negotiations of the period. It may have been the instinctive prejudice of a native of Maine and of one so long a supporter of the
Maine fishing interests. It shows clearly in his discussion of the
treaty of 1871 and the award of 1877. See *Twenty Years of Congress,*
II, Ch. 27.

United States would, of course, insist upon dealing with Great Britain alone. For these reasons he felt that the Canadian proposals offered no basis for negotiations.[33] After some telegraphic correspondence it was agreed that Canada should withdraw her demands, the negotiations should be diplomatic, and between Great Britain, Russia, and the United States, but no conclusions should be assented to without Canadian approval.

It was not, however, until January 28, 1890, that Salisbury sent Pauncefote the terms upon which Great Britain was ready to propose the resumption of negotiations: the negotiations were to be tripartite and at Washington, claims for compensation due the British sealers, arising from the seizures since 1886, should be the subject of separate negotiations, and it was to be understood that Great Britain was to be satisfied on this point before she could come to any settlement about a closed season. The United States must give assurance that there would be no more seizures.[34] Blaine agreed to the terms and asked the approximate amount of the claims but when informed that they amounted to about a half-million dollars, he insisted that, in his opinion, the Government was not liable, and that he could not ask Congress for such an astounding sum unless the liability was proved. He suggested that the claims be arbitrated, and that this be done while the tripartite negotiations were going on.[35] On Febru-

---

[33] *Fur Seal Arbitration*, V, 400.

[34] Salisbury to Pauncefote, January 28, 1890, *ibid.*, 435.

[35] Pauncefote to Salisbury, February 7, 1892, *ibid.*, 440.

ary 10 Pauncefote sent Blaine the formal proposal for the negotiations, and before the end of that month Baron Struve, the Russian minister, was authorized by his Government to take part in them.

While awaiting the formal invitation, Blaine gave to Pauncefote on January 22 a long note taking up the whole question of the seal fisheries, in order to place before him the view of the State Department on all the issues involved. The communication was technically in answer to Salisbury's note of October 2, protesting against the renewal of seizures, and gave the basis of American action in the Bering Sea. It began by stating that "the Canadian vessels arrested and detained in the Behring Sea were engaged in a pursuit which was in itself *contra bonos mores*, a pursuit which of necessity involves a serious and permanent injury to the rights of the Government and people of the United States." The fisheries had been exclusively controlled by Russia without interference or question and by the United States from 1867-1886 with no intrusion from the citizens of other nations. The taking of seals in the open sea would inevitably result in their extinction as had been amply proved in other regions. Only upon land could the age and sex of seals be determined, therefore,

nations not possessing the territory upon which seals can increase their numbers by natural growth, and thus afford an annual supply of skins for the use of mankind, should refrain from the slaughter in the open sea, where the destruction of the species is sure and swift.

He went on to discuss the regulations made by the

United States statutes for the protection of the fisheries and endeavored to show that, since the skins were sent to London to be prepared for the market, the English interest in the preservation of the seals was as great as our own. He expressed surprise that Great Britain had protested at the seizures in 1886 and had defended the course of the Canadians,

in disturbing an industry which had been carefully developed for more than ninety years under the flags of Russia and the United States. . . . Whence did the ships of Canada derive the right to do in 1886 that which they had refrained from doing for more than ninety years? Upon what grounds did Her Majesty's Government defend in the year 1886 a course of conduct in the Behring Sea which she had carefully avoided ever since the discovery of that sea? By what reasoning did Her Majesty's Government conclude that an act may be committed with impunity against the rights of the United States which had never been attempted against the same rights when held by the Russian Empire?

Blaine proceeded to brush away the limitations of the three-mile jurisdiction by reference to the British pearl fisheries in Ceylon and to piracy and violations of common rights of war and wrongs so odious and destructive as to demand remedy regardless of the ordinary rules of international law.

The law of the sea is not lawlessness. Nor can the law of the sea and the liberty which it confers and which it protects, be perverted to justify acts which are criminal in themselves, which inevitably tend to results against the interests and against the welfare of mankind.

He held that the action of the United States in the

Bering Sea had been demanded by the "rights of good morals and of good government the world over."

The note ended with an expression of the agreement of the Harrison with the Cleveland policy by stating:

This government has been ready to concede much in order to adjust all differences in view and has, in the judgment of the President, already proposed a solution not only equitable but generous.

Finally the United States asked only the privileges which were conceded to Russia by all nations before Alaska was ceded to the United States.[36]

This enunciation of the position of the United States did not receive an answer from Lord Salisbury until late in May, and meantime the tripartite negotiation went through its brief and inconclusive course. The meetings began on February 22, when Mr. Blaine and Baron Struve proposed as the area to be affected by a closed season all the region north of 50° north latitude,[37] which was practically the proposal of 1888. This was referred by telegraph to Salisbury and by him to the Colonial Office, which responded that the area was much too large and that it should be confined to a line near to and around the islands.[38] Mr. Charles Tupper, son of Sir Charles, was sent to Washington by the Canadian Government to assist Sir Julian Pauncefote, and Blaine reluctantly agreed that the basis for negotiations should be: first, the proof of the necessity for

[36] Blaine to Pauncefote, January 22, 1890, *U. S. Foreign Relations, 1890*, 366 ff.

[37] *Fur Seal Arbitration*, V, 450.

[38] Colonial Office to the Foreign Office, February 27, 1890, *ibid.*, 451.

a closed season and, only secondly, the extent of the closed season and the area for it.[39] For this purpose Blaine and Pauncefote exchanged evidence as to the facts of seal life and the effect of pelagic sealing, the British evidence being derived from Canadian documents collected to prove that there was no serious danger to the seal herd and that what danger there was lay in the lack of proper safeguards on the islands rather than in the conduct of pelagic sealing by Canadians.[40]

The deadlock between the Russian-American and the Canadian views soon became apparent. Blaine, despairing of arriving at any solution which would be satisfactory to Canada, suggested that Pauncefote work out a plan or counter proposal.[41] The latter set to work on such a proposal but sadly reported to his chief that being anxious to seem liberal and impartial and at the same time to please Canada was a difficult proposition.[42] The draft convention which he succeeded in working out was approved by Salisbury on April 3 and by the Canadian Government on April 18. It was sent to the State Department on April 29, was considered by Blaine during the next month, and was then refused in behalf of the United States and Russia.

[39] *Ibid.*, 454.

[40] *U. S. Foreign Relations*, 1890, 371-407. It is interesting to note that the Canadian argument was largely prepared by George Dawson, assistant director of the Geological Survey of Canada, for Dawson was to be one of the experts appointed by Great Britain to the Joint Commission of 1891-1892.

[41] Pauncefote to Salisbury, March 18, 1890, *Fur Seal Arbitration,* V, 456.

[42] *Ibid.*, 460.

This proposal, which was admitted by Blaine as a basis for future negotiation, offered temporary and provisional restriction, prohibiting pelagic sealing in Bering Sea and the Sea of Ochotsk during the months of May and June and October, November, and December; at other times vessels were to stay at least ten miles from the islands. These restrictions were to operate during negotiations which were to follow the lines of the convention which Pauncefote had prepared. By its first article a mixed commission of experts was to be appointed, which was to report on the following points: (1) Whether regulations properly enforced upon the islands and in the territorial waters were sufficient for the preservation of the seals? (2) If not, how far from the islands was it necessary that such regulations should be enforced? (3) In either of the above cases what should such regulations provide? (4) If a closed season on the islands was required, what months should it embrace? (5) If a closed season outside the territorial waters is necessary, what extent of waters and what months should it cover?

The convention provided that, upon the receipt of the report of the joint commission, the three countries should proceed to a determination of necessary regulations and that, if they could not agree, the matter should be referred to the arbitration of an impartial government. The remaining article referred to the enforcement of the provisional restrictions.[43]

Before Blaine's refusal of the Pauncefote proposal

[43] See *U. S. Foreign Relations*, 1890, 411, for draft of the convention.

reached the British legation, a statement appeared in the newspapers to the effect that it had been decided at a meeting of the Cabinet to reject the proposal, and that instructions had been issued to a United States revenue cutter to arrest pelagic sealers in Bering Sea. Pauncefote immediately protested against the publication of the statement in the press before the proposal had been formally answered and against the issuing of any such instructions to the revenue cutters. Mr. Blaine replied that the press could not be controlled and, in regard to the draft convention, the British proposal seemed entirely inadequate to Russia and to the United States. The regulations to be prescribed for sealing on land were especially objectionable, for the rights of the nations owning these islands had never been called into question. He stated, however, that the proposal might be used as a basis for further negotiations, perhaps for an arbitration agreement.[44]

On the next day, May 23, Pauncefote sent to Blaine a note announcing that since he had confirmed the rumors that orders had been issued to prevent pelagic sealing in non-territorial waters, the British Government would send a formal protest without delay.[45]

In reply Blaine expressed his surprise that Great Britain should protest, since the United States was acting only to preserve seal life by regulations similar to those to which Lord Salisbury had been willing to

[44] Moore, *International Arbitrations*, I, 789.

[45] Pauncefote to Blaine, May 23, 1890, *U. S. Foreign Relations*, 1890, 424.

consent in 1888 in the negotiations which had been broken off because of the objections of Canada. After a review of those negotiations, Blaine said that in his early interviews with Pauncefote there had seemed good reason to look for a settlement, that he and Baron Struve both had copies of a map upon which was drawn a line for a closed-season area, agreed to by Pauncefote, which corresponded to the one used in the 1888 discussion in London. Once again negotiations had been interrupted by the interposition of Canada, and the draft of a convention offered by Pauncefote in April was entirely inadequate and quite different from the earlier plans. Blaine expressed his bitter resentment that the United States should be expected to be content with the fact that "her rights within the Behring Sea and on the islands thereof are not absolute but are to be determined by one of Her Majesty's Provinces." Negotiations would, nevertheless, be kept open, and since it was too late to conclude any agreement in time for the coming season, he proposed that Great Britain agree not to permit vessels to enter the Bering Sea pending the conclusion of negotiations.[46]

Lord Salisbury at once refused to carry out Mr. Blaine's suggestion; he could not even for one hour forbid the passage of British vessels to any parts of the high seas; he had no legal powers to do so for an act of Parliament would be absolutely necessary.[47] He

[46] Blaine to Pauncefote, May 29, 1890, *U. S. Foreign Relations*, 1890, 425.

[47] Pauncefote to Blaine, June 3, 1890, *ibid.*, 430.

had become satisfied that the measures of 1888 were not necessary and thus laid himself open to another philippic from Blaine on the whole problem of the seal fisheries and the iniquities of pelagic sealing.[48] If a prohibition against vessels entering Bering Sea was impossible, Blaine asked that Salisbury, by proclamation, request that British vessels keep out of the sea for the coming season. This request was answered by a note of June 27, stating that such a proclamation presented constitutional difficulties which would prevent his acceding to it except as a part of a general scheme for the settlement of the controversy, and giving the conditions upon which he would feel justified in issuing it. These conditions included an agreement to arbitrate the question of the legality of the action of the United States from 1886 to 1889. Pending such arbitration, all interference with British vessels was to cease, and if the award was adverse to the United States, she would make compensation for all losses.[49]

In his reply of July 2, Mr. Blaine accepted the general principle of arbitration, stated that he had never conceded the legality of British claims but was willing to arbitrate them also. The arbitration project was too late for this season and could not be hurried. The United States, therefore, refused to accept Lord Salisbury's conditions, and the proclamation was not issued.[50] It seems apparent from this correspondence of

[48] Blaine to Pauncefote, June 4, 1890, *ibid.*
[49] Pauncefote to Blaine, June 27, 1890, *ibid.*, 436.
[50] Blaine to Pauncefote, July 2, 1890, *ibid.*, 432.

1890 that Secretary Blaine had, since the failure of the tripartite attempt at settlement in the early spring, been working to obtain an offer for the arbitration of the whole question. Pending that arbitration, he would undoubtedly have liked a closed-season agreement, but the British terms were too high.

Although this diplomatic sparring produced no result, and although the revenue cutters had proceeded to the Bering Sea, there were no seizures during the season of 1890.[51] After the departure of the cutters Sir Julian Pauncefote on June 14 delivered the formal protest of Great Britain against any interference with British vessels upon the high seas, the final clause of which declared that "Her Majesty's Government must hold the Government of the United States responsible

[51] In the *Life of Sir Charles Tupper*, an interesting sidelight is thrown on the reason for the fact that there was no interference in 1890. Tupper was Canadian high commissioner in London and was in constant communication with Knutsford, the colonial secretary, who informed him when news came from Pauncefote of the dispatch of United States cruisers to Bering Sea to capture Canadian sealers. Sir Charles at once went to the Foreign Office where he had a long conversation in which he said that the United States would not go to war, having agreed to arbitrate, and that "if, as matters now stand, the United States should be permitted to seize a Canadian vessel, it will be felt the time has already come when the British flag is not sufficient to protect our rights." Tupper firmly believed that this remark caused instructions to Pauncefote to warn Blaine that seizures would have serious consequences, and says, "within an hour after the reception of this message by Mr. Blaine, the swiftest steamers on the Pacific Coast were sent to countermand the orders for seizures." In any event there were no seizures. *Life and Letters of Sir Charles Tupper*, II, 138-139, and Tupper, *Recollections of Sixty Years*, 209-210.

for the consequences that may ensue from acts which are contrary to the established principles of international law." [52]

The summer of 1890 was taken up by the writing of long dispatches on the history and conditions of the seal industry. Salisbury sent an answer on May 22 to Blaine's note of January 22 stating the bases for the American action. After a careful resumé of Blaine's argument, he proceeded to demolish it by calmly relying on the fact that in international law no country had a right to enforce its municipal legislation outside the three-mile limit except in "cases of piracy or in pursuance of special international agreement." As to pelagic sealing being *contra bonos mores*, Great Britain could admit no such statement, for fur seals had always been regarded as *ferae naturae* and therefore *res nullius*. "No person, therefore, can [could] have property in them until he has actually reduced them into possession by capture." Lord Salisbury then went into an elaborate historical survey to show that since the time of J. Q. Adams, the United States had protested any such claim on the part of Russia to exclusive jurisdiction in Bering Sea, and that from 1867 to 1886, there had been no such claims advanced in her own behalf.[53]

Blaine answered this dispatch on June 30 with an attack upon Salisbury's historical argument, stating that Adams had protested only the extension of Russian authority in the North Pacific and asserting that the

[52] *U. S. Foreign Relations*, 1890, 435.
[53] Salisbury to Pauncefote, May 22, 1890, *ibid.*, 419.

Bering Sea at that time was not considered a part of the Pacific Ocean. A long analysis of the treaties between the United States and Russia and between Great Britain and Russia followed, in which Blaine claimed to find proof that the terms Pacific Ocean, Great Ocean, and South Sea referred to the Pacific only and excluded the Bering Sea. The Bering Sea, he stated, was tacitly excluded from the British-Russian treaties of 1843 and 1859, and the rights of the Russian American Company had been recognized. Since the United States had obtained all Russian rights in Alaska and the Bering Sea, it had a right to the jurisdiction Russia had been asserting there.[54]

Salisbury answered on August 2 with a discussion of Blaine's historical argument. He maintained that England had refused to admit any part of the Russian claim to Bering Sea control, that the treaty of 1825 had always been regarded as a renunciation on the part of Russia of that claim in its entirety, that in 1825 the Bering Sea had been regarded as a part of the Pacific Ocean and was included in the negotiations as such. He stated that Great Britain was making no new claim, that the fact that she had not taken seals in the high seas prior to 1886 did not nullify her right to do so, that the growth of the Canadian Northwest was recent, and that the fishing interests there were only in their infancy. In conclusion he asserted that Great Britain was willing to concede to the United States all she had ever granted to Russia, and since there was a difference

[54] Blaine to Pauncefote, June 30, 1890, *U. S. For. Rel.,* 1890, 437.

of opinion as to what had constituted Russia's rights, he asked for an arbitration agreement.[55]

Mr. Blaine did not answer this dispatch until December 17, when he wrote that legal and diplomatic questions which appeared so complicated were often found to turn on a single point. In the case of the Bering Sea controversy, this point was whether Bering Sea was in 1825 included in the term "Pacific Ocean" or not. He followed this with a long discussion of the historical background, restating his previous arguments. He came, then, to the vital point of Lord Salisbury's note, the offer of arbitration, and stated that it amounted to a submission of the question whether any country had a right to extend its jurisdiction more than one marine league from the shore. He asked if Great Britain would arbitrate the real questions at issue:

(1) What exclusive jurisdiction in the sea now known as the Behring Sea and what exclusive rights in the seal fisheries therein, did Russia assert and exercise prior to and up to the time of the cession of Alaska to the United States?

(2) How far were these claims of jurisdiction as to seal fisheries recognized and conceded by Great Britain?

(3) Was the body of water now known as the Behring Sea included in the phrase "Pacific Ocean," as used by the treaty of 1825 between Great Britain and Russia; and what rights, if any, were given or conceded to Great Britain by the said treaty?

(4) Did not all the rights of Russia as to jurisdiction and as to the seal fisheries in Behring Sea east of the water boundary, in the treaty between the United States and Russia of

[55] Salisbury to Pauncefote, August 2, 1890, *ibid.*, 476.

March 30, 1867, pass unimpaired to the United States under that treaty?

(5)   What are now the rights of the United States as to the fur seal fisheries in the waters of the Behring Sea outside the ordinary territorial limits, whether such rights grow out of the cession by Russia of any special rights or jurisdiction held by her in such fisheries or on the waters of the Behring Sea, or out of the ownership of the breeding islands and the habits of the seals in resorting thither and rearing their young thereon and going out from the islands for food, or out of any other fact or incident connected with the relation of those seal fisheries to the territorial possessions of the United States?

(6)   If the determination of the foregoing questions shall leave the subject in such position that the concurrence of Great Britain is necessary in prescribing regulations for the killing of the fur seals in any part of the waters of the Behring Sea, then it shall be further determined: First, how far, if at all, outside the ordinary territorial limits it is necessary that the United States should exercise an exclusive jurisdiction in order to protect the seals for the time living upon the islands of the United States? Secondly, whether a closed season . . . is necessary to save the seal fishing industry . . . from destruction? And if so, third, what months or parts of months should be included in such season and over what waters should it extend?

The United States disavowed any claim to the Bering Sea as *mare clausum* but did claim the right to protect the fur seals in certain sections of the Bering Sea. If the rules of international law were inadequate, it was time for the formation of new precedents.[56]

[56] Blaine to Pauncefote, December 17, 1890, *U. S. Foreign Relations,* 1890, 477. Mr. Blaine's proposals have been given verbatim because

When Sir Julian Pauncefote announced to his chief the receipt of these proposals from Secretary Blaine, he stated that while the United States Government declined to submit to arbitration the real question at issue, the legality of the seizures outside of territorial waters, it was willing to submit various historical and political questions which he felt would raise false issues and decide nothing, for even if they were decided in favor of the United States, neither the legality of the seizures nor the claims of the United States to the control of the Bering Sea would be proved.[57]

The formal answer to Secretary Blaine's proposals arrived late in February. Lord Salisbury objected to the idea that an inherent right to free passage and free fishing over a vast extent of ocean could be

renounced by mere reticence of omission. The right is one of which we could not be deprived unless we consented to abandon it, and that consent could not be sufficiently inferred from our negotiations having omitted to mention it upon one particular occasion [1825].

He then took up the six proposals for an arbitration agreement. Great Britain was ready to accept the first and the second and the first part of the third with a reservation denying that a decision upon the third would conclude the larger questions. The last half of the third proposal was refused, for Great Britain had

they constitute the basis for negotiations of the arbitration treaty of 1892.

[57] Pauncefote to Salisbury, December 19, 1890, *Fur Seal Arbitration*, V, 627.

never admitted that she conceded any exclusive rights by the treaty of 1825. The fourth proposal was scarcely worth submitting because Great Britain accepted it without discussion. The first clause only of the fifth proposal was acceptable. The sixth could be submitted but it should be the subject of a special reference and should give no special right to the United States. He suggested an additional article submitting the question of claims.[58]

Secretary Blaine modified his proposals to meet Lord Salisbury's objections, leaving articles 1, 2, 4, and 6 the same as before. The latter half of article 3 was changed to "what rights, if any, in the Behring Sea were held and exclusively exercised by Russia after the said treaty?" Article 5 was rewritten entirely, the new statement reading:

Has the United States any right, and if so, what right, of protection of property in the fur seals frequenting the islands of the United States in Behring Sea when such seals are found outside the ordinary three mile limit?

The President was willing to include a damage clause, but if the views of the United States were accepted by the tribunal, there should be a payment at market prices for the fur skins taken by the Canadians.[59] These proposals were followed by a long historical discussion and by the assertion in much more definite terms than

[58] Salisbury to Pauncefote, February 21, 1891, *U. S. Foreign Relations*, 1891, 542.

[59] Blaine to Pauncefote, April 14, 1891, *U. S. Foreign Relations*, 1891, 548.

ever before of the property rights of the United States in the seal herds.[60]

The approach of the sealing season made the Secretary of State anxious for a *modus vivendi* which would prevent difficulties, pending the result of the arbitration, so he proposed that all sealing by land or by sea be stopped for the season of 1891.[61] This proposal was modified later, to permit the North American Company to kill 7500 seals for the natives of the Pribilof Islands.[62] Salisbury accepted the proposal but suggested the appointment of British consuls to the islands to study the situation and desired Russian adherence to the convention.[63] The United States objected to both of these conditions, and the early part of June was taken up with much discussion of these and other points. Salisbury corresponded with the British ambas-

[60] This point, touched upon by Baron Rosen in 1889 (see Appendix, p. 377), was again offered by Secretary of the Navy, B. T. Tracy, whose report on the question was later published in the *North American Review* for May, 1893. It was suggested by Blaine in his dispatches of 1890 and was asserted also in Harrison's Annual Message of December 1, 1890. Richardson, *Messages and Papers*, IX, 111.

[61] This *modus vivendi* project had been urged in a report made by Professor Elliott, a scientist sent to Bering Sea in 1889 to examine the facts of seal life. This report was in Blaine's hands in November, and it gave evidence to prove the necessity for the entire cessation of seal killing. *Fur Seal Arbitration*, V, 693, 767. The failure of Mr. Blaine to publish this report was used as a weapon against the United States in the arbitration, as it was claimed that Elliott proved that the extinction of the seal herds was due to land killing as much as to pelagic killing.

[62] Blaine to Pauncefote, May 4, 1891, *U. S. Foreign Relations*, 1891, 552.

[63] Pauncefote to Blaine, June 4, 1891, *ibid.*, 358.

sadors to Russia and Germany and became confident that no difficulty would arise from other nations. The German Government stated that it had no interests in the Bering Sea, and the Russian Government expressed no interest in measures taken east of the treaty line of 1867 but some apprehension lest vessels driven from the American portion of Bering Sea might swarm west to the detriment of the Russian herd.[64]

On June 8, Parliament passed a bill authorizing the issuance of Orders in Council to prohibit the catching of seals by British ships in Bering Sea and on the 15th an agreement on a *modus vivendi* was finally signed by Pauncefote and Blaine. This *modus* was at once proclaimed by President Harrison and by the British Government. In general it followed the proposals of Mr. Blaine.[65] The Queen appointed Sir George Baden-Powell and, at the suggestion of Canada, Professor George Dawson, as commissioners to study seal life on the islands.[66]

With the establishment of a *modus vivendi*, attention went back to the terms of the arbitration convention which had been last discussed in Secretary Blaine's note of April 14. In June, Lord Salisbury agreed to

[64] *Fur Seal Arbitration*, V, 769-801. This correspondence between Russia and Great Britain led to a proposal from the former that the *modus* be tripartite and apply to the Russian portion of the Bering Sea also. Salisbury was forced to decline this offer because the United States Government could not act in the region west of the treaty line without fresh legislation, which could not be obtained in time since Congress was not in session. *Ibid.*, 839.

[65] *U. S. Foreign Relations*, 1890, 570.

[66] *Fur Seal Arbitration*, V, 793.

articles 1 to 5 but refused consent to article 6, substituting for it a proposition for a joint commission of experts to report on the question:

For the purpose of preserving the fur-seal race in Behring Sea from extermination, what international arrangements, if any, are necessary between Great Britain and the United States and Russia or any other power? [67]

In the absence of Secretary Blaine from Washington in the summer of 1891, the correspondence was carried on by Under-Secretary of State Wharton, who furnished Pauncefote with a new article 6, incorporating the British proposal for a joint commission. By this article the reports of such a commission were to be used by the arbitrators in determining what regulations were necessary in preserving the seal herd, if their preceding decisions rendered concurrent legislation of Great Britain and the United States necessary. Mr. Wharton presented, also, a draft for a seventh article which would submit to arbitration not only the legality of the seizures made by the United States and the question of compensation for damages resulting to Great Britain from the same, but also the question of compensation to the United States for injuries resulting from pelagic sealing, if the arbitrators found the jurisdiction claims of the United States justifiable.[68]

The progress of the convention was, therefore, held up for months because Great Britain refused to submit

[67] Pauncefote to Blaine, June 3, 1891, *U. S. Foreign Relations*, 1891, 559.

[68] Wharton to Pauncefote, June 25, 1891, *U. S. Foreign Relations*, 1891, 574.

to arbitration the question of her liability for acts done by her nationals on the high seas, claiming that such an admission was not warranted by international law; while the United States refused to submit her liability for the seizures without the reciprocal action on the part of Great Britain. There were proposals and counter-proposals, which came to nothing. Finally President Harrison terminated the discussion by suggesting an article 7, which was an admission of the agreement to disagree. This article stated that the respective Governments were solicitous that this subordinate question should not interrupt or longer delay the submission of the main question, that either Government might submit any question of fact in such claims, but that the question of the liability should be the subject of further negotiation.[69]

After Lord Salisbury had agreed to this article late in October, there was further delay because of reservations which he wished to make to the effect that the necessity of any regulations in the seal fisheries was to be left to the arbitrators and, secondly, that the regulations were not to be obligatory upon the two Governments until they had been accepted by other maritime powers.[70] Salisbury yielded, reluctantly, at Blaine's refusal to consider reservations, and the agreement to arbitrate on the basis of the seven articles was at last signed on December 18, 1891.[71]

[69] U. S. Foreign Relations, 1891, 585-604.
[70] Pauncefote to Blaine, ibid., 598.
[71] Pauncefote to Salisbury, December 10, 1891, Fur Seal Arbitration, V, 906-907.

On the same day the Bering Sea Joint-Commission Agreement was signed. Each Government was to appoint two commissioners, who were to investigate conjointly the facts of seal life. They were to make a joint report when they could agree and separate reports where they were in disagreement. These reports were to be secret until they were submitted to the arbitrators.[72] Both Governments appointed as commissioners the men who had been sent to the Bering Sea the preceding year to investigate, as a strictly scientific project, the facts of seal life and the necessity for and nature of protective regulations. The British commissioners were Sir George Baden-Powell and Dr. George Dawson. President Harrison appointed Professor Thomas Corwin Mendenhall and Dr. Clinton Hart Merriman.[73] This Commission met in Washington in February, 1891. There was considerable agreement as to the facts of the life of the seals and as to the fact that the herd was diminishing but complete disagreement as to the causes and measures to remedy that danger of extermination. The American scientists insisted that the cause was pelagic sealing and the remedy was its prohibition, while the British maintained that more adequate restrictions upon killing on the islands would be adequate. Their joint report was, therefore, brief, while their separate reports later submitted to the arbitrators were in complete disagreement.[74]

[72] *U. S. Foreign Relations*, 1891, 606.
[73] *Ibid.*, 608.
[74] Moore, *International Arbitrations*, I, 808. Prof. T. C. Mendenhall, "Expert Testimony in the Behring Sea Controversy," *Popular*

Secretary Blaine had considered that the first thing to be taken up by the Joint Commission was the question of a *modus vivendi* for the coming season, as that of 1891 expired on May 1. Pauncefote maintained that the *modus*, if any were needed, would have to be determined by the two Governments after the signing of the final act of the treaty submitting to arbitration the questions arising out of the seal fisheries. This treaty was signed on February 29, 1892, and contained some fifteen articles providing for the constituting of the board of arbitrators, the date and place of meeting, procedure, etc. It contained also the preliminary convention as to subjects submitted and the joint commission agreement. The contracting parties agreed to consider the findings of the arbitrators binding.[75] The Senate ratified the treaty on March 29.

With the signing of the treaty, Blaine turned once more to the subject of a new *modus vivendi*, asking the same provisions as in the preceding year. Lord Salisbury at first denied that he was influenced by the wishes of the Canadian Government, which persistently refused

Science Monthly, November, 1897. Prof. Mendenhall states that the "American Commissioners alone, and from the beginning, considered the subject from a scientific or judicial standpoint, while their colleagues . . . treated the problem as if it were diplomatic in character." This view may have been prejudiced but the events of the following years proved that the American commissioners were correct in their judgment as to the proper regulations.

[75] Text of the treaty, *U. S. Foreign Relations*, 1891, 615-619. Mr. John W. Foster, later the United States agent at Paris, drew up the treaty and prepared the American case in the illness of Mr. Blaine. He became Secretary of State when Mr. Blaine resigned in June, 1892.

to admit the necessity for any restrictions.[76] The offer of a thirty-mile radius about the islands in which pelagic sealing would be prohibited if the United States limited killing upon the islands to 30,000 was rejected by the United States as inadequate.[77] Salisbury finally agreed to an arrangement similar to that of 1891, provided the United States would agree, if the decision of the arbitrators should be adverse to their claims, that the arbitrators might assess damages for injuries which the prohibitions of the *modus vivendi* might have caused to Canadian sealers. If the decision was adverse to Great Britain, damages should be paid the United States for the limitation of sealing on land.[78] This arrangement was accepted by the President and a *modus vivendi* was signed on April 18, 1892, which was to endure at least until October 31, 1893.

Secretary Blaine resigned in June, 1892, because of his increasing ill-health and was followed in office by John W. Foster. Mr. Foster had been in the diplomatic service for some years and had been throughout 1892 preparing the case of the United States for the arbitration tribunal. He resigned as Secretary of State in order to be the agent of the United States at the Fur Seal Arbitration at Paris in 1893. The procedure provided by the Treaty of February 29, 1892, was duly carried out. The cases and counter-cases were prepared

[76] Stanley of Preston (Governor General of Canada) to Lord Knutsford, February 23, 1892, *Fur Seal Arbitration*, V, 923.

[77] Wharton to Pauncefote, March 8 and 22, 1891, *U. S. Foreign Relations*, 1891, 621-628.

[78] *Ibid.*, 628.

and exchanged, the tribunal met and held its hearings in the summer of 1893, and the award was announced on August 15. On the various questions of right submitted to it by the Treaty of February 29, 1892, the decision was against the United States. The house of cards so carefully constructed by Secretary Blaine had collapsed so completely that the unfavorable decision was not a surprise.

In his report to the State Department, Mr. Foster, the agent of the United States at Paris, wrote that early in the preparation of the case,

the conclusion was reached that it would be difficult to sustain the claims which had been put forward by the United States in the diplomatic correspondence as to the exclusive jurisdiction exercised by Russia over the waters of Bering Sea previous to the cession of Alaska,

and the decision of the tribunal on the first four points was not unexpected. The counsel for the United States had felt themselves on solid ground on the point as to the property right to the seals, since the seals spent more than half of their lives upon the territory of the United States and that power alone could protect them. The tribunal, in the opinion of Mr. Foster, decided against the claim of a property right in seals because it was a novel idea and because it conflicted with the doctrine of freedom of the seas.[79]

Since the arbitration of the facts was coupled with the question of regulation, the tribunal felt that it could save the seals from extermination by regulations, with-

[79] *Fur Seal Arbitration*, VII, 10-13.   Report of Foster.

out undue concession to the United States. The regulations instituted were not a success, and it became more and more clear that the only safe course lay in the complete prohibition of pelagic sealing. As before, no admission of such regulation could be obtained from Canada.[80] So the matter dragged, causing irritation and international difficulties until 1911.

Certain facts emerge from the maze of negotiations, arbitrations, and regulations of the period from 1886 to 1893. In the first place, the United States, through its Secretary of State, did not, in the beginning of the controversy, make any assertion of sovereign rights in the Bering Sea but sought to obtain the protection of the seals by international agreement. Secretary Bayard initiated the first of these diplomatic attempts and the second, in 1889-1890, was carried on by Blaine on exactly the lines laid down in the first. The opposition of Canada twice caused the negotiations to fail, and it was only upon this failure that Secretary Blaine advanced to the position of reliance on the sovereign rights obtained from the cession of Alaska by Russia. The case was a weak one, as he undoubtedly knew, and the additional argument as to property rights in the seal herd was also impossible to maintain, although stronger than the other.[81]

The fact that it was a concession which he must seek and not an acknowledgment of a right made Mr.

[80] Foster, "The Results of the Bering Sea Arbitration," *North American Review*, December, 1895.

[81] Foster, *Diplomatic Memoirs*, II, 28.

Blaine's position a difficult one. Great Britain would undoubtedly have been willing in 1889, as she had been in 1888, to make the necessary concessions, had it not been for the antagonism of Canada but, since the British policy in matters concerning one of the self-governing colonies was determined by the wishes of that colony, Lord Salisbury was forced to refuse. The brilliant, plausible, rather bombastic, far from concili-atory notes of Secretary Blaine may have hindered rather than aided the cause of the United States. His training had been political rather than diplomatic or legal, and arguments which seemed expedient and op-portune lacked the substantial basis which alone would have made them proof against the counter-attacks of his able opponent, Lord Salisbury. The result, how-ever, was the same in 1893 as it would have been had the arbitration occurred in 1888. International law and the tradition of the freedom of the seas, firmly adhered to by all maritime peoples, were on the side of Great Britain. That which could not be obtained by negotia-tion and mutual concession could not be gained by arbi-tration.[82]

President Harrison was criticized, stated John W.

[82] Foster, "Bering Sea Arbitration," *North American Review*, De-cember, 1895. "In no part of that statesman's (Blaine's) career did his devotion to his country more conspicuously rise above partisan-ship than in that correspondence. It is doubtful if any other living American could have made a more brilliant or effective defence of the action of his Government." And yet the *Nation*, August, 1893, stated that the arbitrators "declared Mr. James G. Blaine's history to be fiction; his geography, fancy; and his international law, a whim."

Foster, the American agent at Paris, for allowing the
question to be submitted to an arbitration from which
we gained so little and before which our case was ad-
mittedly so weak. The difficulty lay in discovering any
other way out of the dilemma. All attempts at negotiation had been futile, and the disagreement between the
ideas of what constituted due protection of the seal
herds seemed hopeless. The President could have
abandoned the entire position built up by his own and
the preceding administrations and paid the damages
asked for Canada. This course was one which would
have been disapproved by nearly all Americans of both
parties. He could have ignored the British protests and
continued the seizures, thus forcing the Canadians from
the Bering Sea. This course would not have been approved by public opinion in the United States, for it
would have made inevitable at least the danger of war
with Great Britain. Arbitration furnished the only outlet from the diplomatic tangle into which the combination of a natural and laudable desire to prevent the
extermination of the seal herd and an insufficient legal
basis for such action had brought the Department of
State.[83]

[83] Foster, *Diplomatic Memoirs*, II, 29.

CHAPTER XIV

RELATIONS WITH CANADA

ANY attempt to explain the difficulty of reconciling the points of view of Canada and the United States in the Bering Sea controversy leads one to a consideration of other questions at issue between them in the eighties and nineties. At no time was the Canadian interest in the sealing industry considerable.[1] The support which Canada gave the industry and her bitter determination to prevent Great Britain from taking a conciliatory course were largely due to friction in other matters. Had some of these other difficulties been amicably adjusted, it is possible that Canada might not have been so recalcitrant in regard to the seal fisheries.[2]

In the first place the long and vexing question of the Northeast Fisheries had failed of adjustment when the Senate refused to ratify the treaty negotiated in 1888,

[1] *Canadian Sessional Papers*, Vol. 25, No. 11, 1892, "Report of the Minister of Marine and Fisheries." In 1891 the Victoria fleet of sealing vessels numbered 49 with a total value of $425,000, total tonnage, 3,203, and total crew employed, 1082. There were a few additional schooners from Vancouver appearing that year for the first time.

[2] Thomas Hodgins, *Diplomacy Affecting Canada, 1782-1899*, is one long anathema upon the United States' attitude and actions toward Canada and a criticism of British generosity toward the United States and neglect of Canadian interests. It probably is an expression of the extreme Canadian opinion.

which had been, in the judgment of many men of all parties in the two countries, a very fair arrangement. The Republican protective tariff policy in the United States was regarded by Canada as very detrimental to her growth and prosperity. From 1854 to 1866 and from 1871 to 1885, when there had been a limited reciprocity, there had been great prosperity in Canada, and she was willing to make great efforts to secure again reciprocal commercial concessions. In the Northeast Fisheries Treaty of 1888 such an attempt was made but it failed.

The McKinley tariff, the Canadians believed, would be a heavy blow to their trade, for it placed high duties on their exports to the United States.[3] The Conserva-

[3] Oscar Douglas Skelton, *The Life and Times of Sir Alexander Tilloch Galt*, 570-572. The following letter from Galt is evidence of the feeling of many Canadians. Galt to Gladstone, February 26, 1891:

". . . your position enables you alone to secure acceptance of that policy, which will immediately and permanently counteract the McKinley Tariff, and the political ends which Mr. Blaine is seeking to promote through its agency.

"This Tariff, though primarily and directly aimed at the exclusion of British manufactures from the United States, had also avowedly for its object to create a state of feeling in Canada hostile to the maintenance of the Colonial connection, while the Reciprocal Treaties of Commerce proposed with South America point to most serious interference with British trade there.

"I need not enlarge on these points as they cannot fail to have occurred to your own mind. The American Tariff is therefore a hostile measure — an act of commercial war — and goes far beyond those measures of mere customs duties which in this country are regarded as only injurious to those adopting them. Retaliation is the only argument applicable in the present case, and the United States are so peculiarly vulnerable, that its effect would be immediate, and

tive party, then in power, felt that the change in the tariff was intended so to embarrass Canadian trade as to force the Dominion to ask for annexation to the United States.[4] There was some basis for this apprehension, for the late eighties and early nineties was a period of much discussion on both sides of the boundary of the subject of a commercial union or *Zollverein* with the ultimate possibility of political union. The subject received much attention in Congress in 1889 and 1890. Senator Sherman made a speech asking for mutual good will and stating that the true policy of the United States was one of conciliation, which would lead the Canadian people to desire to be a "part of this Republic." [5] Representative Butterworth advocated a *Zollverein* in the House of Representatives[6] and, most sig-

would necessitate negotiations probably resulting in a great and permanent amelioration in their fiscal system, while the 'object lesson' might not be lost upon France and the other European nations.

"The imposition of the former British duties on grain and agricultural produce, limited strictly to the United States and removable on the conclusion of a Treaty of Commerce, would instantly array the whole farming community of the United States against the McKinley Tariff, and would seriously affect their commercial and railroad interests, while the price of food in this country would not be much enhanced as the markets of the rest of the world would be available."

[4] *Life and Letters of Sir Charles Tupper*, II, 145 ff. See also *Correspondence of Sir John Macdonald*, 478, for a letter of Macdonald's in which he appears afraid of unlimited reciprocity and annexation.

[5] *Life and Letters of Sir Charles Tupper*, II, 146.

[6] The *Congressional Record* for these years contains much reference to the questions of reciprocity. The Fisheries Treaty in 1888 caused much discussion and Mr. Blaine's advocacy of reciprocity in regard to Spanish America added to it. *Sen. Doc.* No. 80, 62 Cong., 1st Session, contains five volumes on reciprocity. Volumes 1-3 are on the historical

nificant of all, the Liberal party in Canada had many prominent members who were outspoken in favor of reciprocity and a few who were commercial unionists. Reciprocity with the United States became the outstanding issue between the Conservative and Liberal parties in Canada in the period 1888-1892, and a separate party known as the Commercial Unionists was formed.[7] Sir John Macdonald and Sir Charles Tupper, the Conservative leaders, were both opposed to any sort of union with the United States and, therefore, insisted upon every possible manifestation of Canadian rights and independence. They were determined to yield no jot or tittle to the United States and perhaps felt that it was necessary to prolong and stimulate the bad feeling between the two Governments.[8]

The Conservatives, however, were forced to take some action by way of compromise in 1890, both because of the alarm in Canada over the McKinley tariff and because of their feeling in regard to the Blaine-Bond Treaty. In October, 1890, Mr. Robert Bond, the colonial secretary of Newfoundland, visited Washington, and after repeated conferences with Secretary

aspects of the question and contain reprints from documents written in 1888-1893 and extracts from the *Congressional Record* for that period. *Senate Report* No. 1530, 51 Cong., 1st Session, is composed of some 1300 pages on "Relations with Canada" in the form of testimony taken before a select committee of the Senate in 1889.

[7] J. S. Willison, *Sir Wilfred Laurier and the Liberal Party. A Political History*, II, 121 ff.

[8] This feeling that the United States was covetous of Canada and that they must defend the Dominion from annexationists without and within shows up in many of the letters of these two leaders.

Blaine, a treaty was drawn up providing for complete reciprocity. This treaty was sent to London for approval and would undoubtedly have received it, had it not been for the action of Canada.[9] Sir Charles Tupper met Lord Knutsford, the colonial secretary, on October 20, and was told that Great Britain would approve the treaty. Tupper protested because of the alleged injury it would bring to Canadian trade with Newfoundland and on the next day was assured by Knutsford that Great Britain would withhold her approval while the Dominion conducted negotiations with the United States.

The Canadian Government, moved by the attitude of Newfoundland and fearful lest the policy of free trade with the United States announced by the Liberal party might spell the ruin of the Conservatives in the elections of 1891, asked Sir Julian Pauncefote to propose to Blaine a formal negotiation in Washington for a treaty providing commercial reciprocity. Secretary Blaine was resentful toward Canada because of the fate of the Blaine-Bond Treaty[10] and was disinclined to move. He was not an advocate of limited reciprocity such as he felt the Conservative Government would offer and had always been convinced that the United States had had the worst of the bargain in the reciprocity treaties of 1854 and 1871.[11]

[9] *Sen. Exec. Doc.* No. 114, 52 Cong., 1st Session, "Report by Blaine to Harrison," April 15, 1892.

[10] Foster, *Diplomatic Memoirs*, II, 178.

[11] Blaine, *Twenty Years of Congress*, II, 620. Blaine resented the

He had always a feeling toward Canada which was a queer combination of a rather suspicious dislike and a conviction that Canada must sometime in the probably far distant future become a part of the United States or of some Union of American States which the United States would dominate. He wrote to President Harrison in September, 1891:

It is of the highest possible importance in my view that there be no treaty of reciprocity [with Canada]. They will aim at natural products, to get all the products of the farm on us in exchange for Heaven knows what. They certainly will not give us manufactured articles, as that will interfere with their own and break down their tariff. This might be pushed by their friends against the natural products, but I would not put the subject to risk by saying we will take the tariff if you will throw in the manufactures, because when the Liberals come into power they will agree to that.

. . . I think it would be one of the worst things among the farmers in a political point of view we could do, and we cannot afford to lose a vote now until after the presidential election. . . . The fact is we do not want any intercourse with Canada except through the medium of a tariff, and she will find she has a hard row to hoe and will, ultimately, I believe, seek admission to the Union.[12]

If annexation were to be the ultimate destiny of Canada, Blaine would most assuredly not desire to take any action which would make the Canadians fully content with any condition short of that destiny. The Con-

fact that all Canadian raw products were admitted free of duty while our manufactured goods must pay a high duty.

[12] Quoted in Hamilton, *Blaine*, 693-694.

servative party, moreover, was acting in regard to the fur seals question in a manner designed to obstruct in every way possible the solution desired by Blaine. Any move which Canada might make in this period was, apparently, foredoomed to failure.

The offer of formal negotiations was therefore declined, but Blaine stated his willingness to have

a full and private conference with the British Minister and one or more agents of Canada and consider with them every subject connected with the relations of the two countries upon which a mutual interest could be founded, with a view to formal negotiations should the proposed conference indicate a probability of agreement on any of the subjects discussed.[13]

Canada thereupon made a proposal through Lord Knutsford of the subjects upon which she was ready to open negotiation. They were: (1) a renewal of the Reciprocity Treaty of 1854, adapted to the changed circumstances; (2) a reconsideration of the treaty drawn up in 1888; (3) the protection of the mackerel and other northeast fisheries; (4) and (5) a relaxation of seacoast and lake coasting laws; (6) mutual salvage and saving of wrecked vessels; (7) the Canada-Alaska boundary.[14]

The electoral campaign opened in Canada in January of 1891, shortly after the consent of Mr. Blaine for an informal conference had been secured, and on the sixth of that month the Toronto *Empire*, a leading

[13] *Sen. Exec. Doc.* No. 114, 52 Cong., 1st Session, 4.
[14] *Life of Tupper*, II, 147-148.

newspaper of the Conservative party in Canada, published a dispatch from its Ottawa correspondent in
which it was stated that he had learned from the very
best sources that the Candian Government had recently
been approached by the United States Government
with a view to the development of trade relations between the two countries, and that Canada had requested
the advice of Great Britain on the subject.[15] This mis-
statement of the facts led to a very caustic note from
Secretary Blaine to Sir Julian Pauncefote and to a further postponement of the conference.[16] The Liberal
party felt that the Conservatives had stolen the one
plank upon which they had decided to base the campaign against the administration, and Blaine was asked,
doubtless in their behalf, by a New York Congressman,
what negotiations were in progress. The prompt answer, declaring that "no negotiations whatever are on
foot for a reciprocity treaty with Canada," may have
understated a little the facts in the case, but at least it
had the effect of puncturing the Conservative scheme.[17]

The campaign was one of "shrieking denunciation
and violence," an appeal to every prejudice and sentiment of the Canadians as members of the British Empire.[18] Blaine's denial that he had initiated negotiations

---

[15] Quoted in Willison, *Life of Laurier*, II, 151.   See also, Oscar
Douglas Skelton, *The Life and Letters of Sir Wilfred Laurier*, I, 411-
412.   Skelton says, "It was an audacious move and as disreputable as
it was audacious."

[16] Blaine to Pauncefote, April 1, 1891, quoted in Willison, *Laurier*,
II, 157.

[17] *Ibid.*, 156.

[18] *Ibid.*, 160.

for a commercial treaty forced the Conservatives to change their tactics to a certain degree. They made as much as possible of the necessity for having any reciprocity measures carried on by a safe and moderate party. They called the Liberals "annexationists in disguise" and endeavored to prove their desire to undermine the empire.[19] The Conservatives won after a close and desperate struggle. Sir Charles Tupper, who was much criticized for having returned in his capacity of high commissioner to assist in the campaign, felt that the whole question of annexation to the United States was at stake. He stated much later in his *Recollections of Sixty Years*, that "he [could] not overestimate the vital importance of the rejection of that reciprocity arrangement." [20]

Apprehensive, no doubt, lest the campaign had entirely alienated the United States, Sir Charles Tupper went to Washington immediately after the election as the guest of Sir Julian Pauncefote. Sir John Thompson and Mr. George Foster were assisting Pauncefote with the other matters under negotiation, and they all called upon Blaine on April 5, only to be told that President Harrison wished to be in Washington when the negotiations went on, and that Secretary Blaine could do nothing until the President's return. Tupper waited for ten days longer and then sailed for England.[21]

[19] Skelton, *Laurier*, I, 412 ff.

[20] Willison, *Laurier*, II, 304-305, referring to the platform of the Liberal party.

[21] *Life of Tupper*, II, 152 ff.

When the negotiations were resumed the next year, he was not a member of the conference.[22]

The date of February 10, 1892, was at last agreed upon as the date when the delegation of the Canadian cabinet should meet Mr. Blaine in the informal conference provided for in December of 1890. Mr. Blaine was not well and had associated with him Mr. John W. Foster, who was taking over more and more of the work of the department, the chief of which he was soon to be.[23] Canada was represented by Sir John Thompson, Mr. George E. Foster, and Mr. MacKenzie Bowell, associated with Sir Julian Pauncefote. The Canadian commissioners proposed a reciprocity treaty similar to that of 1854, confined entirely to natural products. They were informed that the United States was not prepared to agree to any treaty which did not include a list of manufactured good in its schedules of articles for free or favored exchange. Upon inquiry from Canada as to whether such preferential treatment must be limited to the United States or might be extended at the Canadian ports to other powers, Mr. Blaine informed them that it was the desire of the United States to make a treaty which should be exclusive in its application.[24] In other words, Canada was to

[22] Tupper resented this exclusion. It is not clear whether it was due to the campaign of 1891 or to the coolness toward him on the part of the new Canadian Premier. *Ibid.*, 160.

[23] Foster, *Diplomatic Memoirs*, II, 179.

[24] The negotiations and Blaine's report may be found in *Sen. Exec. Doc.* No. 114, 52 Cong., 1st Session. The report of the Canadian commissioners to their Government is found in *Canadian Sessional Papers*,

make a distinction in favor of United States manufactured products as against those of England.

The Canadian commissioners asked for time to consider the proposals of the United States and on the eleventh reported that it would be impossible for them to agree. They gave as their first reason the fact that Canada would have to give preference to United States goods as against those of Great Britain, "with which country she stood in the close and valued relation of a colony to the motherland." The only return Great Britain received for the services rendered the self-governing colonies was the right to enter their ports on the same trade basis as other countries.[25] For that reason, therefore,

they did not consider it competent for the Dominion government to enter into any commercial arrangement with the United States, from the benefits of which Great Britain and its colonies should be excluded.[26]

In the second place, the question of revenue was a serious one, for the free list of manufactured goods from the United States would cause a serious loss to their customs receipts. Not only would they lose the eight million dollars derived from the tax upon goods from the United States but, due to the fact that other countries would be discriminated against and would not

Vol. 26, 1893, No. 11 (No. 52). It contains a full report of each day's work and differs at no essential point from the United States document cited.

[25] *Canadian Sessional Papers* (No. 52), 1893.

[26] *Sen. Exec. Doc.* No. 114, 52 Cong., 1st Session.

be able to compete with the United States in Canadian markets, imports would fall off to such an extent as seriously to deplete the Canadian revenues. Moreover, the infant industries of Canada would receive a paralyzing blow from which it would take generations to recover. Mr. Blaine admitted the truth of all of these statements, but said that the United States could consent to nothing less than unlimited reciprocity, accompanied by discrimination in favor of the United States and the adoption of common tariff barriers.[27] The subject of reciprocity, therefore, was not discussed again in the remaining days of the conference.

The Canadian commissioners asked that Canadian fish and fish products be admitted to the United States free of duty in return for the removal of license fees from the vessels of the United States which used the in-shore privileges of the prolonged *modus vivendi* of 1888. This proposal was at once refused, and the conference discussed informally and without arriving at any conclusion the other subjects upon the list presented by Canada in 1890.[28]

The chief subject for consideration during the last days of the conference was the charge which the United States made that Canada was discriminating against the vessels of the United States, in violation of the Treaty of 1871, which provided that the vessels of both countries should have the use of the canals of the Great Lakes-St. Lawrence system without discrimina-

[27] *Canadian Sessional Papers* (No. 52), 1893.
[28] *Sen. Exec. Doc.* No. 114, 52 Cong., 1st Session.

tion. Canada had, by order in council, made a discrimination in favor of vessels carrying wheat through the Welland Canal to Montreal for trans-shipment, by ordering a drawback of eighteen cents of the twenty cents toll levied on each ton of grain. Vessels carrying wheat to a port of the United States for trans-shipment paid the full twenty cents toll. There were other charges of discrimination in regard to the carrying of coal and other commodities. Technically, Canada was treating the vessels of both countries alike, in that the orders in question made no mention of the nationality of the vessel, but actually there was a discrimination, for in general only Canadian vessels trans-shipped at Montreal.[29]

The Canadian commissioners promised to bring the subject before their Government and departed. In April, instead of removing the discriminatory orders, they were reissued, and this was followed by renewed protests from the United States. There was further correspondence and a second conference but no agreement, for the Canadians asked free navigation of the New York canals and of the Hudson River in return for a withdrawal of the orders.[30] The outcome of the affair was the levying of tolls on the St. Mary's Falls canals in retaliation. This act was followed by the withdrawal of the Canadian orders in council, and the

[29] *Sen. Exec. Doc.* No. 114, 52 Cong. 1st Session, p. 6.

[30] *Ibid.*, 45. Report of John W. Foster to President Harrison, June 6, 1892.

retaliatory tolls on the canals of the United States were dropped.[31]

Mr. John W. Foster, who was practically in charge of all these negotiations, believed that the whole episode of the Commission of 1892 was largely political so far as Canada was concerned.[32] However that may be, the failure of the effort still further estranged the relations of the two countries and made the Canadians less inclined than before to make any concessions to their southern neighbor.[33] The United States felt that, in the words of President Harrison,

in many of the controversies, notably those as to the fisheries on the Atlantic, the sealing interests on the Pacific and the canal tolls, our negotiations with Great Britain have continuously been thwarted or retarded by unreasonable and unfriendly objections and protests from Canada.[34]

The Canadians were equally sure that the United States in its policy toward the Dominion was covetous, jealous, and domineering, and that the future economic prosperity of Canada lay in cementing closer relations with the Empire. The reciprocity negotiations of 1892, instead of drawing Canada closer to the United States, had caused her to look toward England for relief. It is, of course, impossible to state whether an agreement at that time upon a scheme for limited reciprocity would

[31] Richardson, *Messages and Papers of the Presidents*, IX, 313.
[32] Foster, *Diplomatic Memoirs*, II, 182.
[33] *Life of Laurier*, II, 181.
[34] Richardson, IX, 314.

have tended to draw Canada more into the orbit of the United States and to weaken the bonds of the Empire, but it is safe to make the negative assertion that, failing an agreement, Canada and the United States grew farther apart.[35] Instead of reciprocity the succeeding years were to see the growth of the idea of preferential tariffs within the Empire, and the annexationist schemes of political leaders in the United States were given up as impossible of realization. Mr. Blaine's own party, in later years, repudiated his policy and in 1911 came forward as willing to accept the sort of reciprocity he had scorned.

[35] The Conservative leaders in Canada were content that this should be so. In presenting the budget report in the House of Commons on March 22, 1892, Mr. G. E. Foster spoke of the Washington conference and frankly expressed his satisfaction that the long-discussed question of reciprocity was settled. He said that nothing could be hoped for from the United States as long as the present policy and party were in control in the United States and that Canada should settle down to work out its own destiny. The Canadian farmer should "prepare himself to find a market for his wares in other countries where they get more favourable entrance, and he can especially prepare himself to enter fully upon that almost inexhaustible market which awaits him for all his products in Great Britain, our Mother Country." *Debates of the Canadian House of Commons*, Second Session, Seventh Parliament, 1892, I, 334.

CHAPTER XV

CONCLUSION

A STUDY of the foreign policy of any administration or of any one Secretary of State is, at best, an examination and a piecing together of the fragmentary and disjointed episodes and problems with which the diplomatic corps of that period was dealing. It is an analysis and a synthesis, an attempt to study these fragments in the light of American diplomatic history as a whole and to fit them together into a consistent line of action or policy. In such a study one is lead from one country to another, through a maze of unrelated problems and negotiations, few of which fall as units entirely within the period chosen, for most are mere segments of problems faced by the Executive in one guise or another, through long years of development. The problems to be considered by the historian are: Does the statesman in question strike out a new path or does he follow that of his predecessors? Does he carry his party and the public with him or is he out of touch with his time? Does he have a definite objective, a policy of his own? Is there in some part of his work an indication of vision and high endeavor or is it all routine? Is he, in other words, in part at least, a real statesman or always just an office-holder?

James G. Blaine came into the office of Secretary of State in 1881 with rather unusually definite ideas as to what he wanted to do. His many years as a political leader and his extensive training in the legislative branch of the government, his brilliancy in debate, and his shrewdness in dialectic did not, perhaps, furnish the best possible training for the work of a diplomat. Much of the lack of training in diplomacy was offset by his acknowledged exquisite tact and great personal magnetism, but he undoubtedly was lacking in the endless patience, persuasiveness, and grasp of the viewpoint of his opponents, which mark the trained diplomat. His very ability in debate caused his State papers to be, too often, marred by bombastic statements, insistence of manner, and clever, plausible arguments which could not quite stand the searchlight of law and logic. But at the same time the long years in Congress in close touch, not only with legislation but also with the public and its opinions, had given him an insight into American history, desires, and destiny, which is denied to one less closely in contact with events.

In 1881 Mr. Blaine came into office as the choice of a President who was at the same time his devoted friend. Each had a high regard for the other's ability and respect for his opinions.[1] There was a perfect ac-

[1] The delightfulness of the relationship is evidenced by their personal letters. For example, see Hamilton, *Blaine*, 534, for a letter from President Garfield, dated March 27, 1881. "Just as we are starting for church, your note comes. It is like the current of the Gulf Stream conquering the Arctic Sea — and I thank you for it. Above all the worriments and contradictions of politics, arises my

cord between them as to what the policy of the Department of State was to be. There was to be a new interpretation, a positive conception, of the Monroe Doctrine. The States of the Western Hemisphere were to be welded together into a peaceful, amicable relationship under the benevolent leadership of the United States. Communication and commerce between the two continents were to be developed and improved. The Clayton-Bulwer Treaty with its restrictions on the canal zone was to be abrogated or modified. Hawaii was to be recognized as within the American system of states and as subject to ultimate annexation. The same view was taken of the final destiny of Cuba and Canada, although Mr. Blaine recognized that no steps could be taken to accomplish such results for many years, probably for generations. As regards Europe and the Orient, he had little interest except where the safety of the lives or property of United States citizens was concerned. He had, it must be admitted, a peculiar suspicion or prejudice amounting almost to dislike of England and Canada, and he always showed his worst qualities in correspondence with Great Britain. He coupled indifference toward the Orient with an implacable opposition to Chinese immigration.

The administration of Garfield was cut short by the assassination of the President, and Mr. Blaine's career as Secretary of State came to an end within a brief nine months but not before his policy was apparent. The

anxiety for Blaine's health. I cannot do good work with 'the half of my surviving soul' prostrate and in pain."

controversy with England over the Clayton-Bulwer Treaty, the attempts at mediation in Central American boundary disputes and in the War of the Pacific, and the calling of the Peace Conference had exhibited most of the phases of his American policy. The repeated enunciation of his ideas as to the attitude of Latin American States toward each other, toward Europe, and toward the United States had evidenced an impetuosity and a vigor which alarmed Spanish America and frightened the conservative element in the United States. It was felt that he was going too fast and too far. The country was not yet ready for a Latin American policy of so virile a type. "His Pan Americanism was magnificent but it was inconvenient" [2] was doubtless the reason why there was a sigh of relief when he went out of office.

The period was that of the beginnings of modern economic imperialism. European countries were wrangling over markets, spheres of influence, sources for raw products, and colonies. The United States had not quite reached the stage of industrial development where it, too, was to enter this world-wide competitive movement, but the far-sighted could make some estimate of the future. Blaine was twice Secretary of State in a period of transition and rapid development in economic fields. He appears to have comprehended the situation to some extent, and that comprehension is reflected in his policies. The Western Hemisphere was to be with-

[2] A. B. Hart, in a review of Miss Hamilton's *Blaine*, in *American Historical Review*, II, 181.

drawn from too close contact with Europe. There should be no direct European control, and in every way possible the United States was to supplant Europeans in trade with other American States. The Monroe Doctrine was to have an economic as well as a political interpretation. And yet Mr. Blaine was no longer a young man in the eighties. He had grown up in the period of Manifest Destiny and had come into public life in the days of Secretary Seward. His ideas as to the predominant position of the United States in the Western Hemisphere owed as much to the older type of thought as they did to the new, and it cannot be said that he was conscious of, or fully understood, the imperialism which later took advantage of the beginnings which his policy had made.

In the eight years before he became Secretary of State again, much had occurred to temper that impetuous and impatient nature and to disillusion the vivid personality, so that in 1889-1893 Mr. Blaine seemed in many ways a conservative and very restrained man. The vision was still there, the objective had not changed, but he seemed no longer to expect that it could all be accomplished. Professor Hart, who is by no means a gentle critic of Blaine, says, "Had he enjoyed the dozen years of public life which a man of his age might fairly have expected, he might have become again a great force in the nation." [3]

The presidential campaign and the election of 1884 left their mark upon his spirit. The campaign was one

[3] *Ibid.*

of especial virulence, and the election was far closer than usual. A few votes more in one state, and Blaine would have been President.[4] The years between 1881 and 1885 were spent in writing and publishing his interesting and important work, *Twenty Years of Congress*. A long trip abroad and advancing ill health kept him out of public affairs until 1889. His refusal to consider the nomination for the Presidency the year before and his hearty support of Harrison in the campaign made inevitable his selection as Secretary of State. He came back into office with great pleasure but with the knowledge that under President Harrison, there could never be that independence of action he had known in 1881. Mr. Blaine was not at any time during the next three years a well man. The advances of the mortal disease

[4] *The Letters of Mrs. James G. Blaine*, II, 120-121. Mrs. Blaine to Alice, November 30, 1884:

"You need not feel envious of any one who was here during those trying days. It is all a horror to me. I was absolutely certain of the election. . . . Then the fluctuations were so trying to the nerves. It is easy to bear now, but the click, click of the telegraph, the shouting through the telephone in response to its never-to-be satisfied demand, and the increasing murmur of men's voices coming up through the night to my room, will never go out of my memory, — while over and above all, the perspiration and chills, into which the conflicting reports constantly threw the physical part of one, body and soul alike rebelling against the restraint of nature, made an experience not to be voluntarily recalled."

The letters of Mrs. Blaine and the biography of Blaine by a relative, Miss Dodge (Gail Hamilton), furnish an intimate picture of the man himself which can never be neglected in a study of any phase of his career. The concluding chapter of Mr. Stanwood's *Blaine* is frankly eulogistic, but valuable as evidencing the point of view of men who admired Mr. Blaine.

which caused his death in 1893 were apparent to his intimates. In 1890 tragedy came into a previously happy domestic life when his eldest son, who was his close associate, and, within two weeks, his eldest daughter died in Washington.

It is not to be noted with surprise, therefore, that the Secretary of State in 1889-1892 was a different man from the James G. Blaine, "the plumed knight," of 1881. Neither his admirers nor his enemies could have been quite satisfied with the change. He was neither so spectacular nor so vulnerable but, perhaps, as much, if not more, the statesman. During this second period there was not to be the accord with the President which had made the first short term of office so pleasant. President Harrison and Mr. Blaine were not sympathetic by nature and were not apt to see eye to eye on many questions. The President disliked being eclipsed by his brilliant Secretary of State and was determined to keep a controlling hand on foreign affairs. The period, as well as the men, was destined to be different.

The International American Conference came with peculiar appropriateness in this second term of office. Mr. Blaine's conduct of that Conference and his genuine sympathy and understanding of its problems showed that, although he still held the same ideal as to the relations of the American States to each other, he had come to a realization of the complexity of the problems involved. Elihu Root, in an address in 1906, said:

Twenty-five years ago Mr. Blaine, sanguine, resourceful, and gifted with that imagination which enlarges the historian's understanding of the past into the statesman's comprehension of the future, undertook to inaugurate a new era of American relations, which should supplement political sympathy by expanding trade, and by mutual helpfulness. . . .

Nevertheless, Mr. Blaine was in advance of his time. In 1881 and 1889 neither had the United States reached a point where it could turn energies away from its own internal development and direct them outward towards the development of foreign enterprises and foreign trade, nor had the South American countries reached the stage of stability in government and security for property necessary for their industrial development.[5]

The Samoan Conference furnished an abundance of evidence that Blaine did not carry his imperialism beyond the two continents of North and South America, and that the extension of American influence into the South Seas was no part of his policy. On the other hand, it was equally apparent that his views in regard to Hawaii had not changed. Every effort must be made to see that the Sandwich Islands were brought under the control of the United States. They were a "part of the American system of states."

Secretary Blaine was not permitted to solve any of the important questions troubling the relations of the United States and Canada. His handling of the Fur Seal Question was clumsy, lacking in finesse, and was his most conspicuous failure. Canada and Great Britain both felt his dislike of them and returned it without stint. His conduct of this controversy and of the reciprocity negotiation widened the breach between the

[5] Quoted in Mrs. Blaine's *Letters*, II, 13, note.

United States and Canada and postponed the day of Anglo-American friendship. Instead of advancing the day of the annexation of Canada by the United States, he stimulated the development of a closer union between the mother country and the colony.

Many problems came to him as heritage from previous administrations, some of which he was able to settle and some of which were passed on to his successors. There appears to be nothing in this second period that could be considered radical or dangerous in policy.

Mr. Blaine has been likened to Henry Clay, whose great admirer he was. If that comparison goes too far in its praise, it may be balanced by the accusations of charlatanism made against him by other American historians.[6] The truth probably lies neither with his admirers nor with his detractors. He was a Secretary of State with greater vision and greater grasp of the interests and problems of the United States than any who held that office between the time of Seward and that of John Hay. Much of his policy has been adopted, much that he endeavored to accomplish has been achieved by his successors, and the public which acquiesced did not remember that they were the policies of James G. Blaine, twice Secretary of State and a statesman as well as a politician.

[6] See Fish, *American Diplomacy*, 371, 387, 391.

APPENDIX I

UNPUBLISHED LETTER OF
JOHN S. STEVENS

United States Legation
Honolulu, Oct. 8, 1892.

No. 70   Confidential.

Sir:

My dispatches 64 and 65, of Sept. 9, 14, indicated an unsettled and feverish state of things here regarding the Cabinet. The situation has not improved. The new Cabinet, in the place of the old voted out by the Legislature, was constructed without consulting the Legislative majority and in positive disregard of the best public sentiment. It contains the most objectionable man of those voted out, and its choice was clearly in accord with the wish of the Tahitian favorite of the Queen. Two weeks since this new Cabinet was pronounced against by a vote of 24 to 21. But the President of the Legislature, a Welshman, a resident here many years, of unsavory reputation and (?) to relations with the recent king in his worst peculations, decided the vote not carried, because the 24 of the majority is not a majority of the Legislature, which, when full, is composed of 48 members. There were two vacancies, the actual number being 46. The 24 members against the Cabinet are made up of some of the chief men of the little kingdom, and they are backed by the principal people of the Islands, among them all the best of the native Hawaiians. As this Cabinet is less American than any other which has existed for years, the English Minister and his wife intervened openly in its favor, the wife being the more positive personality of the two. Two English members of the Legislature are believed, for the best of reasons, to have been influenced by the English Legation to vote for the new Cabinet, though they had previously stood with the majority of the Legislature. The Premier is known to be strongly English in sympathy and plans, is a member of the commercial house, dealing in liquors largely, through which the English loan was made in the worst days of the recent king by which this Government was cheated out of fifty thousand dollars, more or less, and this shameful transaction was one of the causes which led to the new Constitution of 1887, taking from the king much of his power. This commercial house is in bad repute among the best men of the Islands, and the wife of the English Minister has had compromising relations with it through the Custom House privileges accorded to Foreign Ministers. Hence she was actively on the floor of the Legislature in favor of the Cabinet. She has also certain relations with the Police, growing out of the fact that her son is married to an illegitimate half-white sister of the Princess heir-apparent now in England, and another of her sons is in the Honolulu Post Office. The English Minister and wife have resided here nearly twenty five years, and the latter has an unsavory reputation in all the best circles here. Besides this indicated Anglo member of the Cabinet, the other member most objectionable to the responsible men of the country, is the Attorney General, a German Jew in origin, a cast-off politician of San Francisco, a gambler, and much the ablest member. He is the choice of the Tahitian half-caste Marshal, and believed to be in the pay of the opium ring, whose ramifications reach to Hong Kong, to San Francisco, and to Vancouver, Honolulu being one of the strongholds.

To add to the fever of the present situation there is an organized movement here to force through the Legislature a lottery charter of the Louisiana type. The men at the head of this lottery scheme are supposed to have the design of selling the franchise to the New Orleans gang. Part of this new Cabinet are believed to be in the scheme, with the support of the Tahitian favorite.

The 24 Legislative opponents of this Cabinet are strongly American in sympathy. Probably they will increase in numbers, and that this Ministry so objectionable to the property holders and to the best men of the country, will be voted out in a few days from this. While it is in place perhaps it may send to Washington some dispatch unfriendly to the undersigned, for the American Deputy in the Foreign Office is sick and out of town, and things in that office are "at loose ends" at this time, and the Department is really without a responsible head. I am doing my utmost to blend reticence and prudence with firmness and vigor, and so far as possible shall protect American influence and interests here. I know that this Legation has the confidence and earnest support of a majority of the Legislature and of the chief men of the Islands. I trust the Department of State will not be disturbed by any unfavorable reports that may be in the San Francisco papers for the opium and lottery rings and their supporters in the Cabinet have in their interests some of the most unscrupulous adventurers who correspond for some of the San Francisco papers.

I am, Sir, Your obt. Servant

John S. Stevens

Hon. John W. Foster
Secretary of State

Note

I neglected to state above, that three English born members of the Legislature, two of them Canadians well Americanized, voted with the majority of 24, and paid no regard to the manifest wish of the English Minister and wife.   S.

APPENDIX II

DOCUMENTS PERTAINING TO THE NEGOTIATIONS WITH RUSSIA IN 1889.[1]

First Draft

CONFIDENTIAL

The Undersigned Baron Rosen, Chargé d' Affairs of the Russian Empire and James G. Blaine, Secy. State, the United States duly authorized thereunto have agreed upon the terms and conditions of the following memorandum which is to be communicated by their respective Governments to the principal Maritime Powers of the world.

1. WHEREAS the Governments of the Russian Empire and of the United States of America are the sole owners of the only remaining important breeding places of the fur seal (Callorhinus ursinus), viz; the Commodore Islands in Behring Sea and Robbin Island in the Sea of Okotsk belonging to Russia; and the Pribylow Islands in Behring Sea, belonging to the United States — the right of ownership of the two Governments in the so-called "seal fisheries" at these islands being part of their *right of* [2] indisputable sovereignty:

[1] The Manuscript Notes from the Russian Embassy, Vol. 13, contain five drafts of the proposed Russian-American Treaty, two of which are here produced in exact copy. Baron Rosen's *aides mémoire* are significant and are reproduced in the order in which they occurred in the Notes. These documents relating to the negotiations of 1889, appear never to have been published, nor have they been used in any secondary accounts save in Rosen's *Forty Years of Diplomacy.*

[2] All italicized passages in this Appendix are deleted in the original MS. of the Documents.

2.   AND WHEREAS the two Powers are deeply interested in the maintenance, protection and continuous development of these "seal fisheries," not only as a matter of right, but also as a special means of securing the welfare of the native population of these islands, whose livelihood is entirely dependent on the continued existence of the "seal fisheries":

3.   AND WHEREAS scientific investigation, illustrated and enforced by varied experience in other parts of the world, has conclusively proved that unless the promiscuous killing of seals in the open sea be strictly prohibited, seal life is certain to become extinct within a measurably short period of time:

4.   AND WHEREAS the careful provision made by the two Governments for the protection, perpetuation and increase of seal life on the islands named (hitherto effective) has been, within the last two years, in danger of being rendered nugatory, through the action of parties who have adopted a plan of killing seals in the open sea, by intercepting them on their annual migrations to and from their breeding places and on their excursions in search of food, *destroying by this mode seven seals to one that may be secured, mode a vastly larger number of seals than they secure.* a practice that tends directly and rapidly to the extermination of the "seal fisheries."

5.   AND WHEREAS, on these islands belonging to Russia and to the United States, the exclusive right of killing seals is given by both Governments to responsible corporations whose operations are carried on under official regulations and supervision of the strictest character, with heavy penalties for violating any part of their contract;

6.   AND WHEREAS it is impossible to admit that the inviolability attaching to the flag of a friendly nation, and the indisputable freedom of the high seas open to all nations for legiti-

mate purposes of navigation, trade and commerce, could imply or confer the right of the vessel of any one nation to carry on with impunity operations leading to the destruction of any other nation's lawful and incontestable property. *The law of the sea can never justify lawlessness.*

Therefore, it is that the Governments of Russia and the United States.

7. AND WHEREAS the necessity of preserving and maintaining protective regulations herein referred to is, in the judgment of the two Powers, devolved upon them as an absolute duty:

THEREFORE it is that the Governments of Russia and the United States have resolved to apply to all vessels and all persons engaged in hunting fur seals in the seas surrounding the above named islands the same laws and regulations governing the seal hunting industry in their own respective territories and *Dominions* applied to their own ships, and to their own subjects and citizens.

This measure is resorted to as the only effectual mode of putting an end to unlawful practices that threaten speedy extinction to an industry which furnishes to the world a valuable article of commerce of wide-spread use, and in the continued existence of which all civilized nations have, in varying degrees, a common interest.

In resorting to their measure, the Governments of Russia and the United States, declare it to be their *intention* purpose to carefully avoid all interference with the legitimate trade and commerce of other maritime powers; and they entertain the belief that the necessity, as well as the justice, of the course adopted by them will secure the recognition and acquiesence of all friendly nations.

Rosen's Suggestions.

Preamble

6.   AND WHEREAS it is impossible to admit that the principle of the freedom of the high seas, open to all nations for *all* legitimate purposes of navigation, trade and commerce, could imply the right of vessels of any one nation to carry on with impunity on the high seas operations leading to the destruction of any other nation's lawful and incontestable property under cover of the inviolability attaching on the high seas to the flag of a friendly nation:

8.   THEREFORE it is that the Governments of Russia and the United States have resolved to apply to all vessels and all persons wheresoever found to be engaged in hunting fur seals in the seas surrounding the above named islands, the laws and regulations governing the seal hunting industry in their respective territories and dominions.

9.   This measure is *entirely exceptional and without prejudice of generally recognized principles of maritime international law and* resorted to as the only effectual means of putting an end to practices that threaten speedy extinction to an industry which furnishes the world a valuable article of commerce of wide spread use and in the continued existence of which all civilized nations have in varying degrees, a common, *allied* indirect interest.

10.   In resorting to this exceptional measure the Governments of Russia and the United States declare it to be their intention to carefully avoid all interference with the legitimate trade and commerce of other Maritime Powers and they entertain the hope that the necessity as well as the justice of the course adopted by them will *be generally recognised* secure the *friendly recognition* recognition and acquiesce of all friendly nations.

Aide Mémoire   Rosen's Paper.

CONFIDENTIAL.

The Governments of Russia and of the United States are the owners of the only remaining important breeding places of the fur seal (Callorhinus ursinus), viz. the Commodore Islands in Behring Sea and Robben Island in the Sea of Okhotsk — belonging to Russia, and the Pribylow Islands in Behring Sea — belonging to the United States.

Their right of property in the so called seal fisheries at these islands is part of their right of sovereignty (dominion). They are deeply interested in the maintenance and protection of these "fisheries" not only as a matter of right but also as a matter of solicitude for the welfare of the native population of these islands whose only means of subsistence are entirely dependent on the continued existence of the fisheries.

Scientific investigation, as well as experience in other ports of the world, has shown conclusively that, unless the reckless and promiscuous killing of seals be carefully guarded against, seal life is certain to become extinct within a measurably short period of time.

On the islands belonging to Russia and the United States the right of killing seals is farmed out to a responsible corporation whose operations are carried on under the strictest regulations and supervision.

The careful provision made by the two Governments for the protection and perpetuation of seal life, hitherto effective, is, within the last two years, being rendered nugatory to a considerable extent through the action of illicit hunters who have adopted a plan of killing seals in the open sea intercepting them on their periodical migrations to and from their breeding places and on their daily excursions in search of food.

The depredations caused by these illicit hunters have of late reached a most alarming extent.

That the result of these depredations, if permitted to go on unchecked, would inevitably be the total extinction of seal life on the islands within a very few years, is very concisely and very conclusively demonstrated by Professor Elliott, the highest scientific authority on seal life, in his letter to the Secretary of State dated December 3rd, 1887.

The necessity of putting a stop to what Professor Elliott so aptly terms, "pelagic sealing" is therefore apparent and was, it would seem admitted by the Governments approached on the subject when, in 1887, the Government of the United States proposed an international agreement for the protection of seal life, — a proposal with which the Imperial Government of Russia at once declared itself in the fullest accord.

The negotiations then initiated by the Government of the United States having failed to bring about the desired result, the Governments of Russia and the United States find themselves compelled to take such exceptional steps as the exceptional necessities of the case require and as the exceptional nature of the property to be protected justly warrants. They have therefore resolved to instruct the commanders of their cruisers charged with the protection of the seal industry to seize all vessels engaged in the pursuit of illicit killing of seals wherever found in the seas surrounding the above named islands.

This measure is entirely exceptional and without prejudice of generally recognized principles of maritime international law and is resorted to as the only effectual means of putting a stop to practices that threaten speedy extinction to an industry which furnishes to the world a valuable article of commerce of wide spread use and in the continued existence of which all civilized nations have a common albeit indirect, interest.

In resorting to this exceptional measure the Governments of Russia and the United States declare it to be their intention to carefully avoid all interference with legitimate trade and they entertain the hope that the necessity as well as the justice of the course adopted by them will not be questioned and that the Government of —————— will lend them its cooperation with a view to preventing avoidable injury to private interests by warning its subjects or citizens against entering the seas where the above named islands are situated for the purpose of unlawfully killing fur seals.

The substance of what is said above might be embodied in an identical note to be addressed by the Governments of Russia and the United States to the principal Governments interested in the question.

The advantages of such a course, if adopted by the two Governments, would seem to be as follows;

it would place the question of seizing on the high seas vessels engaged in illicit sealing on the basis of their unquestionable right of property in the seal fisheries and of their right to take for the protection of this property the steps which necessity dictates and which experience has shown to be alone effectual;

it would allay apprehension felt in regard to imputed vague claims of general maritime jurisdiction over the whole expanse of Behring's Sea, which claims would be sure to be strenuously resisted;

and it would probably either lead to acquiescence in the course adopted by the two Governments, or it would hasten the conclusion of the international agreement proposed by the United States in 1887, either of which results would appear to be highly desirable, as it would put an end to the present state of uncertainty and would in the future preclude the possibility of complaints and claims with their attendant embarrassment and irritation.

FINAL DRAFT

WHEREAS the Governments of the Russian Empire and of the United States of America are the sole owners of the only remaining important breeding places of the fur seal (Callorhinus ursinus), viz; the Commodore Islands in Behring Sea and Robber Island in the Sea of Okotsh, belonging to Russia; and the Pribylow Islands in Behring Sea, belonging to the United States — the right of ownership of the two Governments in the so-called "seal fisheries" at these islands being part of their right of indisputable sovereignty:

AND WHEREAS the two Powers are deeply interested in the maintenance protection and continuous development and increase of these "seal fisheries," not only as a matter of right, but also as a special means of securing the welfare of the native population of these islands, whose livelihood is entirely dependent on the continued existence of the "seal fisheries:"

AND WHEREAS scientific investigation, illustrated and enforced by varied experience in other parts of the world, has conclusively proved that unless the promiscuous killing of seals in the open sea be strictly prohibited, seal life is certain to become extinct within a measurably short period of time:

AND WHEREAS the careful provisions made by the two Governments for the protection, perpetuation and increase of seal life on the islands named (hitherto effective), has been, within the last two years, in danger of being rendered nugatory, through the action of parties who have adopted a plan of killing seals in the open sea by intercepting them on their annual migrations to and from their breeding places and on their excursions in search of food, — destroying by this mode seven seals to one that may be secured:

AND WHEREAS, on these islands belonging to Russia and the United States, the right of killing seals is given by both Governments to a responsible corporation, whose operations are carried on under official regulations and supervision of the strictest character, with heavy penalties for violating any part of their contract:

AND WHEREAS the necessity of preserving and maintaining these protective regulations is, in the judgment of the two Powers, devolved upon them as an absolute duty:

THEREFORE, it is that the Governments of Russia and the United States, after full and friendly consultation, have determined, with careful avoidance of all interference with the legitimate trade and commerce of other Maritime Powers, to exercise their indisputable right to preserve and protect this valuable seal industry.

To this end, the two Governments, either jointly or separately, will from time to time, as circumstances may develop the necessity therefor, publish such orders and regulations as will secure the following results:

First. The limitation of the number of seal skins which may be lawfully taken each year from the islands herein named;

Second. The killing of seals shall be rigorously confined within the season which long experience and scientific investigation have proved to be necessary for the preservation of the seal during the period of breeding;

Third. The cruel killing of seals in their periodic migrations through the sea to their feeding grounds and upon their return to their breeding places, with the waste and destruction attendant thereon, is absolutely forbidden and will be prevented by the two Powers with the use of force, if necessary.

In the full belief that the other Maritime Powers of the world will respect this measure of protecting a valuable property from wanton destruction, the Governments of Russia and the United States, through their respective representatives duly authorized and empowered thereunto, make proclamation of the same for the information and guidance of all whom it may concern.

Rosen's Paper.

With reference to the analogy that might be said to exist between the Fisheries on the Bank of Newfoundland and the so called "Seal Fisheries" it would appear that whatever argument could be put forward in support of the exclusive right of fishing on the Grand Bank — participation in which was secured to France by the treaty of Utrecht and to the United States by the treaty of 1783, and was totally and forever renounced by Spain in the treaty of Paris in 1763 — would apply to the case of the Seal Fisheries and that with infinitely greater force, inasmuch as:

1. the location of the so called Seal Fisheries is not as in the other case an immense expanse of open ocean, but the very shores of the islands belonging to the two governments, where alone the killing of fur seals can be carried on legitimately and in a manner calculated to ensure the continued existence of seal life;

2. the title to these Seal Fisheries, vested in the two Governments and acquired by one of them through discovery and first occupation and by the other through cession by treaty — can not be questioned, much less disputed;

3. the supply of fur seals is not, as in the supply of fish on the Grand Bank, practically inexhaustible, but on the contrary, as experience has amply demonstrated, is particularly liable to speedy and total extinction, unless properly protected.

The whole question therefore resolves itself simply to this: is there anything in the principles of international law that could compel two Nations to witness in helpless inaction the wanton destruction of a most valuable property through the action, and for the sole and temporary benefit of a few illicit traders whose mode of operation besides is such as to ensure, if suffered to go on unchecked, the speedy destruction not only of the legitimate seal killing industry, but also of the very source of their own illicit gains, and this for the sole reason that these nefarious operations are carried on beyond the limits of their territorial waters.

To this question, evidently, only one answer is possible, and that an emphatic No.

International Law recognized not only the right but the solemn duty of a Nation to work for the perfection and security of its estate and the right derived therefrom to resort to all such actions as are apt to prevent not only the total ruin thereof, but also any injury or prejudice thereto.

This principle is very clearly enunciated in de Wolff's great, though somewhat antiquated work on the Law of Nature and of Nations.

Then again, from the generally recognized principles that the high seas are open to all nations for all legitimate purposes, it does not by any means follow, one should think, that vessels of one nations may with impunity carry on on the high seas operations destructive of the lawful property of another nation and then, when interfered with in their nefarious pursuit, invoke the inviolability attaching to the flag of a friendly nation on the high seas.

> Copy of subsequent communication from Rosen to his Government believed to have been sent Spring of 1890.

The Secretary of State tells me that information has reached him, from a source, which he is not at liberty to disclose, to the effect that our hesitation to accept the proposed memorandum is due to a desire to associate these with the British Government and that negotiations on the subject are on foot between that Government and ours. Although not absolutely certain of the correctness of this information he asks me to tell you that the Government of the United States are determined not to replace the question on the basis of the London negotiations of last year, the very object of the proposed memorandum being to avoid rendering the defense of incontestably legitimate and exclusively American and Russian interests dependent upon an international agreement with other Powers, and that the only international arrangement which they would consider acceptable would be an agreement to the effect of simply recognizing the right of the United States (and of course that of Russia on her side) to police the high seas in the neighborhood of their seal islands for the strictly defined purpose of supressing the illicit killing of fur seals. But it is convinced that this right will not be conceded, either tacitly or explicitly, till after we have affirmed it and declared our intention to exercise it. He concluded by saying that he was fully aware that a joint action of the United States and Russia would more than double the strength of the position in this matter of each of the two Powers, and that he did not at the same time conceal from himself that a lack of unity in the views and action of the two Powers, whose interests in this matter are identical, would be an element of weakness in an isolated action, of any one of them, but that the Cabinet of Washington, much as *they would hav* for these reasons they would have appreciated our cooperation, are nevertheless determined, in the event of our not joining them, to maintain the position taken in the proposed memorandum for the reason that they consider it the only one suited to the interests of the United States and apt to lead to a satisfactory result.

Manuscript Instructions Russia, 1890.

Blaine to Smith, May 10, 1890, (Telegram).

It is of the utmost importance that we cordially cooperate with Russia in the policy touching our joint interest in the Behring Sea. Omit no proper opportunity to impress this view upon the Russian Government any difference between the two powers will inure to the advantage of Great Britain.

BIBLIOGRAPHY

The works listed in this bibliography are those used in the preparation of this study. Reference to most of them has been made in the footnotes. No attempt has been made to include materials examined which did not prove to be of value for this subject.

I. MANUSCRIPTS

The Archives of the Department of State contain considerable unpublished material for the period of James G. Blaine. The dispatches from the United States ministers abroad and the instructions to them were examined for the periods 1880-1883 and 1888-1893, as well as the volumes of notes to and from the foreign embassies in Washington. The footnotes contain many references to materials obtained from the Archives. Special mention might be made of the material relating to a few episodes no part of the correspondence on which has ever appeared in print.

The Berlin Conference. An entire volume relating to the Conference at Berlin on Samoa in 1889. The correspondence consists of the confidential correspondence to and from the United States delegation.

The Russian-American Treaty negotiated by Baron Rosen and Mr. Blaine in 1889. The drafts of the treaty and Baron Rosen's *aides mémoire* are contained in Volume 13 of the Notes from the Russian Embassy. This negotiation was secret and informal and the treaty was never presented to the Senate.

  This seems to be the only unpublished material of importance on the Fur Seal Controversy.

The Gherardi correspondence on the attempt at acquiring the Môle St. Nicholas. The correspondence is contained in Dispatches, Haiti, Volume 25.

Commodore Shufeldt's reports and Mr. Blaine's instructions to him.

These are contained in the dispatches from and instructions to China for 1881 and furnish evidence of Blaine's Far Eastern policy.

II. PUBLISHED DOCUMENTARY MATERIAL

A. UNITED STATES

The Congressional Record.

The Senate and House Executive Documents.

The Senate and House Miscellaneous Documents.

The Senate and House Reports.

> The Executive Documents, especially the volumes entitled *Foreign Relations*, which appeared for each year as House Executive Document No. 1, furnished the most fruitful source for material upon foreign policy. Detailed reference to the documents has been made in the footnotes. Special reference, therefore, is made here to only a few of outstanding importance.

The Fur Seal Arbitration, 15 vols. Senate Executive Document No. 177, 53 Congress, 2nd Session, Serial No. 3166.

> Since this document contains the British as well as the American correspondence it is invaluable for any study of the Fur Seal Controversy.

Hawaii. A very complete collection of all correspondence on Hawaii published as Appendix II of *Foreign Relations*, 1894, Serial No. 3294.

The Interoceanic Canal Correspondence. Senate Document No. 237, 56 Congress, 1st Session, Serial No. 3853.

> Contains reprints of all important government documents on the canal question as well as new material, making it complete to 1900.

MOORE, JOHN BASSETT, *Digest of International Law*, 8 vols. House Document No. 551, 56 Congress, 2nd Session, Serial No. 4206. Published separately (Washington, 1906).

> An indispensable aid in any study of American foreign relations.

————, *History and Digest of the International Arbitrations to which the United States has been a party . . .*, 6 vols. House Miscellaneous Document No. 212, 53 Congress, 2nd Session, Serial No. 3267. Published separately (Washington, 1898).

Morrison, Hugh A., *A list of books and articles in periodicals relating to the interoceanic canal and railway routes*, with an appendix consisting of a bibliography of United States public documents on the subject. This very helpful work appeared as Senate Document No. 59, 56 Congress, 1st Session, Serial No. 3848. Published separately (Washington, 1900).

Richardson, J. D., Editor, *A Compilation of the Messages and Papers of the Presidents*, 10 vols. Published as House Miscellaneous Document No. 210, 53 Congress, 2nd Session, Serial No. 3265. Published separately (Washington, 1899).

The War in the Pacific. Senate Executive Document No. 79, 47 Congress, 1st Session, Serial No. 1989.
> This is a collection in one volume of all the correspondence on the subject of the war between Chile and Peru and Bolivia from 1879 to the date of its publication, 1882.

Venezuelan Arbitration of 1903. Senate Executive Document No. 119, 58 Congress, 3rd Session, Serial No. 4769.

Wharton, Francis, *International Law Digest*. Senate Miscellaneous Document No. 162, 49 Congress, 1st Session, Serial No. 2350-2352. Published separately (Washington, 1887).

B. FOREIGN

British and Foreign State Papers. Published annually from 1812 on.

Canadian Parliament, Official Reports of the Debates of the House of Commons (Ottawa, 1867).

Canadian Parliament Sessional Papers (Ottawa), published annually from 1867 on.

Hansard's *Parliamentary Debates* (London, 1804 on).

Die grosse Politik der europäischen Kabinette (Berlin, 1922 on).
> This monumental publication contains very little pertaining to the United States for the Blaine period. It was of value in the study of British-German colonial disputes.

III. UNOFFICIAL PUBLICATIONS CONTAINING DOCUMENTARY MATERIAL

International American Conference, Reports of Committees and Discussions Thereon, 4 vols. (Washington, 1890).
> The official collection of source material on the first Pan

American Congress. Also published in the Congressional Document Series as Senate Executive Document No. 232, 51 Congress, 1st Session.

Maritime Canal Company of Nicaragua, *The Nicaragua Canal Construction Company: The Interoceanic Canal of Nicaragua; its history, physical condition, plans and prospects.* Published by the Canal Construction Company (New York, 1891).

Valuable for the documents contained in the appendices.

SULLIVAN, J. T., *Report on the History and Technical Information Relating to the Problem of Interoceanic Communication by Way of the American Isthmus* (Washington, 1883).

Especially good on the Wyse Concession and the Paris Conference in 1879.

IV. SERIAL PUBLICATIONS

The Annual Register (London, 1761 on).

Appleton's Annual Cyclopedia and Register of Important Events (New York, 1862-1903).

Archives diplomatiques (Paris, 1861-1913).

Das Staatsarchiv (Leipzig, 1861-1913).

V. MEMOIRS, AUTOBIOGRAPHIES, CORRESPONDENCE, SPEECHES, AND THE "LIFE AND LETTERS" BIOGRAPHIES

The biographies included in this list contain, in the form of letters or extracts from diaries, source material of value, which is unobtainable elsewhere.

BEALE, HARRIET BLAINE, Editor, *The Letters of Mrs. James G. Blaine,* 2 vols. (New York, 1908).

Extremely valuable for its intimate picture of Mr. Blaine and for its many shrewd comments upon men and policies of the period.

BLAINE, JAMES G., *Discussions Legislative, Diplomatic, and Political* (Norwich, Conn., 1886).

A collection of speeches and dispatches on many subjects of public interest.

————, *Twenty Years of Congress: from Lincoln to Garfield*, 2 vols. (Norwich, Conn., 1884-1886).

> Contains indispensable material on the conditions of the period and on Blaine's attitude toward them.

ECKARDSTEIN, HERMANN, FREIHERR V., *Lebenserinnerungen und politische Denkwürdigkeiten*, 3 vols. (Leipzig, 1919-1921).

EVANS, ROBLEY D., *A Sailor's Log: Recollections of Forty Years of Naval Life* (New York, 1901).

> Evans was stationed in Valparaiso harbor throughout the winter of 1891-1892 and kept a diary which contains valuable information on the Chilean situation.

FITZMAURICE, EDMUND GEORGE PETTY, *Life of Granville, George Leveson Gower, second Earl Granville, K. G. 1815-1891* (London, 1905).

> Granville was secretary of state for foreign affairs in 1881 and conducted the British side of the negotiations in Mr. Blaine's attempt to abrogate the Clayton-Bulwer Treaty.

FOSTER, JOHN W., *Diplomatic Memoirs*, 2 vols. (New York, 1909).

> Mr. Foster was an intimate friend and associate of Mr. Blaine and was in close touch with the Department of State throughout the period, being in the diplomatic service much of the time. In 1892 he was himself Secretary of State. His *Memoirs*, therefore, are of great value.

GRESHAM, MATILDA, *Life of Walter Quintin Gresham, 1832-1895*, 2 vols. (Chicago, 1919).

> Mrs. Gresham's biography of her husband is valuable rather for its impressions of men and measures than for accounts of foreign policy and diplomatic episode.

GWYNN, STEPHEN LUCIUS, and TUCKWELL, GERTRUDE, *Life of the Right Honorable Sir Charles Dilke, bart., M.P.*, 2 vols. (London, 1917).

> Dilke was an under-secretary in the British Foreign Office when Blaine was in office in 1881. He was always well informed and made comments of interest on various matters of foreign policy.

HAMILTON, GAIL (ABIGAIL DODGE), *The Biography of James G. Blaine* (Norwich, Conn., 1895).

> The most useful biography of Blaine. It is of the nature of an intimate family account and valuable for the mass of detail which it contains that could have been accumulated only by

a member of the family. It contains many letters to and from Mr. Blaine and other members of the family and friends, which are not elsewhere obtainable. For that reason it is an invaluable aid in a study of any phase of the life of Blaine.

JAMES, HENRY, *Richard Olney and his Public Services* (New York, 1923).

Useful for the Venezuela boundary dispute.

MCELROY, ROBERT M., *Grover Cleveland, the Man and the Statesman* (New York, 1923).

Contains material in relation to Hawaii and Venezuela.

POPE, SIR JOSEPH, Editor, *The Correspondence of Sir John Macdonald* (Toronto, 1916).

Of some value in an estimate of Canadian attitude toward the United States.

ROSEN, BARON, *Forty Years of Diplomacy* (New York, 1922).

Contains the only secondary account of the Russian-American negotiations of 1889.

SAUNDERS, E. M., Editor, *The Life and Letters of the Right Honorable Sir Charles Tupper*, 2 vols. (Toronto, 1916).

Tupper was Canadian high commissioner in London in 1890 and was a leader in Canada's Conservative party.

SCHURZ, CARL, *Speeches, Correspondence and Political Papers*, FREDERIC BANCROFT, Editor, 6 vols. (New York, 1913).

Contains some reference to Blaine, to whom Schurz was exceedingly antagonistic.

SKELTON, OSCAR DOUGLAS, *The Life and Times of Sir Alexander Tilloch Galt* (Toronto, 1920).

Valuable for information on Canadian views and the attitude of Canada toward the United States. Galt was Canadian high commissioner at one time and kept up his contact with British leaders in politics.

————, *The Life and Letters of Sir Wilfred Laurier* (Toronto, 1921).

Extremely useful for the Canadian election of 1891 and for the attitude of the Liberal party toward reciprocity and kindred questions.

SMITH, THEODORE CLARK, *James Abram Garfield — Life and Letters*, 2 vols. (Yale Press, 1925).

Based largely upon Garfield's diaries and letters, this work is practically source material. It was of great value in the light it threw upon the relations of Garfield and Blaine and the influence of Garfield upon foreign policy in 1881.

STANWOOD, EDWARD, *James G. Blaine* (New York, 1905).

One of the two good lives of Blaine. It is unannotated and does not contain source material, but it is the work of an intimate friend and of an historian.

THAYER, WILLIAM ROSCOE, *The Life and Letters of John Hay*, 2 vols. (Boston, 1915).

A valuable work but with slight bearing upon this study.

TUPPER, SIR CHARLES, *The Recollections of Sixty Years* (Toronto, 1914).

Valuable for Canadian views on the fur seal question and on reciprocity.

WILLISON, J. S., *Sir Wilfred Laurier and the Liberal Party. A Political History*, 2 vols. (Toronto, 1903).

Contains an account of the reciprocity negotiations of the period and of the attitude of Canadian Liberals toward the United States.

VI. CAMPAIGN PAMPHLETS AND BIOGRAPHIES PUBLISHED BEFORE THE CAMPAIGN OF 1884 OR AS EULOGIES PUBLISHED IN 1893 AFTER MR. BLAINE'S DEATH

America's Egypt: Mr. Blaine's Foreign Policy (New York, 1884).

A campaign work and almost valueless. An attack upon Blaine's policy toward Mexico.

BALCH, WILLIAM RALSTON, *The Life and Public Services of James G. Blaine* (Philadelphia, 1884).

Campaign biography.

Mr. Blaine and his Foreign Policy. An examination of his most important dispatches while Secretary of State, American History Pamphlets, Vol. I (Boston, 1884).

Very condemnatory of Blaine's policy.

BOYD, JAMES P., *The Life and Public Services of the Hon. James G. Blaine* (New York, 1893).

Of no value to the student.

CONWELL, RUSSELL H., *The Life and Public Services of James G. Blaine* (Augusta, Maine, 1884).

Campaign biography.

CRAWFORD, THERON CLARK, *James G. Blaine. A Study of his life and career, from the standpoint of a principal witness of the events of his history* (Philadelphia, 1893).

A eulogistic account but better than the campaign biographies.

HURLBURT, WILLIAM HENRY, *Meddling and Muddling: Mr. Blaine's Foreign Policy* (New York, 1884).

This pamphlet, originally printed as a letter to the editor of the New York *Herald*, is an extremely unfair campaign criticism of Blaine's nine months in office. But, due to the fact that the author was the brother of General Hurlburt whom Blaine sent as minister to Peru, it contains some material not found elsewhere.

JOHNSON, WILLIS FLETCHER, *The Life of James G. Blaine, "The Plumed Knight"* (Atlantic Publishing Company, 1893).

A subscription biography of eulogistic nature.

RAMSDELL, HENRY J., *Life and public service of Hon. James G. Blaine, the brilliant orator and sagacious statesman, the bosom friend of the lamented Garfield, and now the choice of the nation for President of the United States; by his intimate friend and associate* (Philadelphia, 1884).

Campaign biography.

RIDPATH, JOHN CLARK, and others, *The Life and Work of James G. Blaine* (Philadelphia, 1893).

Profusely illustrated, eulogistic, and interesting but of little value to the serious student.

VII. OTHER MATERIALS, SECONDARY IN NATURE

BANCROFT, HUBERT H., *The New Pacific* (New York, 1913).

Contains a good bibliography on the canal question.

BRYCE, JAMES, *South America* (New York, 1912).

CARPENTER, EDMUND JAMES, *America in Hawaii. A History of the United States Influence in the Hawaiian Islands* (London, 1899).

CLEVELAND, GROVER, *Presidential Problems* (New York, 1904).

One of the problems discussed is the Venezuela-British Guiana boundary question. Valuable both as an outline of the controversy and as Cleveland's view.

COOLIDGE, ARCHIBALD CARY, *The United States as a World Power* (New York, 1908).

CURTIS, WILLIAM E., *From the Andes to the Ocean* (New York, 1907).
    Contains some interesting material on the Chilean Revolution
    of 1891. Curtis traveled extensively in South America about
    this time.

DENNETT, TYLER, *Americans in Eastern Asia: A critical study of the
    policy of the United States with reference to China, Japan and
    Korea in the Nineteenth Century* (New York, 1922).
    The most recent and most authoritative account of Far East-
    ern relations. Based largely upon unpublished sources.

DEWEY, DAVID R., *National Problems, 1885-1897*, Vol. 24, American
    Nation Series (New York, 1907).
    Contains a good bibliography.

ELLIOTT, G. F. SCOTT, *Chile: Its History and Development, Natural
    Features, Products, Commerce and Present Conditions* (London,
    1911).
    Not detailed on historical side, probably a standard English
    work on the subject.

FENWICK, CHARLES G., *International Law* (New York, 1924).

FISH, CARL RUSSELL, *American Diplomacy* (New York, 1915).

FOSTER, JOHN W., *American Diplomacy in the Orient* (New York,
    1903).

HANCOCK, ANSON URIEL, *A History of Chile* (Chicago, 1893).
    Standard history of Chile published in the United States.

HART, ALBERT BUSHNELL, *The Foundations of American Foreign Policy*
    (New York, 1901).
    Contains a good bibliography.
———, *The Monroe Doctrine, an Interpretation* (Boston, 1916).
    Contains a good bibliography.
———, *Practical Essays in American Government* (New York, 1905).
    Especially the essay on the "Chilean Controversy."

HENDERSON, JOHN B., *American Diplomatic Questions* (New York,
    1901).
    Unannotated but useful summary of some of the important
    diplomatic problems of United States history.

HODGINS, THOMAS, *British and American Diplomacy affecting Canada,
    1782-1899* (Toronto, 1900).
    A very Canadian point of view. It probably represents a con-
    siderable body of opinion in Canada in the nineteenth century.
    It is bitterly antagonistic toward the United States.

HYDE, CHARLES C., *International Law: Chiefly as Applied by the United States*, 2 vols. (Boston, 1922).

> Valuable for this study for its account of the Barrundia affair and for its summary of the rights of American citizens abroad.

JOHNSON, WILLIS FLETCHER, *American Foreign Relations* (New York, 1916).

———, *Four Centuries of the Panama Canal* (New York, 1906).

> Both general, popularly written accounts.

KEASBEY, LINDLEY MILLER, *The Nicaragua Canal and the Monroe Doctrine: A political history of isthmus transit, with special reference to the Nicaragua Canal project and the attitude of the United States thereto* (New York, 1896).

> Aside from its strong anti-British bias, this book is extremely useful and contains much material not easily available. It is a plea for the Nicaragua route.

KEIM, JEANNETTE, *Forty Years of German-American Political Relations* (Philadelphia, 1919).

> A doctoral dissertation. The chapter on Samoa was useful for the account of events preceding the Samoan Congress.

KRAUS, HERBERT, *Die Monroedoktrin* (Berlin, 1913).

> The best German work on the subject and one of the best in any language. Contains an appendix of documents.

LATANÉ, JOHN H., *The Diplomatic Relations of the United States and Spanish America* (Baltimore, 1900).

———, *The United States and Latin America* (New York, 1920).

> Based on his earlier work.

LAWRENCE, T. J., *Essays on Some Disputed Questions in Modern International Law* (Cambridge, 1885).

> Contains a chapter on the interoceanic canal. British in viewpoint. Upholds the Clayton-Bulwer Treaty.

MOWAT, R. B., *The Diplomatic Relations of Great Britain and the United States* (New York, 1925).

> Interesting summary of Anglo-American relations.

PECK, HARRY THURSTON, *Twenty Years of the Republic, 1885-1905* (New York, 1913).

PÉTIN, HECTOR, *Les États Unis et la doctrine de Monroe* (Paris, 1900).

> An interesting French treatise on the Monroe Doctrine. The chapter on the interoceanic canal contains considerable mate-

rial upon the Wyse Concession and the French activities at Panama.

RHODES, JAMES FORD, *History of the United States from the Compromise of 1850*, 8 vols. (New York, 1893-1922).

RIPPY, J. FRED, *The United States and Mexico* (New York, 1926).

ROBERTSON, WILLIAM SPENCE, *Hispanic-American Relations with the United States* (New York, 1923).

RODRIGUES, J. C., *The Panama Canal, its History, its Political Aspects and Financial Difficulties* (London, 1885).

> Rodrigues was a journalist and newspaper correspondent. He was in Panama when De Lesseps began operations and gives an interesting account of the French enterprise.

SCRUGGS, W. L., *The Colombian and Venezuelan Republics with Notes on other parts of Central and South America* (Boston, 1901).

> Scruggs was at different times United States minister to various Latin American Republics and knew them intimately.

SPARKS, EDWIN E., *National Development, 1877-1885*, Vol. 23, American Nation Series (New York, 1907).

> Contains a good bibliography.

STANWOOD, EDWARD, *American Tariff Controversies in the Nineteenth Century*, 2 vols. (New York, 1903).

> Particularly detailed for the part played by Blaine in the making of the McKinley Tariff in 1890.

STEVENSON, ROBERT LOUIS, *A Footnote to History: Eight Years of Trouble in Samoa* (New York, 1895).

> Of great value in any study of Samoan difficulties. An intimate account of one almost an eye-witness and well acquainted with native life in Samoa. It is a contribution to both history and literature.

STROBEL, EDWARD H., *Blaine and His Foreign Policy* (Boston, 1884).

> Campaign material.

STUART, GRAHAM H., *Latin America and the United States* (New York, 1922).

> An extremely useful summary of the relations of the United States to Latin America. Practically every phase of Mr. Blaine's American policy is touched upon.

TOWNSEND, MARY EVELYN, *Origins of Modern German Colonialism, 1871-1885*, Columbia University Studies in History, Economics, and Public Law, Vol. 9 (New York, 1921).

Of use in obtaining the background for German activities in Samoa.

TRAVIS, IRA D., *The History of the Clayton-Bulwer Treaty*, Publications of the Michigan Political Science Association, Vol. 3 (Ann Arbor, 1900).

A very useful study of the history of the treaty with most of its emphasis upon the period prior to 1860.

VIALLATE, ACHILLE, *Essais d'histoire diplomatique americaine* (Paris, 1905).

Contains an essay entitled, "Les États-Unis et la canal interoceanic."

WILLIAMS, MARY W., *Anglo-American Isthmian Diplomacy, 1815-1915* (Washington, 1916).

The most authoritative account of the subject. The work, however, covers so long a period that the amount of space devoted to the work of Blaine is slight.

ZIMMERMANN, ALFRED, *Geschichte der deutschen Kolonialpolitik* (Berlin, 1914).

VIII. PERIODICAL MATERIAL

BUSTAMANTE, ANTOINE S. DE, "Le Canal de Panama et la droit international," *Revue de droit international* (Paris, 1885).

COLQUHOUN, R. H. U., "Reciprocity Trips to Washington: A Page from Political History," *Canadian Magazine*, March, 1897.

DOUGLASS, FREDERICK, "Haiti and the United States: Inside History of the Negotiations for the Môle St. Nicholas," *North American Review*, September, 1891.

The only secondary account of the affair based upon knowledge of the source material. Douglass was United States minister to Haiti at the time.

FOSTER, JOHN W., "The Bering Sea Arbitration," *North American Review*, December, 1893.

Written after the meeting of the tribunal. Foster was the United States agent and had prepared the case for his Government.

HARDY, OSGOOD, "The Itata Incident," *Hispanic American Historical Review*, Vol. V.

A valuable contribution to historical research in this period.

> Mr. Hardy has used much newspaper and manuscript material inaccessible to most students.

HURLBURT, WILLIAM HENRY, "Reciprocity with Canada," *North American Review*, October, 1891.

KEASBEY, LINDLEY M., "The National Canal Policy," *American Historical Association Report*, 1902, Vol. I.

——, "The Nicaragua Canal and the Monroe Doctrine," *Annals of the American Academy of Political and Social Science*, January, 1896.

——, "The Terms and Tenor of the Clayton-Bulwer Treaty," *Annals of the American Academy of Political and Social Science*, November, 1899.

MENDENHALL, T. C., "Expert Testimony on the Behring Sea Controversy," *Popular Science Monthly*, November, 1897.
> Mendenhall was one of the commission of experts which visited Bering Sea and reported upon seal life and the regulations necessary for its preservation.

MOORE, JOHN BASSETT, "The Chilean Affair," *Political Science Quarterly*, September, 1893.
> A juristic account.

MUNSON, L. E., "A Commercial Union with Canada," *New Englander and Yale Review*, July, 1894.

The *Nation*. There are numberless editorials in the *Nation*, usually by Godkin, in the Blaine period. They are uniformly condemnatory of Blaine's policy and violent in their bias against him.

PECK, H. T., "A Spirited Foreign Policy," The *Bookman*, XXI (June, 1905).
> A chapter of his book, *Twenty Years of the Republic*.

ROMERO, MATIAS, "Blaine and the Boundary Question between Mexico and Guatemala," "The Settlement of the Mexican-Guatemalan Boundary Question, 1882," *American Geographical Society Journal*, XXIX.
> Romero was for· some time Mexican minister to the United States. He had a wide knowledge of the Guatemalan affair and was well acquainted with all persons involved.

——, "The Pan-American Conference," *North American Review*, September, 1890, and October, 1890.
> Romero was a delegate to the Conference and gives a first-hand account of its work.

SHELDON, JOSEPH, "Canadian Reciprocity within the Union — Not Free Trade and False Pretences," *New Englander and Yale Review*, June, 1891.

TRACY, B. F., "The Behring Sea Question," *North American Review*, May, 1893.

> Tracy was Secretary of the Navy under Harrison.

WILGUS, A. CURTIS, "James G. Blaine and the Pan-American Movement," *Hispanic American Historical Review*, Vol. V.

> A profusely annotated account of the first Pan American Congress and the preliminaries to it.

WIMAN, ERASTUS, "What is the Destiny of Canada," *North American Review*, June, 1889.

> Wiman was an ardent believer in commercial union with an eventual, peaceable consummation of political union.

WOOLSEY, T. S., "Suez and Panama — A Parallel," *American Historical Association Annual Report*, 1902, Vol. I (Washington, 1902).

NOTE: The great mass of periodical and newspaper comment upon Blaine and his policy was so colored by the attitude of the authors toward Blaine that it did not prove very useful in a study of foreign policy. Only such articles are cited as were of some use in an estimate of policy.

INDEX